GET ROMMEL

Books By Michael Asher

FICTION

The Eye of Ra

Firebird

Rare Earth

Sandstorm

NON-FICTION

In Search of the Forty Days Road

A Desert Dies

Impossible Journey – Two Against the Sahara

Shoot To Kill – A Soldier's Journey Through Violence

Thesiger – A Biography

Last of the Bedu – In Search of the Myth

Lawrence – the Uncrowned King of Arabia

The Real Bravo Two Zero

Sahara (with Kazoyoshi Nomachi)

Phoenix Rising – The UAE, Past, Present & Future
(with Werner Form)

GET ROMMEL

The Secret British Mission
to Kill Hitler's Greatest General

Michael Asher

WEIDENFELD & NICOLSON

Weidenfeld & Nicolson

The Orion Publishing Group Ltd
Orion House, 5 Upper Saint Martin's Lane, London WC2H 9EA

British Library Cataloguing-in-Publication Data. A catalogue
record for this book is available from the British Library.

ISBN 0-297-84685-X (cased edition)
ISBN 0-297-84636-1 (export trade paperback edition)

Cartography by Peter Harper

Printed and bound in Great Britain by Clays Ltd, St Ives plc

This book is dedicated to the memory of my father,
Sergeant Frederick William Asher, 3rd (Cheshire)
Field Squadron, Royal Engineers, who served with the
Eighth Army throughout the North Africa Campaign,
and to the memory of my father-in-law, Lieutenant
(later Brigadier General) Pasquale Peru, who
commanded a company of the Brescia Division at Tobruk,
and was captured by the British. Enemies for a time,
but now united for eternity. Per Ardua Ad Astra.

How can I live among this gentle

obsolescent breed of heroes, and not weep?

Unicorns, almost,

for they are falling into two legends

in which their stupidity and chivalry

are celebrated, Each fool and hero will be

an immortal ...

Keith Douglas *Selected Poems*

Contents

Acknowledgements

I would like to give special thanks to Dr Rolf Wichmann of the UN High Commission on Human Settlement, Nairobi, for translating the German documents, and for his encyclopaedic knowledge of German forces in the Second World War. I would also extend a similar deep thanks to David List of the BBC, for his intimate knowledge of the Second World War Special Forces, his patient assistance, and particularly for helping me compile the initial nominal roll. I am extremely grateful for the crucial help of Ronald Youngman of the Commando Association, and the advice of Henry Brown, formerly of the Commando Association.

A great debt of gratitude and admiration is due to those who took part in the raid or its preparation: Jim Gornall MM, Charles Lock, Frederick Birch and Sir Thomas Macpherson MC, for their personal accounts. I would also like to thank the survivors of 11 (Scottish) Commando, and other Second World War special forces, who wrote to me and sent me various documents, including George, the Earl Jellicoe DSO, Sir Carol Mather MC, Robin McCunn, Walter Marshall, Eric Garland MC, D.D. Drummond, Adam B. Archibald and Jimmy Foot.

I would like to add an additional thank-you to Lord Roger Keyes, second Baron Keyes of Zeebrugge, for both the personal interview and for crucial family documents.

Further deep thanks go to Mary Louise Guiver and Charles Lock junior, the children of Charles Lock, for giving me access to their father's diaries and letters; to Mrs Ruth Lock for her personal account of life on

Arran; Mrs June McCunn for her letters relaying her husband's experiences in 11 Commando; Paul Hughes, grandson of Malcolm 'Spike' Hughes, and his aunt, née Alice Hughes; John Terry, son of Jack Terry DCM; William Briggs of the *Glasgow Herald*, for archive material, and for his assistance in finding survivors of the raid; Alan McSherry of the Cameronland Museum; Bert Riggs, Archivist, Centre for Newfoundland Studies, University of Newfoundland, for details of Joseph Kearney's letters; Hans Edelmaier and his publisher for sending me a copy of *Das Rommel Unternehmen*; David and Margaret Short of the Spean Bridge Hotel, Scotland, which houses the Commando Museum, and John Condon, who sent me the background material on John Haselden.

I am grateful for the assistance of the staff of the Public Records Office, Kew (now the National Archives), and to the staff of the Liddell-Hart Centre For Military Archives at King's College, London. I owe a deep debt of gratitude to my editor at Weidenfeld & Nicolson, Ian Drury, for his advice and suggestions, and further special thanks to my agent, Anthony Goff, and his assistant Georgia Glover, without whose help my research would not have been possible. Last but not least, I would like to thank my wife, Mariantonietta, and my two children, Burton and Jade, for their encouragement while I was researching and writing this book.

Michael Asher
Langata, Nairobi, 2004

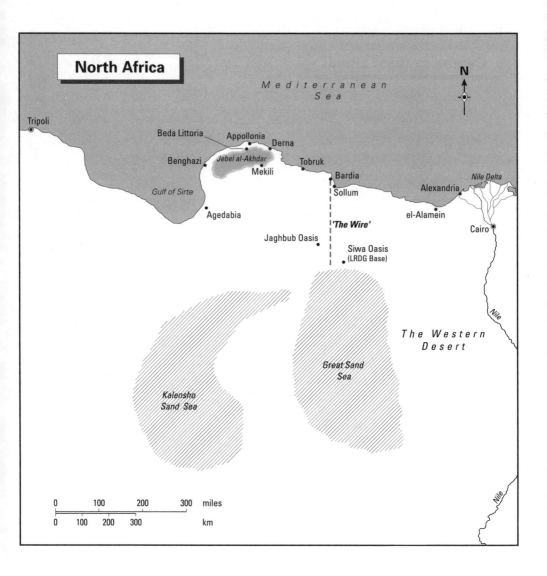

North Africa

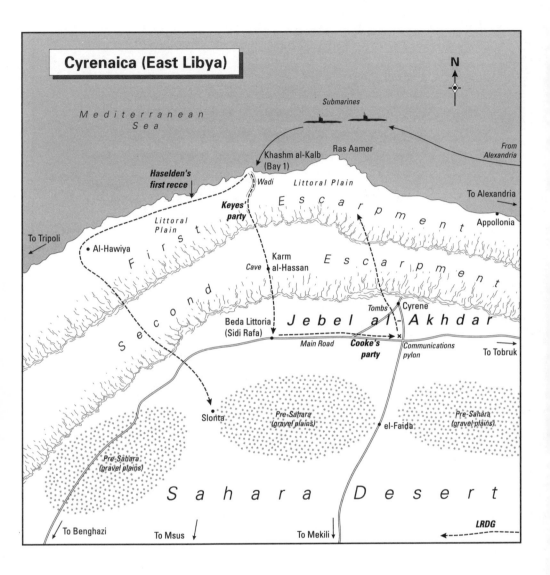

Cyrenaica (East Libya)

N

Mediterranean Sea

Submarines

From Alexandria

To Alexandria

Khashm al-Kalb (Bay 1)

Ras Aamer

Haselden's first recce

Wadi

Littoral Plain

Keyes' party

E s c a r p m e n t

Appollonia

Littoral Plain

• Al-Hawiya

F i r s t

To Tripoli

E s c a r p m e n t

Cave

Karm al-Hassan

S e c o n d

Tombs

Cyrene

Jebel al Akhdar

Beda Littoria (Sidi Rafa)

Main Road

Cooke's party

Communications pylon

To Tobruk

Slonta

Pre-Sahara (gravel plains)

el-Faida

Pre-Sahara (gravel plains)

Pre-Sahara (gravel plains)

S a h a r a   D e s e r t

To Benghazi

To Msus

To Mekili

LRDG

DAY 2

19 November 1941 1345–1400 hours

It felt like a horse kicking him from behind. He went down, sprawling into the sand. Lieutenant John M. Pryor of the Special Boat Section lay on the beach, his thigh pumping blood, while enemy rounds licked up spurts of dust all around him. The bullet had been fired by one of the forty Italian colonial *carabinieri* who were now skirmishing towards him downhill under a hail of covering fire. The wound looked bad, but curiously, there was no pain. 'I lay there and thought, well, I've often hit a rabbit in the back legs,' said Pryor. 'I hope it doesn't hurt more than that, because that was nothing.'[1]

Minutes earlier, armed only with a Webley .38 revolver and a No. 36 Mills grenade, John 'Farmer' Pryor had advanced to within 150 yards of the enemy in a vain attempt to convince them that an outflanking movement was in progress. In fact, the only man with him – a commando private whose name he never knew – was pinned behind a rock, his Thompson sub-machine-gun jammed. Pryor had assured his one-man team that the *carabinieri* they were up against couldn't hit a barn door at twenty paces, but closer up he had spotted a section of steel-helmeted Italian regulars on the hill behind the Arabs, taking careful aim. At that point he decided he'd got close enough. As he turned and tried to make his way back towards the command post as fast as he could, the bullet had taken him.

Now he crawled behind a flat stone and set it on its edge for cover, but when two ricochets pinged off it, he realized that he would soon be exposed to the advancing enemy. His legs were drenched in blood but, with a last titanic effort, he dragged himself on to his knees and managed to crawl ahead of the Italians a quarter of a mile back to where the men of 11 Commando lay in a defensive formation around the caves they had withdrawn to the previous night.

It was now some minutes past one in the afternoon and *Operation Flipper*, already a failure, was fast turning into a débâcle. The raiding party had returned to the beach the previous day minus its leader, Lieutenant Colonel Geoffrey Keyes, who was confirmed dead. His Second-in-Command, Captain Robin F. Campbell, had been badly wounded and captured by the Germans. Another officer, Lieutenant Roy Royston Cooke, and six men, were missing in action. Now the survivors of the raid were stranded on the beach of Khashm al-Kalb, a remote headland on the Libyan coast two hundred and fifty miles behind Axis lines, with no radio, no back-up, no air support, and little chance of escape.

Rifle fire was pouring into the position from the west, but the men were well dug in – some were actually inside the caves – and taking no casualties. They had been under fire by the *carabinieri* for two hours, but though their shooting was accurate enough, they had no automatic weapons: so far, the enemy had been cautious. A few of the commandos were armed with Thompson .45 sub-machine-guns, close-quarter weapons with a maximum effective range of only 175 yards, but most had Lee-Enfield .303 Mark IV rifles, accurate to 400 yards and over. They had one .303-calibre Bren light machine-gun and some pistols and grenades, but no heavy machine-guns or mortars.

Lieutenant Colonel Robert E. Laycock, commanding *Operation Flipper*, had been confident that his force could hold the enemy off until last light, when they would withdraw to the beach for evacuation by *Torbay*, a submarine of the Royal Navy's 1st Submarine Flotilla. Now, as Laycock examined the wound in Pryor's thigh, he was not so certain. There was a lot of blood; it was probable that a main artery had been hit. 'Damn it,' he said. 'That's no good. We'd better bugger off!'

Bob 'Lucky' Laycock was thirty-three years old, and known as a tough nut – with his wide-apart eyes and boxer's nose, he had a perpetual 'punchy' look. Married, with five children, he had attended Eton and Sandhurst: he was one of the British Army's *Wunderkind*, later the model for Evelyn Waugh's character Lieutenant Colonel Tommy Blackhouse in his novel *Officers & Gentlemen*. He had been commissioned in the élite Royal Horse Guards, but had done time at a desk in the War Office before being invited, in 1940, to form and head 8 Commando, one of the world's first modern special forces units. Though he had not been in action before that year, he was believed to be a man of initiative, imagination and daring, and to possess what his wife Angie called a rare combination of upper-class nonchalant panache and professional efficiency. Within three years he would become Director of Combined Operations and, at thirty-six, the British Army's youngest major general.

Scanning the landscape with his field-glasses, Laycock noticed that more red-turbaned *carabinieri* were arriving from the west, and a company of German infantry was approaching down a wadi from the north. To cap it all, another large force of Italian regulars had appeared on the brow of a hill about a mile away. He lowered the binos and glanced at his watch. It was almost 1400 hours on the afternoon of 19 November 1941, and the second major British offensive in North Africa, *Operation Crusader*, had been underway for 32 hours. If all had gone according to plan, the armoured and mobile infantry columns of Lieutenant General Sir Alan Cunningham's Eighth Army would soon be pushing deep into Cyrenaica.

Laycock knew that there was no chance now of holding the Axis off until nightfall. Their only hope lay in those advancing British columns. If the raiding party broke up into small groups, they might be able to hold out, hiding in the brush on the slopes of Jebel al-Akhdar and evading the enemy until Cunningham's units picked them up.

At 1400 hours precisely Laycock told the nearest of his men to pass on the order to bug out – to run for it – and then he looked again at 'Farmer' Pryor. Laycock guessed that Pryor's reckless action had been compensation for mysteriously 'losing' their rubber dinghies the day previously; the commandos were to have used them to regain the submarine. Pryor looked pallid and was bleeding profusely and Laycock feared he would soon bleed to death. He asked Pryor if he could walk. 'I was a bit knocked up,' Pryor said, 'and I dare say I looked worse than I was, with a lot of blood about.' Laycock instructed Private Edward C. Atkins, a medical orderly from Manchester, to staunch the bleeding and told both to surrender to the Italians. Then, 'under a storm of excited and inaccurate shots from the Eyeties,' Pryor said, '[he] dashed off into the surrounding scrub.'[2]

Atkins was unhappy about being sacrificed to the enemy when his CO was not willing to do the same. As the Italians approached, he erected a makeshift white flag and studied it dubiously. 'Do you think they'll shoot us, sir?' he asked Pryor.

Thinking this was hardly a decent bedside manner to adopt for a wounded man feeling cold and miserable, Pryor answered him trucu-lently, 'Yes, I'm sure they will.' Atkins's face was a picture.

It was an ignominious end to the most audacious raid ever carried out by British commandos, an operation which, had it succeeded, could have been the biggest propaganda coup of the Second World War.

Just five days earlier, the men of 11 (Scottish) Commando, with an escort of SBS canoeists, had been landed by the submarines *Torbay* and *Talisman* on this same beach. Their orders, revealed only after the subs had put to sea, were to disrupt communications behind enemy lines – and to kill or capture the commander of the *Panzergruppe Afrika*, Lieu-tenant General Erwin Rommel himself.

2 OPERATION CRUSADER

MINUS 18 MONTHS
June 1940

Twenty-two commandos on the beach at Khashm al-Kalb were virtually all that remained of *Layforce*, the 2,000-strong Special Service Brigade named after its chief, Bob Laycock, which had been assembled in Egypt in March 1941. The commando concept itself had been born nine months earlier out of Winston Churchill's determination that the British Army, in the wake of its devastating defeat by the Germans on the plains of Europe in May 1940, would not lapse into the kind of defensive mentality he believed had sunk the French. To that end, only a week after the evacuation of 333,000 Allied troops from the beaches of Dunkirk, he had sanctioned the raising of a dozen self-contained, thoroughly equipped raiding units of up to a thousand men apiece, to harry the Germans along the Channel coasts.

'Enterprises must be prepared with specially trained troops of the hunter class,' he wrote to the Chiefs of Staff on 3 June 1940, 'who can develop a reign of terror … against the whole German occupied coastline.'[1]

No one was quite sure how this was to be done, but the idea of putting an existing infantry division through special training was rejected early on, as all available regular troops were needed for defence of the islands, and in any case, the kind of warfare Churchill had envisaged required a new and different mentality. Ten Independent Companies had been raised from Territorial Army volunteers earlier in the year to wage a guerrilla war against the Germans in Norway, but these wouldn't exactly fit the bill either, since they were 'stay behind' parties, trained to fight alone rather than in concert. Instead, the Chiefs of Staff decided to ask for volunteers from each regional command of the United Kingdom. Each was requested to supply the names of forty officers and a thousand other ranks for unspecified mobile operations.

The day after the first requests had gone out, General Sir John Dill, Chief of the Imperial General Staff, found himself saddled with a decision on how this new strike force was to be used. He delegated the task to his Military Assistant, GSO1 Lieutenant Colonel Dudley Clarke, a Royal Artillery officer gifted with unusual imagination, and the creator of what would later come to be called psyops.

Clarke had grown up in South Africa and had served in Palestine in the 1930s during the Arab Rebellion, where he had seen bands of Arab guerrillas tie down an entire corps of British Army regulars assisted by thousands of auxiliaries. He took the name 'commando' from a book of the same title by South African author Denys Reitz, about the lightly armed and fast-moving Boer *Kommando* companies who had held back British forces for months during the South African campaign. Despite grumblings from the old guard in the War Office, the name stuck. The commandos, Clarke said, should first of all be volunteers, and as physically fit as the finest athletes; they should be trained to the highest standards in the use of infantry weapons, and capable of killing or capturing the enemy quickly and silently. They should be able to operate in darkness rather than daylight, and should be familiar with ships and the sea. A commando soldier should be able to work in small groups or on his own, and to use independent initiative – he should think of warfare solely in terms of attack.

It has often been said that special forces – undoubtedly a British creation – grew out of an individualism inherent in the national character, but this is untrue: in fact, as Correlli Barnett has shown, the generation to which the officer corps of the Second World War belonged was the most hidebound and orthodox in the Empire's history. The British

Army of 1940, Barnett wrote, was an anachronism. 'Although the army of a twentieth-century social democracy and a first-class industrial power, it was nevertheless spiritually a peasant levy led by the gentry and aristocracy. Its habits of mind and work, its mental and emotional life were those of a social order based on birth and lands that had passed from supremacy in the national life by the end of the nineteenth century.'[2]

Indeed, it was the Germans rather than the British who trained their officers to be flexible and self-reliant, and Rommel himself criticized British officers for their 'lack of independent initiative and somewhat stereotyped and over-systematic tactical methods.' An OKH (German High Command) assessment to which Rommel contributed significantly characterized British command as *Schwerfällig* or sluggish, citing 'rigidity of mind and reluctance to change positions as swiftly and readily as situations demanded ... great fussiness and over-elaboration of detail in orders which thus became inhibiting, inappropriate and excessively long, with subordinate leaders given little freedom of action or decision.'[3]

David Hunt, a British intelligence officer, was told during his training that the Germans were fiendishly clever, but inflexible, and unable to operate if their ingenious schemes went wrong, whereas the British were at their best when forced to improvise. In practice, Hunt found that the opposite was true. German subalterns were allowed far greater scope for thought and action than their British counterparts – their training encouraged them to believe that *any* action was better than no action at all. German officer cadets like Rommel usually served in the ranks for a year before entering the military academy; they knew the jobs of private soldiers and NCOs as well as their own. Their training included not only platoon tactics, but battalion tactics too, so that each subaltern could theoretically step into a battalion commander's shoes if necessary. British officer cadets received only the rudiments of platoon-commanders' training, and learned nothing of battalion tactics.

The concept of special forces grew not out of national character, but out of a geographical and historical necessity: the British Army had been crippled at Dunkirk – small, lightly equipped units carrying out tip-and-run raids across the Channel was, at that stage, the only way it *could* fight. 'Guerrilla warfare,' Dudley Clarke declared, 'was always, in fact, the answer of the ill-equipped patriot in the face of a vaster though ponderous military machine; and that seemed to me to be precisely the position in which the British Army found itself in June 1940.'[4]

11 (Scottish) Commando was raised at Galashiels in the Borders region, where, in early August 1940, Lieutenant Colonel Dick Pedder, 35, an irascible martinet of the Highland Light Infantry, and Major Bruce Ramsay, of the Cameron Highlanders, set up their HQ in the Douglas Hotel. The commando establishment allowed for ten troops of about fifty men, each with a troop commander and one or two other officers. 11 Commando was one of several commando units raised, all over the country, at this time.

One of Pedder's first troop commanders was Captain Geoffrey Keyes, of the Royal Scots Greys – although not obvious special forces material, he was an asset: his father, Sir Roger John Brownlow Keyes, was, in effect, Pedder's boss.

Born in India in 1872, Geoffrey's father, Admiral of the Fleet Sir Roger John Brownlow Keyes, had joined the Royal Navy as a midshipman at the age of just thirteen. He was promoted to commander after successfully blowing up and storming a Chinese fort during the Boxer Rebellion in 1899 and was a rear admiral by the time he was 45. It was while working as Director of Plans at the Admiralty in 1918 that Roger Keyes had come up with a dazzling solution to the German U-boat threat that had a stranglehold on vital British supply convoys in the Atlantic. The German subs were slipping through the Bruges ship canal and into the Straits of Dover before circling the British Isles and heading for Atlantic waters. Keyes realized that if the canal could be blocked at both its mouths – Zeebrugge and Ostende – by specially constructed 'block-boats' made of concrete, the U-boat menace would be discouraged, if not permanently plugged.

It was the kind of idea that rarely comes more than once in a lifetime. The raid, carried out on St George's Day 1918, and led by Roger Keyes personally, accounted for no fewer than eleven VCs, twenty-one DSOs, twenty-nine DSCs and scores of other decorations. The *Zeebrugge Operation*, one of the few unconventional missions of the First World War, was the kind of heroic failure the British loved – for the Germans had promptly removed the obstructions and the U-boat threat had continued unabated. But it had brought Roger Keyes public adulation, a knighthood, and the lifelong friendship of Winston Churchill.

'Keyes has frequently been compared with Nelson,' Barrie Pitt has written 'and possibly if he had died at Zeebrugge he would by now have been as deeply venerated.'[5]

Comparison with Nelson was a hard act to follow. All his life, Geoffrey Keyes had striven to emulate his father and to live up to his reputation, a particularly difficult task for him because he was not cast in the robust mould from which heroes are supposed to be made. Suffering from poor hearing and eyesight, he had been obliged to give up boxing at Eton because of potential damage to his ears, and to ditch rowing because of curvature of the spine. His mother, a woman who believed that to show affection to a child was to spoil it, obliged him to wear various contraptions – all of them unsuccessful – to cure this ailment, which only added to his sense of inadequacy. During his first term at Sandhurst he was rated below average physically, and he was never more than a mediocre shot.

In fact, Geoffrey's talents lay on the intellectual rather than the athletic side, a quality that caused his father more consternation than pride. Sir Roger, 46 years old when Geoffrey was born, still held to the Victorian notion that manliness meant athleticism, and intellectual ability was to be equated with effeminacy and even 'un-Englishness'. He once confided in a school friend of Geoffrey's that he was worried because his son's school reports were *too good*, and enquired anxiously – and perfectly seriously – if the friend thought Geoffrey would *be all right*.

From childhood, Geoffrey had desperately wanted to be a naval officer like his father. When he was told at Eton that his eyesight was below the standard required, he plumped instead for the army, taking a commission in his uncle's regiment, the Royal Scots Greys. But even this had been a disappointment to his father, for the Greys was officered largely by the sons of businessmen and traders – Sir Roger would have preferred him to have been commissioned into the socially élite 'Blues', the Life Guards.

Even so, Sir Roger was soon able to exert some influence over his son's career. Six years after he had retired from the Royal Navy with the rank of Admiral of the Fleet and become the Honorable Member of Parliament for Portsmouth, Winston Churchill brought his old friend out of mothballs to become Director of Combined Operations – with responsibility for the recruitment and deployment of the commandos. One of Sir Roger's first acts as DCO was to wire Scottish Command and request that his son, Acting Captain Geoffrey Keyes, then serving with the 3rd Cavalry Training Regiment at Redford Barracks in Edinburgh, be posted to the new commando force.

Naturally, Geoffrey Keyes always resented the idea that his posting to the commandos had depended on his father's patronage and he insisted that he had been selected thirty-six hours before Sir Roger's wire of recommendation arrived from the War Office. This may be technically true; though his interview for the commandos took place on 24 July 1940, a full week *after* his father had been appointed DCO, the influence of the British ruling class worked in ways more subtle than official wires. The interviewing officer, Major Bruce Ramsay, was of First World War vintage, and even if he had not received a wire, and did not yet know that Admiral of the Fleet Sir Roger Keyes had just become his chief, he was certainly aware that he was interviewing a national hero's eldest son.

Keyes had brought with him to Galashiels a contingent of men, including a number of seasoned NCO instructors he had filched with great difficulty from his regiment: 'First class chaps,' he described them, 'and they ought to be the right type.'[6]

As Keyes and his men arrived, would-be commandos from all over Scotland were converging by train on the small town, some of them regulars, some Territorial Army volunteers, others conscripts fresh out of basic training. John Mackay, a farm labourer from Thurso, was only 18 years old, but had already been serving in the 5th (Caithness & Sutherland) Battalion, the Seaforth Highlanders, for two years. He had enlisted in the Territorial Army at 16, giving a false occupation as well as a false age, and a year later, on 2 September 1939, his TA battalion had been mobilized. Mackay and his comrade, David Gunn from Wick, had expected to be sent abroad, but instead they had spent tedious months guarding docks and airfields – so-called key installations – in biting cold and teeming rain.[7] To make matters worse, their sister battalions, the 4th and 5th Seaforths, *had* been sent to France, with the 51st Highland Division, and had been captured by Rommel at St Valery on 12 June.

Itching to get away from the cold and the boredom, to strike a blow in revenge for their regiment and do the job they had signed up for, Mackay and Gunn had volunteered for the 'Special Service' unit that had been advertised on their Part One Orders, and taken the train together to Galashiels. Here, together with an older Thurso man, 27-year-old William Campbell, who had been serving with the Black Watch (Royal Highland Regiment), they were told by their new CO, Dick Pedder, that they could stay together and form part of the 6th (Seaforth) Troop of the Commando, providing they passed what Pedder referred to ominously as 'The Test'.

D.D. Drummond, aged 25, was also from the Seaforths. A professional gardener from Peebles, 18 miles from Galashiels, he joined 11 Commando 'to get excitement'. He had put his name down for Special Service weeks previously while with his regiment at Torres in the north of Scotland.

'We were on Church Parade one Sunday,' he said, 'and when we came back, the officer in charge said, "We want volunteers for a special unit. You must be immune from sea-sickness, able to swim, and drive any kind of car." Well I could only swim a wee bit so that was me out, but all my mates handed in their names before 3 o'clock. About ten to three I put my name down.'[8]

There was a substantial contingent from the Black Watch, including John Herd from Arran, Sergeant John McCulloch from Lancaster and 35-year-old Sergeant Charles Bruce, who had been brought up in Australia and had worked there as a miner before returning to Scotland to join the army.

Lance Bombardier Joseph Kearney was a Canadian from St John's in Newfoundland; in civilian life he had worked first as a customs clerk for the Newfoundland Civil Service, then for the Department of Natural Resources. He had enlisted in the Royal Artillery in March 1940, using a false birth certificate, and had arrived in Britain in April with the 57th (Newfoundland) Heavy Regiment. R.A. Kearney was one of 20 prospective recruits for 11 Commando from Newfoundland, only five of whom were to stay the course.

Sergeant Jack Terry and Charles Lock were English, the former a regular soldier from Nottingham who had been evacuated with his Royal Artillery battery from Dunkirk. Terry, who had also lied about his age, had been a butcher's boy in Civvie Street; he was 16 when he enlisted in the army to get away from a stepfather he despised. Lock, 29, was from Canterbury; he played rugby for the city and his father owned a shop selling musical instruments. Lock joined the London Scottish, a Territorial battalion of the Gordon Highlanders, and was sent for basic training to the Gordon Highlanders' Depot in Aberdeen. Among his 90 comrades were the huge Robert Tait, and John Anderson, a Londoner originally from Aberdeen. Though Anderson believed he had taken the right step by returning to his home town, August 1940 saw him, together with Tait and Lock, volunteering for Special Service and bound for Galashiels with another Gordon, Jimmy Bogle from Glasgow.

Malcolm Edward 'Spike' Hughes was 40, a reserved, stern-faced man from Chiddingford in Surrey, who had served in the Royal Flying Corps in the First World War and subsequently in the Grenadier Guards. Spike had married a London Irish girl in 1923, and they had four children. He was working as a London postman and sorter when the Second World War broke out. Despite his age, he had volunteered, telling his wife, 'If the bloody Germans are coming I want a gun in my hand.'[9] He had been posted to the Manchester Regiment after basic training and volunteered for 11 Commando, together with his friend Neil Sproule, also from the Manchesters.

Peter Barrand belonged to the London Rifles and had been brought along by his officer, Lieutenant Robin Farmiloe, who was soon to become 11 Commando's adjutant. George Dunn of the Royal Artillery was another Londoner; a sign-writer in civilian life, he was a marksman with the Bren gun. His friend, Jim Gornall, was the son of a Preston trawler-man and RNVR skipper; he had joined the Royal Artillery only to find himself manning a searchlight battery in the Orkneys – the most frustrating job in the army, because there was no way of fighting back. Gornall was originally posted to Keyes' No. 2 Troop, but felt out of place among the cavalrymen, whom he considered snooty. He was relieved when Pedder moved him to No. 3 Troop with fellow Gunners George Dunn and Lance Bombardier Terry O'Hagen.

Adam B. Archibald was 20, and came from Musselburgh, north of Edinburgh. He had received his call-up papers in April and had completed his basic training with the Royal Scots at Glencorse Barracks near Penicuik.

'When the training was finished,' Archibald said, 'the CO had us assemble on the parade ground, and asked if any of us would like to volunteer for 11 (Scottish) Commando, if so please take a step forward. I stepped forward along with others – that is how I joined. The reason was that the CO told us we would receive 6s/8d a day extra. What he did not say was that it was to pay for the civilian digs we were billeted in.'[10]

Denis Coulthread was another Royal Scot, a married man from Clyde-bank, who eventually joined No. 2 Troop and became Geoffrey Keyes' batman. Jimmy Lappin was a conscript from Dumbarton who had just completed his basic training with the 5th Battalion, the Cameron High-landers, at Nairn. After a week's leave, he and his friend, Hugh Canavan, a Glaswegian, took a train to Galashiels with a bunch of fellow 5th Bat-talion recruits, including Bill Pryde from Falkirk, John Phiminster, a married man from Campbeltown, Bob Fowler from Sterling, Charlie Paxton from Inverness, and many others who would go on to form 10 Troop of the Commando.

At Netherdale Mills, an ancient, dark, disused textile plant that had been assigned to 11 Commando as temporary billets, they rubbed shoul-ders with more recruits destined for 10 Troop, including a large contingent of Englishmen from the 9th Battalion the Sherwood Foresters, a Nottinghamshire regiment, among whom were Frank Varney from Nottingham City and Andy Simpson from Retford.

Bob Murray was an Aberdonian from the Highland Light Infantry who was fed up with square-bashing and liked the sound of 'special duties'. When he arrived at the Douglas Hotel, Pedder had asked him whether he could swim or drive a car.

'I said I couldn't do either,' he told his new comrades wryly, 'but he still took me. I suppose they have to take what they can get.'

Among the officers at the Douglas Hotel with Keyes were Second Lieutenant William Fraser, a Scotsman, the son and grandson of Gordon Highlander sergeants who was immensely proud to be the first of his line to serve as a officer, and two Irishmen, Second Lieutenants Blair Mayne, 23, a former rugby international, and Eoin McGonigal, 19, who had served together in the Royal Ulster Rifles; they had both been solic-itors before the war. They were as unlike as Laurel and Hardy – Mayne, a Protestant, huge and fair, and the Catholic McGonigal, compact and dark – yet they were close friends. Lieutenant Robin McCunn, 20, was a Londoner of Scottish descent whose father had been a captain in the

King's Own Yorkshire Light Infantry. A Cameron Highlander himself, he had attended Charterhouse School and Sandhurst where, as a keen all-round sportsman and athlete, he had won a soccer blue and set the pole-vault record. A fellow Cameron, 19-year-old Second Lieutenant R.T.S. 'Tommy' Macpherson, was a volunteer from a TA battalion who had recently left school at Fettes in Edinburgh. Like McCunn, he was a keen sportsman, fanatically fit, with a passion for rugby. Lieutenant Eric 'Judy' Garland was an officer of the Yorkshire & Lancashire Regiment; he had already won the Military Cross at Dunkirk.

Second Lieutenant Richard Carr of the Royal Artillery was a Londoner, a member of the Huntley & Palmer biscuit family, while Captain Charles Napier of the Gordon Highlanders was one of the famous Napier military clan.

There were, altogether, thirty-three officers. Fourteen were from Scots infantry regiments, six from English infantry regiments, two from the Royal Artillery, three from the Royal Engineers, two from Irish regiments and five from the cavalry.

Although of various ages and disparate origins, these men had this in common: a need to get out of the stagnation of the British Army under the threat of German invasion, and a desire to strike back at the enemy, hard. Dunkirk had bitten deep into the national psyche; the Germans, a defeated nation in living memory, had punched through a regular British corps like a fist through wet paper. The defeat had shattered many fond illusions the British had held about their army and the nature of war. The Commando idea was an attempt to dispense with antiquated traditions and get back to basics: an active counter to the monster of *Blitzkrieg*, for those who were not ready to wait passively about for Adolf Hitler's stormtroopers to appear.

For most of August 1940 Pedder and his instructors put the officers and men of 11 Commando through a gruelling boot-camp course. Immediately after reveille at 0630 hours, the squads fell in for a mile run and physical training. After a parade and inspection at 0900 hours, there would be a battle-march of eight to ten miles in full kit, with some fieldcraft, cross-country work, map-reading and navigation thrown in. The afternoon was taken up with swimming and more physical jerks, with a 45-minute lecture by Pedder to finish up.

Pedder's intention was to produce men who could march and run seven miles an hour in fighting order and be ready for action at the end of it, a unit which could cover up to 35 miles in 14 hours, in full battle order, and be ready to fight after two hours' rest. It was a stiff demand, and he ruthlessly weeded out those who were not up to it, whether officers or men. As his fellow officers departed with monotonous regularity, Keyes, never a star of the route march or PT session to begin with, began to wonder whether his own days were numbered.

'I am just working off my stiffness and getting fit,' he wrote to his parents on 16 August. 'We march and swim and do other violent things, so one goes to bed very weary and sleeps like a dog.'[11]

On 28 August Pedder paraded the boot-camp survivors and ordered them to march to Ayr, 100 miles distant. They had six days to get there, ready for transfer on 4 September, by train and ferry, to Lamlash on the isle of Arran. This was to be their final test, the one he had warned them about at the beginning.

The commandos were not dependent on support and logistics services: this was one of the radical aspects of the unit. They were free from the rear-echelon staff that weighed down regular units. There were no barracks, no permanent HQ offices, no cooks and no cookhouses. As Adam Archibald had discovered, each man was paid six shillings and eight pence a day (officers 13s/4d) to find his own bed and rations. That meant that the force was entirely mobile – it could be dismissed one evening and told to reassemble the following morning somewhere completely different, without timetables, movement orders or meals.

Neither were there provost staff or guard-houses. One of the traditions that would be continued by later special forces units was that no soldier of the Commando was officially 'on the books'; each belonged to his parent unit and continued to wear his own cap-badge. Since all were volunteers, the only sanction necessary was 'Return to Unit' – RTU – a disgrace the commandos came to consider worse than death.

The march to Ayr was a killing one. The instructors set the pace.

'We marched 20 or 30 miles a day and slept in the hedgerows,' Jimmy Lappin wrote. 'I changed my socks at every stop and washed through the pair I had taken off in a burn [stream]. Many of the men developed blisters and when they could not walk any more they got to ride in the transport that carried our kit. I remember them crowing as they passed. When we got to Ayr they were all RTU'd.'[12]

One of the casualties was Geoffrey Keyes, who dropped out on the first day, but whose social position prevented him from suffering the same fate. 'The first day's walk was rather a shocker,' he wrote home, 'as we started off from scratch with 11 miles nonstop in 3 hours, 20 minutes' halt for lunch, then another 4 miles in one hour. No joke: I finished rather lame as did most of my cavalrymen ... The CO sent me on the next day to arrange the night's bivouac, despite my efforts to be allowed to march. I felt pretty lousy leaving my chaps ... That afternoon ... I was sent on with the Second-in-Command right down the route.'[13]

At Lamlash, on Arran, the men found their own billets with local families while Keyes and two other officers rented a cottage near the White House, a mansion belonging to the Duchess of Montrose, which they also took as an officers' mess.

Lamlash was little more than a hamlet, and the men could be summoned easily from their billets by a bugle call or the blast of a whistle. Now Pedder started commando training in earnest. He continued the battle-marches, but day by day he made them longer, faster, and with heavier loads, until the commandos were bashing ten miles in only 90 minutes, in full fighting order. He trained them in advanced fieldcraft, infiltration behind enemy lines, street-fighting, occupation of terrain, concealment, crossing obstacles, rock climbing and cliff-scaling, with and without ropes, river-crossing and swimming in full kit. All ranks were taught navigation, map-reading and route selection; they were trained in night sense and night confidence.

Pedder and his instructors taught the men semaphore, Morse code and the use of the wireless. They learned first aid and the evacuation of wounded. He had them coached to excellence in infantry weapons – the Lee-Enfield .303 rifle, the Colt .45 automatic pistol, the Bren .303 light machine-gun, and most of all, the Thompson .45 sub-machine-gun. The Commandos were the first special forces troops to do live firing exercises, when ball ammunition was substituted for blanks, to give them the feel of a real battle. While they practised skirmishing, their officers and instructors would fire live bullets over their heads. Geoffrey Keyes was enthusiastic about this aspect of training: 'We … fire live rounds at our Soldiery now,' he wrote gleefully in a letter to a friend in November 1940, 'to impress upon them the horrors of war, and make them utilize the best cover. Most instructive and effective, and brightens training no end.'[14]

Keyes was not so gleeful when the tables were turned on him, as Gunner Jim Gornall, from Preston, recounted: 'If you showed yourself unnecessarily, Keyes used to put a bullet near you,' he said. 'So one day I put one near him. He didn't know it was me, but he knew it was somebody in the area I was … I thought, right you bugger, if you're going to shoot at me I'll give you one back!'[15]

Actually, Keyes was in a far safer position than Gornall, for he was a poor shot, while Gornall was an excellent one.

Keyes was too unpredictable and inconsistent in temperament to be much liked by his men, but Pedder was feared and detested. 'He was a hard man,' D.D. Drummond remembered. 'You had to have certain things in your battledress pockets: pay book, toilet paper, first aid bandage and a length of cheese wire. If the CO stopped you and asked you to turn out your pockets, and you didn't have these items, God help you!'[16]

There were cross-country runs, combat survival exercises, initiative tests and arduous climbs of Arran's highest peak, the 5,000-foot-high

Goat Fell. 'I think the CO loved Goat Fell,' Drummond recalled, 'the number of times we tackled it. You would be wet and miserable and glad to get back to the billet, when the CO's bugler sounded "fall in", and you started all over again. You would get back to the billets around 0300 hours, and be up again for PT at 0700.'[17]

Towards the winter they began practising seaborne landings in small boats off Clauchlands Point at the end of Lamlash Bay. Approaching hostile shores, securing a beach-head, re-embarkation: all these drills were repeated time and time again until they were perfect, initially in Troops, eventually with the whole Commando together, first by day and later by night. Eventually their small boats would be replaced by ALCs – Assault Landing Craft – which were flat-bottomed craft specially designed to carry the commando units. Each ALC carried a half-troop, about thirty men.

Although Pedder aimed to produce soldiers who were highly proficient in martial skills, and as fit as professional athletes, physical excellence was only part of the object. Fighting without the back-up of air support or artillery, and without heavy mortars, machine-guns or anti-tank weapons, his commandos had to be able to endure tremendous fatigue, to face overwhelming odds without flinching, and to persevere to the very end.

Since all the commandos were volunteers, and therefore committed soldiers, they did not require traditional discipline to perform well. While fostering an *esprit de corps* that came from shared hardship, and the mystique of belonging to a crack force, the commando course also emphasized a self-reliance and individualism for all ranks that had no counterpart in the traditional army. These men were not trained to be supermen, nor to *think* they were supermen, but they were encouraged to have supreme confidence in themselves, and to rely on their own initiative, rather than to depend on the leadership qualities of their officers.

This was revolutionary for the British Army of the 1940s. Here, on the wild shores of Arran, a whole new concept was being born: an idea whose aim was to break the mould of a thousand years of tradition. Consciously or unconsciously, it tended to erode the old values, the rigidity of mind, the blind faith in the old ways that had led to the defeat of Britain's army on the plains of Europe in May 1940. Of course, it was as yet merely scratching the surface; relationships carved in stone over countless centuries could not be jettisoned overnight. But for all its flaws, for all the ways in which it obviously fell short of its own idealism, nothing quite like the Commando had ever been seen before.

MINUS 11 MONTHS

January 1941

In January 1941, before 11 Commando had completed its training, the situation that had sparked its formation had changed beyond recognition. The Battle of Britain had been won and the threat of invasion had receded. The Prime Minister, Winston Churchill, having seen how poorly the first raids had gone off, had experienced a volte-face about 'the hunter class'. Now he favoured large-scale amphibious raids, using between five thousand and ten thousand men, to be planned for the winter: the existing commandos would be grouped together in a larger formation, known as the Special Service Brigade, for these attacks.

In the meantime, the Special Operations Executive had come into its own. An even more esoteric guerrilla force than the commandos, governed by the Ministry of Economic Warfare, it was tasked to insert individual agents – both men and women – inside occupied Europe. SOE's function was to raise networks of resistance fighters to gather intelligence, carry out sabotage and spread propaganda against the Axis powers. Churchill did not want the commandos treading on SOE's toes.

And, thirdly, though prospects in Europe were still grim, the situation in North Africa offered a ray of light at the end of the tunnel. In September 1940, Italian dictator Benito Mussolini had invaded Egypt; his massive force, under the leadership of General Rodolfo 'The Butcher' Graziani, had halted at Sidi Barrani, only fifty miles across the frontier. The British Commander-in-Chief in Cairo, Lieutenant General Sir

Archibald Wavell, responsible for defending not only Egypt, but the entire Middle East, the Mediterranean, the Balkans and East Africa, had been unable to oppose the Italian offensive for lack of troops. Wavell had bluffed it out and bided his time until, in December 1940, his commander in the Western Desert, Lieutenant General Richard 'Dick' O'Connor, had taken the field. O'Connor, a small, shy, birdlike, intellectual man, was currently fighting a campaign of dazzling brilliance. What had started out as a five-day reconnaissance had turned into a 500-mile advance, during which O'Connor's *Desforce* would eventually capture all Italian-held Cyrenaica, take 130,000 prisoners and annihilate no fewer than ten divisions. It looked as if Libya would soon fall too.

In these circumstances, a brigade of highly trained commandos might now be of more value securing key Mediterranean islands to support O'Connor's advance than on the European coasts as initially planned.

In October, Geoffrey Keyes' father, DCO Admiral Sir Roger Keyes, proposed a landing by the commandos on Pantelleria, an island off the coast of Sicily, which might be turned into a naval base and aircraft staging post to disrupt Italian lines of communication to Libya. The Pantelleria plan was shelved in favour of an even more urgent necessity: an assault on the island of Rhodes, off mainland Turkey, to prevent the Italians from striking at the main British naval base at Alexandria and to maintain British control of the Eastern Mediterranean.

On 31 January 1941, 1,500 men of the Special Service Brigade, code-named 'Force Z' and comprising 7, 8 and 11 Commandos and part of 3 Commando, were dispatched from the Isle of Arran to Egypt in two commando landing ships, *Glengyle* and *Glenroy*, fast merchantmen converted to carry the davits needed for hoisting ALCs.

It was on this voyage that the men of 11 (Scottish) Commando had their first contact with other commando units, and they were not impressed. 'No. 7 Commando here too,' Geoffrey Keyes wrote in his diary the day his men boarded *Glengyle*. 'A very undisciplined, badly officered mob.'[1]

No. 8 Commando's officers were, if anything, even worse. As one of them – Evelyn Waugh – himself wrote, 'each commando took its character from its CO'. 8 Commando did indeed take its character from its CO, Bob Laycock, who had been something of an adventurer in his youth. He had sailed from Copenhagen to East Africa on a windjammer; on another occasion he'd travelled to Australia and back on a Finnish grain clipper. Much bar-stool kudos was reaped from these experiences, but though Laycock talked a great deal about the initiative and self-reliance they could engender, in practice he belonged to the old school of officer privilege. His axiom – that one should be careful to choose the right man for the right job – actually meant choosing someone who had attended the right school.

Laycock did not believe in meritocracy. 8 Commando was supposed to have been raised from the whole of Eastern Command, but Laycock snobbishly chose his officers as far as possible from the Brigade of Guards. He recruited many of them literally in the bar of White's, believing, as Tommy Blackhouse, the character in Waugh's *Officers & Gentlemen* (supposedly based on Laycock), declares: 'It's going to be a long war. The great thing is to spend it among friends.'[2]

The problem was that many of Laycock's friends were also paid-up members of what the enlisted men came to call the Silver Circle Club, an informal assembly of 'wealthy, smooth-talking, playboy-cum-gambling young blades who appeared to have jumped on the bandwagon when [8] Commando was formed.'[3] These included the Prime Minister's own son, Randolph Churchill, a subaltern of the 3rd Hussars who smoked large Cuban cigars in his father's style, gambled and lost up to £400 a night (11 years' pay for an enlisted man), burst into tears when frustrated, and was unable to get on with anyone except Lieutenant Evelyn Waugh, Royal Marines, with whom he nevertheless bickered endlessly; Lieutenant Edward Fitzclarence, later the sixth Earl of Munster, who boasted on Arran of how he was going to shoot Germans down like rats but once in Cairo got himself a staff job, telling Waugh, 'You know, old boy, I don't like this idea of a spot being "forever England"';[4] Lord Peter Milton, Life Guards, who would distinguish himself by drunkenly shooting a pigeon through the window of Shepheard's Hotel, Cairo, shattering the glass, hitting a house on the opposite side of the street and causing a great furore at GHQ, and Lieutenant David Stirling, Scots Guards, who neglected his duties, gambled ferociously with poor card players like Randolph Churchill, and slept so prodigiously that he was known to his brother officers as 'The Great Sloth'.

Most of these men did not lack courage, and some later distinguished themselves when the chips were down, but many were incompetent and poor material for the special forces. Waugh himself wrote, 'The indolence and ignorance of the [8 Commando] officers seemed remarkable … there was very high gambling … boisterous, xenophobic, extravagant …'[5]

The 'Bar of White's' became a legend and cliché among the upper-class officers, reflecting precisely the right brand of 'easy-going non-professionalism' they wanted to affect. Laycock's specifications for commando training – that there should be 'comradeship between officers, NCOs and men' and that 'the soldier must think for himself, study the whole problem and make his own solution which he discusses with his superiors … Every soldier has the right to state his own views … and can give his own opinion'[6] fell on stony ground as far as the Silver Circle Club were concerned. Despite the knowledge that they were supposed to be in the process of 'unlearning their guardsman-like ways', old traditions died hard and many of Laycock's officers had no real conception of the new kind of force they were supposed to be helping create.

'For the officer must at all times set an example to the men,' wrote one of Laycock's White's Club cronies, Old Harrovian Lieutenant Carol Mather of the Welsh Guards, 'in turnout as well as in bearing, and he must be relieved of mundane chores to achieve this end if he is to concentrate upon the real business of leadership, where men's lives may be saved as well as lost.'[7] Mather wrote affectionately of a brother officer of

8 Commando, Captain Frank Usher, who once refused to go to bed in the desert because his servant, a giant guardsman he called Ethel, had not brought him his hot water-bottle.

That 8 Commando was entirely different from Dick Pedder's keen-as-mustard, hard-disciplined 11 (Scottish) Commando, was a fact that even Waugh, who was soon to become Laycock's intelligence officer, noticed. '11 Commando were very young and quiet,' he wrote in his diary, 'over-disciplined, unlike ourselves in every way, but quite companionable. They trained indefatigably ...'[8]

On the day the Special Service Brigade left British waters, Bob Laycock was appointed its acting brigadier. Redesignated *Layforce* in his honour, the Brigade arrived at Suez on 7 March 1941.

MINUS 8 MONTHS
April 1941

Mussolini's Tenth Army had surrendered to Lieutenant General Dick O'Connor at Beda Fomm on the Gulf of Sirte on 7 February, a week after *Layforce* had left Arran. A day earlier, on 6 February, Major General Erwin Rommel had been summoned to Berlin. At a personal meeting with Field Marshal Walther von Brauchitsch, Chief of the General Staff, he was told that he was to be sent to Libya. He set foot on African soil for the first time six days later, on 12 February.

Half of his *Deutsches Afrika Korps* – the 5th Light Division – had begun to disembark at Tripoli two days later, and had gone into action – against a British reconnaissance patrol of the King's Dragoon Guards – within ten days of landing. Rommel had been instructed to attempt no offensive until the 15th Panzer Division landed in May, but skulking in the desert for three months was not his style. He had persuaded his Italian boss, General Italo Gariboldi, to push his Brescia, Pavia and Ariete Divisions out east to face British lines at the Gulf of Sirte twenty-four hours before his *Afrika Korps* units had started to disembark.

As the German-Italian units pressed forward, with Rommel taking a bird's eye view from the Fieseler Storch spotter-plane he often piloted himself, he noted that British resistance lacked its expected fortitude. He could not know that they had been ordered to withdraw if attacked, but with that apparent sixth sense his men called *Fingerspitzengefühl*, he sensed weakness. He knew they would yield to a smashing blow.

On 24 March, while *Layforce* was still acclimatizing at Geneifa in the

Suez Canal Zone, Rommel's spearhead unit – the 3rd Reconnaissance Battalion – attacked the British forward position at al-Aghayla. As the wall of panzers and light tanks thundered towards them out of the haze of heat and dust, the Royal Artillery opened up with twenty-five pounder howitzers, and a battalion of infantry from the Tower Hamlets Rifles sallied forth in Bren-gun carriers, only to be virtually wiped out in minutes by a close combination of armour and screaming Stuka dive-bombers. It was the first time the British had come up against close air-support, and it was a sobering experience.

They pulled out east to the next post, Mersa el-Brega, and dug in, but a week later they were encircled by the 5th Light Division. Mersa el-Brega folded, and the next day German spotter-planes revealed the British withdrawing in confusion. Rommel unleashed all his muscle, German and Italian, on Cyrenaica for the knockout blow. It was 2 April. *Ultra* intelligence decrypts – the codename for the intelligence gleaned from the Enigma and Geheimschreiber signals – had suggested that he would not even begin to move until 1 May.

Rommel now divided his troops into three columns. The left thrust north along the coast of Cyrenaica to Benghazi, the right veered across the desert to savage isolated posts and sever the British escape-route at Derna and Tobruk. The central column – including the crack 5th Panzer Regiment – went for the jugular, rolling due east on Mekili and Msus.

It was not simply the speed of the advance that awed the British, but the shock of confronting a technique of warfare that was entirely new to them. British technical ingenuity had produced the tank in 1915, and by 1934 the Royal Tank Corps had developed a modus operandi for armoured units so complete that Germany's tank supremo, Heinz Guderian, used it as the basis for his panzer forces.

The theoretical techniques of mobile warfare that would become the German *Blitzkrieg* were developed by an Englishman, Major General John Frederick Charles Fuller, but while Hitler was building a new panzer army partly on borrowed British principles, in Britain itself Fuller's ideas were sneered at – except by Royal Tank Corps officers who were themselves despised as grease-monkeys by the great and noble. The tactics and strategy they had worked out were given short shrift. Instead of creating an entirely new armoured formation, the War Office had made the fundamental mistake of simply armour-plating the cavalry, lock, stock and barrel, in the fallacious belief that there was an analogy between the traditional roles of horsemen and those of modern armour.

'In rapidity of decision and velocity of movement the Germans completely outclassed their enemy,' wrote Fuller. 'It was not that the British generals were less able than the German. 'It was that their education was out of date. It was built on the trench warfare of 1914–18 and not on the armoured warfare they were called upon to direct.'[1]

While the British Army remained spiritually in the feudal era, German panzer divisions of the type commanded by Rommel were a mass *corps d'élite* recruited from a mixture of social classes, truly representative of an industrial country where technology was not a dirty word. German armoured units were not dominated by obsolete regimental traditions, nor by officers to whom tanks were nothing but armour-plated horses. The German panzer division was a highly flexible formation in which tanks, artillery and infantry were wielded in conjunction.

The British-held posts along the Cyrenaica coast went down like skittles under the German-Italian impact. When Mekili, an Ottoman fort on a desert caravan cross-roads, was taken, so were 2,000 British prisoners. Rommel himself was not there to witness this final triumph, as his Storch had piled into a sand-dune while landing him to inspect an 88 mm anti-tank gun. The gun, it turned out, was out of action, and the general was very nearly nabbed by British columns. He made it to Mekili in a commandeered truck in time to snaffle a pair of sand-goggles that had belonged to Lieutenant General Michael Gambier-Parry, commanding the 2nd Armoured Division. They were henceforth to become Rommel's trademark.

The withdrawal had become a rout. By 28 April the British were back behind the wire on Egyptian soil, from where they had ventured six months previously. Rommel, hard on their heels, was forced to stop short of Cairo and Alexandria only because he had outrun his supply columns, but he was already dreaming a dream that must have seemed impossible only a month previously. It was *Plan Orient*, a secret agenda close to Hitler's own heart, in which two German corps formed the arms of a vast pincer movement – one through Russia, the other through Palestine, Syria and Iraq. Such a movement would ensure the Germans' control of the Arabian and Caspian oilfields, and give them mastery of the entire Middle East.

5 OPERATION CRUSADER

MINUS 7 MONTHS
May 1941

April–May 1941 was a bad time for British Commander-in-Chief General Sir Archibald Wavell. The day after *Desforce* re-crossed the Egyptian border, his expeditionary corps in Greece was kicked out with the loss of a fifth of its strength. A week later there was a pro-German revolution in Iraq. The Middle East was becoming dangerously unstable and Wavell had no choice but to prepare an invasion of Syria, where the country's Vichy French masters were offering their airfields to the *Luftwaffe*. Then, on 20 May, thirteen German parachute battalions dropped onto the island of Crete, in the largest airborne operation yet attempted.

The Rhodes operation had long since been abandoned and Pedder's 11 Commando – now officially named C Battalion, *Layforce* – had been moved to Cyprus in April, earmarked for the Syrian invasion. Three other Special Service Battalions remained with *Layforce* in Egypt and at the end of May, two of these – A and D – were deployed on Crete, under Bob Laycock, to help contain the German assault.

Ordered to carry out raids against the Axis airhead at Maleme, *Layforce* landed to find that the combined British, Commonwealth and Greek armies – *Creforce* – were in full retreat. The commandos' role shifted abruptly to covering the evacuation of eighteen thousand troops. Night after night they fought a desperate rearguard action, going out in seven- or eight-man patrols, at one point reduced to fighting with bayonets. In the confusion the command post was overrun; Bob Laycock, with his brigade major, Freddie Graham, forced the Germans back by commandeering a tank. On 30 May, New Zealander Lieutenant General Bernard Freyberg VC, DSO and two bars, the grizzled First World War veteran commanding *Creforce*, gave orders that *Layforce* must remain until all the other fighting units were safely packed up on the naval transports. Laycock's men were not to fight to the last man, nor wait for stragglers, but they were not to move until Freyberg or his deputy, Major General Weston, gave the order.

Laycock himself was charged with presenting the British surrender to the German command, an order that, in effect, meant resigning himself to becoming a prisoner of war. It was the same order that Laycock would give to the medic, Private Atkins, on the beach of Khashm al-Kalb half a year later, but one Laycock thought quite inappropriate to follow himself. He tackled Freyberg's deputy later, protesting that he still had two battalions of commandos in North Africa and Cyprus depending on his command.

But all of the units on Crete had been fighting longer than *Layforce*, and the order stood. 'You were the last to arrive and will be the last to leave,' Freyberg told him.

At 2300 hours on 31 May Laycock stood on the beach at Sphakia with his Intelligence Officer, Evelyn Waugh, Brigade Major Freddie Graham and the rest of his HQ staff, anxiously surveying the embarkation of the defeated *Creforce* troops. An hour earlier, Waugh had recorded in the *Layforce* War Diary that as all fighting forces were ready to go, and there was no contact with the Germans, Laycock considered himself justified in ordering his commandos to withdraw to the beach, ready for their own embarkation. His instruction, sent by Waugh's batman, Private Tanner, did not reach Lieutenant Colonel George Young, commanding *Layforce*'s D Battalion, until almost midnight, and by then it was too late. Tanner himself returned to the beach to find that Laycock, Waugh, and the others had already skedaddled; he managed to get on board a landing craft by the skin of his teeth. Laycock's last act had been to dispatch the surrender document to Young, an officer of the Royal Engineers who

1955, is dedicated to Laycock, but when Ann Fleming, a friend of Waugh's, suggested the dedication was ironic, and that Laycock was the basis for his character Ivor Claire, a Household Cavalry officer who deserts his soldiers on Crete, Waugh was quick to deny the charge, telling her bluntly, 'Fuck You.'

'If she breathes a suspicion of this cruel fact,' he wrote in his diary, 'it will be the end of our friendship.'[3]

Six hundred of the eight hundred commandos under Laycock's command were killed or captured on Crete. Of the 156 men who escaped, 23 were officers.

MINUS 6 MONTHS
June 1941

On the day Laycock and Waugh stood on the beach at Sphakia watching the retreat, Dick Pedder was in Palestine, being briefed on 11 Commando's role in Commander-in-Chief Wavell's forthcoming invasion of Syria. Four days later, Geoffrey Keyes, now Pedder's Second-in-Command, received a coded message. He and 485 men of the Commando were instructed to embark on the British destroyers *Ilex* and *Hotspur* in the early hours of 4 June. They were bound for Port Said; the operation was due to kick off four days later, on 8 June.

The landing, on the Litani River in Syria (modern Lebanon), was 11 Commando's baptism of fire; it was also the first opposed landing ever attempted by commandos and was viewed with foreboding by the officers; this had not been part of their training on Arran. The original plan was for Pedder's men to set down on the beaches just north of the mouth of the Litani and secure the vital Qasmiyya Bridge for the Australian 21st Infantry Brigade advancing from Palestine to the south. The bridge was protected by a redoubt – an enemy machine-gun position, surrounded by barbed wire – and a little further north, at Aiteniyya, there was a second redoubt. To the north-east of the bridge, in the hills, was a military barracks from which reinforcements might be expected. The commandos were to hit all these positions from the rear.

The landing was supposed to go ahead in the early hours of 8 June, when 11 Commando's ALCs would be unwinched from *Glengyle*, but at the last minute *Glengyle*'s skipper, Captain Petrie RN, cancelled the landing. He was worried that the boats would broach in the heavy surf. Pedder argued that the risk was worth taking to preserve the element of surprise, but he was overruled by the navy. Instead, the landing took place the following day, by which time the enemy – two French colonial battalions – had blown the Qasmiyya Bridge and were on the alert for an attack.

The plan now was for one group of commandos to capture the French positions on the Litani River and hold them long enough for the advancing Australian Brigade's sappers to build a pontoon while, at the same time, another party would capture the intact Kafr Badda Bridge on another river five miles to the north.

The commandos were divided into three groups, one commanded by Dick Pedder, the second by Geoffrey Keyes and the third by Pedder's adjutant, Captain George More of the Royal Engineers. The commandos embarked on their ALCs at 0400 hours on 9 June with a full moon behind them and landed at first light with the rising sun in their eyes, in full view of the enemy.

George More's group, with two Troops commanded by Lieutenants Eoin McGonigal, Royal Ulster Rifles, and Tommy Macpherson, Cameron Highlanders, were allocated the most northerly beach, but as the ALCs carrying them closed to the land, two of them hit sandbars and foundered, forcing the commandos to clamber out into neck-deep water. Both of More's wireless sets were wrecked, putting him out of contact with the other two groups.

'We waded ashore in a heavy sea,' recalled Corporal H. Butler, a Bren-gunner with McGonigal's No. 4 Troop, 'over rocks, and each wave breaking over our heads and shoulders. We covered the last 40 yards to shore under machine-gun fire and advanced 150 yards inland without casualties, took cover and discarded lifebelts and haversacks as previously planned. Then we advanced in open formation due east ... I spotted a machine-gun nest at our rear and took aim. The Bren refused to fire, so I made for cover and stripped it down, found it full of water and sand.

Laid low for almost half an hour cleaning it. When clean I reassembled it and found the French MG post had moved.'[1]

Tommy Macpherson's Troop had been ordered to capture the still-intact Kafr Badda Bridge, north of the Litani. 'The terrain was absolutely dead flat,' Macpherson remembered, 'and the bridge itself was exactly at the point where the hills began. There was very little option but to make a frontal assault with such covering fire as we could give from our Bren guns. The distance was about three-quarters of a mile but it seemed much further. We advanced as we'd rehearsed in a widely spread order of individual, diagonal rushes.'[2]

It was lucky for Macpherson's Troop – and the various strays who had joined in the attack – that the French troops manning the bridge got cold feet and pulled out to a better defensive position three hundred yards to the rear. Macpherson captured the bridge with only a couple of casualties – Ben Hurst, a 26-year-old private of the King's Own Royal Lancaster Regiment, and Corporal Bob Mackay of the Cameron Highlanders, 28, who were both shot dead during the skirmishing. Macpherson himself was wounded in the wrist when a Senegalese soldier, emerging from a foxhole as the commando approached, stabbed him with a bayonet. Macpherson's sergeant, Charlie Bruce, Black Watch, the ex-miner from Australia, shot the Senegalese at point-blank range with his Tommy gun.

Once on the bridge, Macpherson's Troop worked their way to the defended position. 'The opposition ... was forced to evacuate,' he said, 'and disappeared in transport, leaving behind a number of casualties and all their heavier weapons ... during the assault an ambulance came up from the north side ... we thought they were evacuating casualties, but in fact it unloaded a heavy mortar. We soon dealt with it, but we were too near for the mortar to be any use, anyway.'[3]

But by 1600 hours the enemy was back in force, with no fewer than fourteen armoured cars. When they engaged 4 Troop with two-pounder guns and medium machine-guns, McGonigal's men withdrew fighting.

No. 8 Troop, commanded by Lieutenant Ian Glennie of the Gordon

Highlanders, had lost touch with Pedder's group on landing and had thrown in their lot with More's men. Advancing towards the Kafr Badda Bridge with Macpherson's party, they came under heavy fire from Axis armoured cars. Lance Corporal Bob Tait, London Scottish, was the first man of 11 Commando to put one out of action. Tait, the Number One in the Troop's 'Bomber Party', was carrying a Boys .55 anti-tank rifle with five rounds of ammunition. Taking careful aim, he squeezed the trigger and hit the armoured car square on: it immediately burst into satisfying gouts of flame.

Sergeant Jack Terry, Royal Artillery – the ex-butcher's boy from Nottingham – had also strayed from Pedder's group. Terry, only 19 years old, had taken command of a section of No. 1 Troop that had got cut off from Pedder and, together with some of More's party, captured a battery of 155 mm howitzers defending the Kafr Badda Bridge; the howitzers had never even opened fire.

As Dick Pedder's landing craft came in, south of More's, machine-guns started rattling from a point three hundred yards to the south. 11 Commando's Regimental Sergeant Major, Lewis Tevendale, Gordon Highlanders, a cool-headed professional soldier, saw orange tracer fire whizzing past the ALC. There were ragged salvos of rifle-fire, and suddenly the chilling wheeze of mortar bombs falling around them, exploding in spouts of surf.

'Immediately the firing started,' Tevendale recalled, 'the landing craft made back to sea, which resulted in about 75 per cent of the men having to swim ashore, or at least wade in water up to the neck.'[4]

Pedder's group was supposed to help assault the enemy barracks, then remain in reserve while Keyes' group attacked the positions on the Litani. On the beach, though, Pedder realized that Keyes' three Troops had vanished entirely.

Lieutenant Gerald Bryan, Royal Engineers, commanding A Section of No. 1 Troop, remembered racing up the beach and throwing himself into the cover of a dune. 'The men behind me were still scrambling out of the ALC,' he wrote, 'and dashing over the 20 yards of open beach. Away on the right we could hear the rattle of machine-guns and the overhead whine of bullets, but they seemed fairly high … Colonel Pedder was shouting to us to push on as quickly as possible … '[5]

Pinned down by machine-guns, Pedder's men monkey-crawled up a gully and ran across the main road without being spotted, cutting telegraph and field telephone wires as they went. They made for the barracks on the bluffs, overlooked by a battery of four 75 mm guns manned by crews from the Senegalese French Colonial troops. Great whorls of smoke could be seen belching from the guns, despite their camouflage screens, but their fire was directed not at the commandos, but at the Australian 21st Brigade, beyond the Litani River to the south.

Pedder's men advanced north of the barracks, capturing two ammunition dumps on the way. Private Jack B. Adams of the Black Watch brought Pedder the French flag that had adorned one of the buildings, but shortly afterwards was hit by a sniper and killed. He was 22 years old.

At 0715 hours, Lewis Tevendale, and one of the officers, Robin Farmiloe, 28, of the London Rifle Brigade, crawled to a ridge to spot the French positions. From the cover of the ridge, Tevendale saw A and B Sections of No. 1 Troop, led by Lieutenant Gerald Bryan and another sapper officer, Lieutenant Alastair Coode, carrying out an attack on one of the 75 mm field-guns. Sergeant Fred G. Worrall, Royal Artillery, and a handful of other men lobbed three No. 36 grenades at the gunners cowering in a ditch, so fast and well-placed that they exploded almost together in spouts of dust and smoke.

Worrall then led his few men in a screaming charge, bayoneting, or drilling the remaining Senegalese with Tommy-gun fire. Worrall, having learned which fuse to use from a surviving *Sénégalais*, opened the gun's breech, shoved a 75 mm shell in, slammed it closed and had the piece swivelled round towards the rest of the battery. With the help of his officer, Gerald Bryan, Worrall adjusted the pitch of the barrel, ranged the gun and fired. There was an earsplitting *whumf*, smoke, and a spear of flame.

'The result was amazing,' Bryan recalled. 'There was one hell of an explosion in the other gun site, and the gun was flung up in the air like a toy. We must have hit their ammo dump.'

Worrall was already ejecting the shell-case and ramming another into the breech. 'There was a flash and a puff of smoke,' Bryan said, 'in the dome of a chapel about half a mile up the hillside. A thick Scottish voice said, "That'll make the buggers pray!"'[6]

Worrall adjusted the elevation and fired again, this time rather low. It was too close for comfort for the enemy gun crew, who started to run. They were mowed down by Bryan's Bren-gunner. Worrall fired four or five more times and hit the two remaining French guns, wiping out the Senegalese crews. Within minutes the entire battery had been silenced. Tevendale and Farmiloe jogged back to the command post to tell Pedder that the battery had been taken out.

When Bryan called Worrall to move back to Pedder's command post, he spiked the 75 mm field-gun by breaking off the firing pin with the butt of his rifle. The two sections ran back to the CP, where Pedder told Bryan to give covering fire while the other sections advanced. The French had spotted them and were putting down a shrill barrage of rounds. Bullets whizzed past their heads and every time Bryan's Bren-gunner tried to open up, he was engaged by an enemy machine-gun post.

Alastair Coode, 23, told Bryan he'd located the machine-gunner, and grabbed a .303 rifle. As he was taking aim, a bullet whapped into his chest and bowled him down like a ninepin, coughing blood. Seconds later, when Sergeant Worrall was hit in the shoulder by an enemy sniper firing from a different direction entirely, Bryan realized they were under attack on two fronts. He ordered a withdrawal to the cover of some scrub a hundred yards away. Worrall broke cover and ran for it, but was gunned down – Bryan saw him fall with his face covered in blood. Almost simultaneously he felt something crash into him and knew he'd been hit himself. 'When I opened my eyes,' Bryan said, 'I saw that it was in the legs and decided not to die. I dragged myself into a bit of a dip and tried to get fairly comfortable, but every time I moved they opened up on us. I could hear an NCO yelling to me to keep down or I would be killed. I kept down. After a time, when the initial shock had worn off, the pain in my legs became hellish. My right calf was shot off and was bleeding, but I could do nothing about it, and the left leg had gone rigid … I was damned thirsty but could not get a drink as I had to expose myself to get the water-bottle, and each time I tried I got about twenty rounds all to myself, so I put up with the thirst and lay there, hoping I would lose consciousness.'[7]

Both Bryan and Worrall were captured by the French and taken to Beirut, where they were liberated by the British six weeks later. By that time, though, Bryan had lost a leg.

Dick Pedder, with Robin Farmiloe, RSM Lewis Tevendale and HQ Troop, had reached a ridge about 800 yards from the barracks when they were blitzed by machine-guns in nests they couldn't see. Tracer fire whizzed past them from sharp-shooters hidden among the trees that surrounded the ridge.

'The situation,' Tevendale commented, 'became very serious.'[8]

Dick Pedder told Farmiloe to run to Alastair Coode with the order to bug out to a more secure position, but Farmiloe came back with the news that Coode was already dead. Fire descended upon them from all sides, ripping up the earth around the mouth of the hollows and ridges where they had taken cover. Pedder told his men to pull out to the gully they had advanced up, intending to try and find Keyes' missing party, but as they withdrew, Pedder screamed, 'I'm hit!'

RSM Tevendale, not twenty yards away, dashed over to him, but found him dead from a bullet in the back; there was a huge exit-wound in his chest.

Tevendale went through Pedder's pockets for important documents, then finding nothing, sprinted back to Robin Farmiloe, who was now in command. Farmiloe had meanwhile marked the ridge from where much of the enemy fire was coming. He ordered Tevendale to take three riflemen and rush it. Tevendale attacked ferociously and had just cleared the ridge when a runner arrived to say that Farmiloe had himself been shot. The RSM returned with the runner, who pointed out Farmiloe's body, lying in open ground that was being strafed by machine-gun fire. Ignoring the constant fire, Tevendale worked his way out to Farmiloe, only to find the man was already dead, with half his right temple shot away.

Command now devolved on Tevendale. He got the remains of Coode's Troop – down to just seven men – and HQ Troop onto a ridge overlooking the road leading to the barracks. At 1300 hours, when the Australian Brigade's artillery started blasting back from south of the Litani River, Tevendale's party found themselves in the path of French troops withdrawing out of range. From the cover of their ridge they launched into the retreating enemy, Tommy guns and Brens blazing. Dozens of Frenchmen went down, but by 1700 hours, Tevendale and his men had been encircled and were forced to surrender.

Not long afterwards, the position came under heavy fire from British destroyers riding shotgun off the coast. Tevendale was glad none of the enemy was hit. 'Our captor was a very polite Frenchman,' he recalled. 'When our own forces started shelling the position, [he] told us, "Today you are my prisoners, tomorrow I may be yours." He was, but [at the time] I knew I would be shot if any of the Frenchmen were killed.'[9]

No. 7 Troop, part of Pedder's group, commanded by McGonigal's friend, the rugby-playing giant Lieutenant Blair Mayne of the Royal Ulster Rifles, had lost their first commando as they splashed out of the surf. 'We saw a lot of men and transport at about 600 yards,' Mayne recalled. 'I couldn't understand it as they seemed to be firing the wrong way, but might have been Aussies. There was quite a lot of cover – kind of hayfield – I crawled up to 30 yards or so of them and heard them talking French. So I started whaling grenades at them and my men opened fire. After about five minutes, up went the white flag. There were about 40 of them – two machine-guns and a mortar – a nice bag to start with.'[10]

Mayne and his men advanced inland towards the barracks and entered, taking possession of weapons, ammunition, grenades and a large stock of food and beer, to which they helped themselves liberally. As they were eating, the telephone rang. 'We didn't answer it,' Mayne wrote, 'but followed the wire and got another bull – four machine-guns, two light machine-guns, two mortars and fifty more prisoners.'[11]

Next Mayne's group turned due south towards the Litani, where they came under fire from the Australian 21st Infantry Brigade on the opposite side of the river. They withdrew, making a long detour, but that afternoon, as the Troop approached the river again, they were shot up by the Australians a second time. Tragically, another man was killed.

Meanwhile Keyes' group had been landed on the wrong side of the Litani entirely – the southern side. Gunner Jim Gornall, Royal Artillery, of 3 Troop, who was seated close behind Lieutenant Eric 'Judy' Garland of the Yorkshire & Lancashire Regiment, first realized something was up as the ALC neared the shore at sunrise. Garland, an astute officer who had won an MC on the retreat to Dunkirk in 1940, stuck his head up above the side of the craft and, after studying the landscape, told the Royal Navy sub-lieutenant in charge, 'You're landing us on the wrong beach!'

With true Senior Service condescension, the sub-lieutenant replied, 'I am in charge of this flotilla, and you'll go ashore where I put you!'

'If the navy-type had looked at the map,' Jim Gornall later commented, 'he'd have seen that on the north side of the river was a big farmstead and a big silo. And lo and behold, on the south side of the river – pretty much equidistant – there was *also* a big farmhouse and a silo. The bloody idiot had lined up on the wrong one!'[12]

Keyes had a fairly dry landing and didn't realize anything was wrong until he reached the top of the beach and noticed the masts of native sailing vessels to the north, rather than the south, where they should have been. It was deathly quiet and still as the three Troops deployed. Keyes, in action for the first time, was in a dilemma. The plan had been for the commandos to assault the enemy from the rear, under cover of darkness, taking them by surprise. Now they could either do nothing, or advance to contact in a classic frontal attack, against troops who were dug in behind barbed wire with artillery and machine-guns. This was not exactly what the commandos had been trained for: a frontal attack in daylight smacked more of the outdated tactics of the First World War than commando ideology. Then there was the river to cross: if they had attacked from the other side, that would have been unnecessary. But Keyes was geared up for action and was not prepared to give in so easily, even though it was obvious that the commandos would take casualties. 'It certainly was most dangerous,' he wrote later. 'I had to make a decision whether to try and cross or go home!'[13] He ordered his Troops to advance to contact.

Very soon they had the curious experience of passing through the lines of the 2/16th Australian infantry battalion, for whom they had been meant to clear the way, but who had actually arrived before them. The Australian CO was astonished to see them. Keyes took the opportunity to enquire if they had a boat the commandos could borrow; the CO was glad to oblige, but showed no sign of joining the attack.

Only minutes after passing the Australians, the carnage started. 'We were going through the Aussie lines,' Jim Gornall recalled, 'and the Aussies were saying, "Go on, Jock, give 'em hell!" And then we got a couple of hundred yards in front of them, and all hell was let loose – on *us*! We had no artillery support. The Aussies had artillery, but there was no one to coordinate it, because we weren't expected – we'd been landed by mistake.'[14]

The way Keyes himself recalled it, in his diary, was that a section of his own No. 2 Troop, commanded by Lieutenant Iain Robinson of the Gordon Highlanders, was on point and had advanced almost to the river when a red flare went up from the barbed-wire redoubt on the other side.

For a split second the commandos froze. Then they went to ground as the sky lit up with the flash and smoke of field guns, the clatter of heavy machine-guns, the eerie whiz and whistle of 81 mm mortar shells. The dirt around them erupted into mushrooms of dust and smoke as the mortars and 75 mm field guns found their range. Corporal John Padbury, aged 27, and his friend Corporal Harold Jones, 32, both Scots Greys who had been with No. 2 Troop since Galashiels, were killed instantly by machine-gun fire. Sapper Desmond Woodnutt of the Royal Engineers, aged 28, also of 2 Troop, was hit, and Private Norman Wilkinson severely wounded. Keyes threw himself behind a bush-covered bank with the sections commanded by Captain George Highland of the Seaforth Highlanders and Lieutenant Richard Davidson of the Royal Scots. Davidson and his men moved thirty yards ahead, but were soon pinned down by snipers.

No. 3 Troop, under Eric Garland and George Highland, skirmished forward about sixty yards, but could go no further because the ground was as flat as a billiard table. Jim Gornall described the scene: 'You could hear the salvos coming as you advanced. The drill was, down, BANG! – then up and off. We got near enough to the river, and the artillery stopped. There was a chap called Tom Kelly behind me, and there was a big machine-gun emplacement, and a 20 mm cannon, and two more machine-gun positions opposite us. Anyway … a head and shoulders appeared, and I thought, "I'll have you." As I came up a bullet pinged past my ear, and Kelly shouted, "They got me!" and he was on his back, rolling about, moaning like God knows what! I thought, "Bloody hell!" What had happened though, was that the bullet that had passed me had taken the heel off his boot. He'd had his heels up in the air when he threw himself flat, and one of them had been shot off.'[15]

And then two French destroyers that had steamed up the coast to the mouth of the Litani joined the attack. For a brief time they added their ordnance to the weight of shells that were falling on the commandos' position before they were promptly chased off by two British destroyers after a brief skirmish in which one of the Britishers was holed.

Keyes confessed himself 'Loath to leave bush for George [Highland's] position, as ground very open and sniped at.'[16] He sent Lieutenant George Duncan of the Black Watch back to locate No. 9 Troop, under Captain 'Johnnie' Johnson of the Highland Light Infantry, which had vanished. In fact, Johnson had been told that Keyes and all his men had been wiped out; he was preparing to go into action with the Australian Brigade. Duncan didn't return, but instead four gallant Australian infantrymen appeared, lugging the boat Keyes had been promised. They managed to get it as far as Richard Davidson's position, thirty yards ahead of Keyes, before one of them was shot dead.

Keyes started to crawl forward towards the boat, down a minute fold in the ground, with his batman, Private Ness, level with him. It took them 28 minutes to reach Davidson, and by that time Keyes had had enough of crawling. 'Ness and I start running,' he wrote in his diary, 'but I trip up after about 3 paces ... Fall down on the bank and Ness, the idiot, gets down too, even more exposed. We got badly sniped so I told him to run on to George, which he does safely. I give them about ten minutes to forget me, and do it in two bursts. Inspect Woodnutt and Jones on the way, both dead.'[17]

Keyes found Highland's No. 3 Troop 'quite cheerful and aggressive', occupying a little dell from which they were trying to deal with the snipers. Eric Garland, himself manning a Bren, was playing the dangerous game of drawing fire by sticking his head up over the edge. Having noted the position of a sniper who had already taken out several of his men, Garland promptly shot him with the Bren.

Jim Gornall and his friend, Billy Morris of the Black Watch, with whom Gornall had shared a billet on Arran, were firing off well-aimed shots from their Lee-Enfields across the river. 'There was another sniper on our side of the river,' Gornall recalled, 'and he'd already picked off quite a few. George Dunn, our Bren-gunner, had his Bren set up, and this chap was spotted by his Number Two, Lance Corporal Larry J. Codd, had helped create the Special Operations Executive, but who, of course, did not belong to Laycock's White's Club set. Young was, at least, awarded the DSO; Tanner, who had risked his life carrying Laycock's redundant and self-justifying message, got a begrudging MID.

The worst of it, though, was that the War Diary entry was phony: all fighting units were *not* yet away – the men of the Australian 2/7th Battalion, in particular, were patiently queueing up to get on the landing craft when the flotilla weighed anchor. They had been assured a place on the evacuation ships, but they never got off the island. Their CO, Lieutenant Colonel Theo Walker, never forgave Laycock: by diving in before them, he had clearly disobeyed orders. This was not out of cowardice – both Laycock and Waugh fought bravely against the Germans during the operation – but out of an inflated sense of his own worth.

Laycock never apologized. 'My orders were to go with the men,' he admitted later. 'But I am not sure that in cases like that a commanding officer should behave in the same way as the captain of a ship and be the last to leave. I attribute the fact that so many were left behind to bad beach organization.'[1]

Nor were Laycock, Waugh and Graham the only ones to abandon their men: there was no officer above the rank of lieutenant colonel among the 5,000 troops left behind. 'Not so much *sauve qui peut,*' one POW wrote bitterly, 'as a damnable and disgraceful scramble for priority, a claim to the privilege of escape based on rank and seniority.'[2]

Lieutenant Evelyn Waugh, though, never forgave himself for what had happened; he went on to portray the withdrawal from Crete in *Officers & Gentlemen* as symbolic of the collapse of the British ruling class. In a sense, it was. His own application for a commission in a Guards regiment had been rejected, it was said, because he wore suede shoes at the interview, but it was actually because he lacked the correct social credentials. He loved rubbing shoulders with Laycock's 'great and noble', but he knew he could never really be one of them, and his attitude to Bob Laycock was always ambiguous. *Officers & Gentlemen,* written in

Royal Signals. George shouted where he was, and hit him with a burst – splattered him all over the place. He did him really well.'[18]

Another 3 Troop Bren was out of action, its parts clogged with sand. While the gunner stayed where he was, his Number Two, Alan Reed of the Royal Signals, carried the clogged parts to a less exposed place, cleaned them carefully and brought them back, snipers' bullets reaming past his ears. No sooner was the Bren cocked than the gunner was drilled through the head and Reed brought the gun into action himself.

Keyes sent Jim Gornall to look for George Duncan, who had not come back from his mission to find Johnnie Johnson and 9 Troop. Gornall couldn't find Duncan, and decided he was not going all the way back to the Aussie lines. By the time he got back to 3 Troop's position, the cogs of command had finally got moving in the Australian ranks and their artillery had opened up. Keyes gave the order to advance the two hundred yards to the river under the cover of the belated barrage and by the time they had reached the phragmites reeds on the river bank the Aussie shells were falling no more than eighty to a hundred and twenty yards in front of them.

But by now they were only the sad remnants of the 150-strong force that had landed on the beach not six hours earlier. Of the Scots Greys Keyes had brought with him from Redford Barracks to Galashiels the previous August, Sergeant Ken Burton, 29, Lance Corporal Bill Ainslie, 28, and Lance Corporal John Lang, 20, as well as Woodnutt, Padbury and Jones, had all been killed. Private Ike Cohen – a Jewish medical orderly of the Cameron Highlanders, from Manchester – was also dead. Ten more had been wounded, some badly, and two were missing. Norman Wilkinson told Keyes later that when Ken Burton had been hit, Ike Cohen had rushed to help him, despite Burton yelling at him to 'stay where you are!' They had been shot and killed together.

Highland's No. 3 Troop had fared little better: they had fourteen casualties, including six dead. During a lull in the firing, possibly caused by the appearance of Blair Mayne's Troop on the opposite side of the river, Garland and six of his Troop got aboard the boat that had been carried up by the four Australians and paddled across to the other side. When they were ashore two Australians brought the boat back, but just as it arrived a French 75 mm field gun opened up, missing the boat but blasting a native sailing vessel moored nearby. The handful of commandos on the south bank was also enfiladed by fire, from a wall on the beach, but this stopped abruptly when Johnson's 9 Troop suddenly appeared in support. Garland and five of his commandos began cutting through the barbed wire of the redoubt with wire-cutters, while one man fired off No. 36 grenades from a launcher fitted to his rifle. Meanwhile Keyes, Highland and their men were lying almost in the river, being shelled whenever they moved. Another of Keyes' Troop, 19-year-old driver Alex Hamilton of the Royal Signals, was killed. One of the Australians, Corporal Dilworth – the NCO in charge of the boat – grabbed his rifle and started shooting back. Dilworth had already behaved with remarkable coolness, not only bringing up the boat, but getting it twice across the Litani under heavy fire.

At 1100 hours, a white flag went up over the redoubt. It was another forty-five minutes before George Highland and six men crossed the river to support Garland and take the position's surrender. By the time Johnson and the Australian commander arrived at Keyes' position on the south bank, it was all over. Garland was shouting across the river to Keyes that he had taken 35 prisoners, but needed reinforcements as he expected a counter-attack.

The Australian Brigade began to cross the Litani that night.

Keyes had come up against the monster of combat for the first time, and had handled himself well. He was not gung-ho by nature, but he had overcome fear by the deliberate exercise of willpower. He had also been ready to sacrifice his men. 11 Commando had fought with great tenacity and courage, but they had paid too a high price for what had been achieved. The element of surprise – crucial to commando ops – had been lost, thanks to the equivocal attitude of the Royal Navy, who had landed the main assault party in the wrong place, and too late. The navy's incompetence was, according to Tommy Macpherson, 'compounded by progressive snags that developed as a result of the long round-trip caused by the postponement. The landing was late and the landing craft hit the beaches in clear visibility after dawn instead of an hour or 90 minutes before.' All in all, Macpherson concluded, the Litani River action was 'a rather tragic farce.'[19]

Out of the 379 men who had landed, 130 were casualties – almost a third of the party – but by far the majority of these casualties had resulted from Keyes' order to advance to contact against a defended position in broad daylight.

'Keyes was the officer commanding our unit,' Jim Gornall – one of the few who crossed the Litani – commented. 'He had no artillery support. He hadn't recce'd any of the area. He knew nothing of the south bank of the river. And yet he made a frontal attack. There were three Troops of us landed on the beach – about 150 men – but only 14 of us crossed that bloody river. Not all of the rest were casualties, but a lot of them were. And that was down to Keyes and his frontal attack.'[20]

That frontal attack played no small part in the decision to disband *Layforce*. On 23 June, when the Commando was back on Cyprus – with Keyes now promoted to Acting Lieutenant Colonel, and commanding officer in Pedder's place, Bob Laycock paid a visit. He described what had happened on Crete, telling Keyes that *Layforce* had been stitched up and made the scapegoat for the bungled evacuation and that, because it had been so reduced by the reverses of Crete and Syria, it was to be disbanded on 1 July.

Keyes' 11 Commando would itself enjoy a reprieve, as it was needed to defend Cyprus, but if the invasion threat receded, it would suffer the same fate as the rest.

In July, Laycock flew back to Britain to plead with Winston Churchill for the reconstitution of a commando force in the Middle East. He carried with him a letter from Geoffrey Keyes to his father, Sir Roger, asking him to preserve the remnants of his commando troops.

7 OPERATION CRUSADER

Summer 1941: I

In mid-June, Rommel had defeated *Operation Battleaxe* – Commander-in-Chief Wavell's hastily prepared counter-offensive – after only three days of fighting around Sollum on the Egyptian frontier. Wavell, who had been pushed into the attack by Winston Churchill, had harboured grave doubts about the ability of British Matilda tanks to stand up to German panzers and 88 mm anti-tank guns. The result was devastating – by the end of the battle, 87 tanks were captured or destroyed, putting two-thirds of Wavell's force out of action. On 18 June, in a letter to his wife Lucie, Rommel wrote that the three-day battle had ended in 'complete victory', adding, in another note on 23 June, 'The joy of the "Afrika" troops over this latest victory is tremendous. The British thought they could overwhelm us with their 400 tanks. We couldn't put that amount of armour against them. But our grouping and the stubborn resistance of German and Italian troops ... enabled us to make the decisive operation with all the forces we still had mobile ... '[1]

Shortly afterwards, he heard unofficially that he had been promoted to Panzer General, and that his *Afrika Korps* was to form part of a much larger Italo-German force, the *Panzergruppe Afrika*, of which he was to be the commander. 'I am very pleased about my new appointment,' he wrote to Lucie. 'Everybody else in that position is a Colonel-General. If things here go as I should like them, I too will probably get that rank when the war is over.'[2]

Erwin Rommel had already come a long way for a man of his modest background. Born in 1891 in Heidenheim, near Ulm, the son of a local schoolteacher, he joined the army in July 1910 and had served for a year in the ranks of his regiment, the 124th Wurtemberg Infantry, rising from private to corporal then sergeant before being posted to the Military Academy at Danzig. It was here that he had met Lucie, a dark-haired Catholic beauty of Polish and Italian extraction. Her family were Prussian landowners; she was in Danzig studying languages. They married in 1916, but their only child, Manfred, was not born until 1928. Loyal by nature, Rommel remained devoted to Lucie throughout their thirty-year marriage, writing to her every day that circumstances allowed.

Rommel was a meritocrat; he made his way up the ladder by excellence. The British never produced anyone like him in the Second World War because their outdated military social structure would never have allowed such a man to reach the top. In the British Army original thinkers like Basil Liddell-Hart, J.F.C. Fuller, Percy 'Hobo' Hobart and Eric 'Chink' Dorman-Smith were feared, despised and sometimes – as in Dorman-Smith's case – knifed in the back. Cleverness was despised because it was a threat to a status quo where pecking order was determined by birth. Instead, there was a cult of anti-intellectualism among the Military Establishment, a 'Colonel Blimp' mentality that exalted the virtues of class, wealth, conformity and submission. 'Few poor men of great ability chose the army as a rewarding outlet for their talents,' Correlli Barnett has written, '... Therefore in a true sense most regular officers in the British Army were amateurs as well as gentlemen ... Cleverness, push, ruthlessness, self-interest and ambition were considerably less prized than modesty, good manners, courage, a sense of duty, chivalry, and a certain affectation of easy-going non-professionalism.'[3]

Such millstones did not hamper Rommel's progress. He was anything but an amateur – indeed, his colleague Franz Halder characterized him as possessing 'morbid ambition, ambition as a disease.'[4] (Rommel, in turn, called Halder 'a bloody fool'.) Rommel was an unashamed modernist, a soldier's soldier, a leader-from-the-front, a seasoned veteran who had not only survived two of the worst battles of the First World War, but had emerged with credit. As a subaltern aged 23, he had fought at Verdun in 1914, where he had taken on a five-man French patrol single-handed, shooting three and charging the remaining two with bayonet fixed. One of the French soldiers had put a fist-size wound in his thigh that had ended his charge abruptly, but Rommel had lived to receive his first decoration: the Iron Cross Second Class. Rejoining his regiment just four months later, at Ypres in Flanders, he led his company in what Winston Churchill dubbed a 'butcher and bolt' – kill and run – raid on a French-held blockhouse, to keep their heads down while he and his men caught up with the rest of the battalion, which had withdrawn without them. His initiative resulted in Rommel being the first subaltern in his battalion to receive the award of the Iron Cross First Class.

In October 1917, while serving with a Mountain Battalion in the Italian Alps, Rommel brought off his most celebrated coups. He scaled the 6,000-foot-high massif of Mount Matajur with a 380-man battle-group and captured it from the Italians. Later, he took the Italian HQ of Longorone near Trieste, capturing an entire division in a day, and was awarded Germany's highest decoration for bravery, *Pour le Mérite* – the equivalent of the British Victoria Cross.

Rommel emerged from the Great War a staff captain with an outstanding reputation for decisiveness, toughness and bravery. He was already being attributed mystical abilities: 'A 'feel' for battle, for the enemy's likely plans and reactions, for what might or might not work, which all recognized as being ... something peculiar, something apart ... it infused utter faith into the men he led. "Where Rommel is," they said, "there is the front."'[5]

Rommel joined his brother officers in swearing an oath of allegiance to Adolf Hitler in 1934: he was a personal admirer of the Führer, with whom he felt he shared a bond. Both had been infantrymen in the war, both had fought and survived Ypres, where Hitler, as a lance corporal runner with the 16th Bavarian Infantry Regiment, had risked his life repeatedly; he won the Iron Cross Second and First Class. Rommel also shared Hitler's contempt for the landowning aristocracy who had dominated the German Army in the First World War.

Hitler and Rommel became acquainted through Rommel's swashbuckling book of his exploits as an infantry officer in the war, *Infanterie greift an* (*Infantry Attacks*), published in 1937, which appealed to Hitler's nostalgia for his own *Fronterfahrung* – the battle-experience that he considered the formative influence of his life. Shortly after reading it, the Führer posted Rommel to his private staff, where he became friendly with Propaganda Minister Josef Goebbels and Holocaust architect Heinrich Himmler. These connections stood Rommel in good stead, socially as well as professionally, and when war was declared in 1939 he accompanied the Führer as he followed his troops' advance into Poland by private train.

But Rommel chafed at the bit for combat. In 1940, now a major general, he asked for command of an armoured division. Grasping the principles of *Blitzkrieg* as if born to them, he headed the 7th Panzer Division in the German advance across France, manoeuvring it so fast and skilfully, turning up behind enemy lines so unexpectedly, that it acquired the sobriquet 'Ghost Division'. Capturing no fewer than 97,000 prisoners, including 10,000 British troops of the 51st Highland Division, Rommel took the Channel port of Cherbourg on 19 June 1940. A general armistice with France followed four days later.

The success of the 7th Panzer Division was excellent publicity for propaganda-chief Goebbels, and Rommel was lauded by his superior, General Hermann Hoth, for exploring 'new paths in the control of panzer divisions.'[6] Hoth added a second mystical quality to Rommel's growing table of attributes: *Fronterfahrung*, a sense of the decisive point in battle. Other officers, less generous or less gullible, found his cavalier attitude to the rules irritating and confusing, and considered him individualist to the point of egomania – or, as General Franz Halder put it, a 'general gone raving mad'.[7]

It was too late, however. Rommel's star was in the ascendant and raving mad or simply unorthodox, he was the Führer's blue-eyed boy, and the sense of assurance and omniscience he exuded made him highly popular with the men. Articulate and reflective as well as practical, supple of mind, possessed of both physical toughness and an iron will, Rommel also firmly believed that the commander on the ground should be able to exercise independent judgment, exploiting weaknesses and opportunities as they arose in the fluid context of battle. Neither anti-Nazi nor anti-Hitler, Rommel had a real compassion for the suffering of his men that is the mark of the truly great commander.

8 OPERATION CRUSADER

Summer 1941: II

Erwin Rommel had been sent to Libya only to strengthen the Italian defences, yet by mid-June 1941 he had completely reversed the situation there. Infuriated, Winston Churchill sacked his Commander-in-Chief, Lieutenant General Sir Archibald Wavell, and on 5 July replaced him with Lieutenant General Sir Claude 'The Auk' Auchinleck, lately C-in-C in India.

'The Auk' had spent much of his active career with the Indian Army. He was 58 but looked younger: a big, square-jawed, tough-looking, dignified man with a direct and unaffected manner. An Ulsterman by birth, he had attended Wellington College and Sandhurst, obtaining a commission in the 62nd Punjab Regiment in 1903. He had fought in Mesopotamia and Egypt during the First World War, winning both the DSO and the *Croix de Guerre*. Although Churchill tried to goad Auchinleck into starting a new offensive as soon as he took up his post, the new C-in-C resisted, determined not to make the same mistake as his predecessor. Recalled to London to face the Prime Minister's wrath, he stuck to his guns, refusing to attack Rommel until he had built a new corps in Egypt – the Eighth Army – consisting of at least two armoured and one motorized division. Churchill declared himself unconvinced by 'The Auk's' argument, but the Chiefs of Staff *were* swayed and the C-in-C returned to Cairo having secured two agreements: first, that the new offensive, codenamed *Crusader*, would not begin before 1 November, and second, that the Eighth Army's new field commander would be Lieutenant General Sir Alan Cunningham, who had, in February, defeated the Italians in East Africa, and restored the Ethiopian Emperor, Haile Selassie, to his throne.

As he set about building the Eighth Army, Auchinleck began to understand that apart from a strategic crisis, he had also inherited a psychological one: there was a 'Rommel Cult' among his own soldiers. Not only did they think more of the enemy general than their own, home-grown commanders, they also regarded his ability to run rings round them as humorous. Rommel had become almost an object of affection.[1] One enlisted man commented: 'We all thought [he] was a bloody good bloke.' In late July, Auchinleck sent a directive to all his commanders and chiefs of staff, warning them of the real danger that Rommel's aura of invincibility was affecting British morale:

'He is by no means a superman, although he is undoubtedly very energetic and able. Even if he were a superman, it would still be highly undesirable that our men should credit him with supernatural powers. I wish you to dispel by all possible means the idea that Rommel represents anything more than an ordinary German general. The important thing now is to see to it that we do not always talk of Rommel when we mean the enemy in Libya. We must refer to "the Germans" or "the Axis powers" or "the enemy" and not always keep harping on Rommel. Please ensure that this order is put into effect immediately and impress on all commanders that, from a psychological point of view, it is a matter of the highest importance.'[2]

What Auchinleck feared most, though, was that Rommel would take Tobruk, the one Libyan port that had not fallen to the Axis during the *Sonnenblume* offensive in April. With Tobruk behind him as a resupply base, Rommel could then push directly into Egypt and seize Alexandria, Cairo and the Suez Canal; Cyprus could be nabbed easily in a Crete-style airborne attack. Auchinleck's Ninth Army under Major General 'Jumbo' Wilson in Palestine was feeble and would go down like a house of cards and there would be no stopping the *Afrika Korps* from over-running Palestine and Syria and acquiring the oilfields in the Gulf.

Rommel was, in fact, planning just that. At the end of July he was in Hitler's *Wolf's Lair* in East Prussia, presenting his proposal to the Führer and all his top commanders. But the angels were on Auchinleck's side that day, for his plan was rejected out of hand by Hitler's staff, who were preoccupied with the offensive in Russia and considered the North African campaign of minor importance. It was obvious, they believed, that Auchinleck was planning an offensive for winter 1941. Rommel's first job would be to repulse that offensive; when that was done, he could safely invest Tobruk without the risk of being attacked from the rear. They were against Rommel making any move against Tobruk until January 1942.

But Rommel was obsessed with Tobruk, and convinced that Auchinleck would make no move in Libya until the outcome of the Russian campaign had been decided. He had already received intelligence reports suggesting that the British C-in-C was shaving off troops from his Western Desert Force to strengthen his Ninth Army, based in Jerusalem. This news came from a highly reliable source: the 'Gauleiter of Mannheim', a German spy who had parachuted into Palestine in June, who was now working as a waiter in the Ninth Army HQ's officers' mess in Jerusalem. The Gauleiter's reports of troop movements from Egypt into Palestine were confirmed by an official visit by Auchinleck.

Hitler and his generals were quite right: Auchinleck *was* planning a major offensive in Libya in November, and what was more, he knew that Rommel was contemplating an attack on Tobruk then through *Ultra* decrypts, the intelligence garnered from the decoding of the German Enigma and Geheimschreiber signals at the British Government's Code and Cypher School at Bletchley. What the Desert Fox didn't know was that he was to be the victim of a Middle East sting operation painstakingly constructed by British Intelligence in the persons of Brigadier John Shearer, the Director of Military Intelligence in Cairo, and the brilliant Lieutenant Colonel Dudley Clarke, whose deception service, 'A' Force, was operating in the theatre.

The source in Jerusalem was in fact a double-agent – he had been picked up immediately on landing and 'turned' by Clarke's men in a Jerusalem holding-centre. Like the best intelligence deceptions, this one worked because it confirmed what Rommel wanted to believe. His pre-occupation with Tobruk led him eventually to dismiss all further reports of preparations for a British offensive in the Western Desert as a cover for the real action in the Middle East. Though Hitler had gone so far as to forbid any move against Tobruk before January 1942, Rommel, convinced that there would be no British attack on Libya that winter, decided that he would not take no for an answer.

As for Auchinleck: he needed to get rid of this troublesome opponent. Though he himself never considered a 'final solution' to the Rommel question, when it came, the idea at least fell on fertile ground.

9 OPERATION CRUSADER

Summer 1941: III

On 15 June, the day *Battleaxe* got rolling at Sollum, five men prepared to jump (with parachutes) from the door of a Vickers Valentia near Fuka in northern Egypt. The jump-altitude was 2,000 feet, yet the men had no helmets and were wearing only khaki drill shirts and shorts.

The Valentia was a mail-delivery plane, hardly suited to parachuting: the static lines that pulled the canopies open had to be attached to seat legs inside the aircraft, and the tail-plane was so low that a developing canopy was likely to get snagged on it. The first two out, Lieutenant John S. 'Jock' Lewes of the Welsh Guards and his batman, Guardsman Davies, landed with no mishaps, but on the second run, Private D'Arcy, of the Irish Guards, was checking his canopy in mid-flight when his partner, Lieutenant David Stirling, Scots Guards – the Great Sloth to his fellow officers – came hurtling past him in the air with his chute only partially developed. He hit the ground with such a crump that he was knocked unconscious; both legs were paralyzed. The fifth man, Sergeant Jimmie Storie, another Scots Guard, made a perfect landing.

The five men, all of 8 Commando, had just made history: they had completed the first recorded parachute descent on the African continent.

It was over the next few days, while recovering from his paralysis in the Scottish Military Hospital in Alexandria, that Stirling had his great epiphany: an idea which, while not entirely original, would eventually change military thinking all over the world. Stirling claimed later that the inspiration came to him while studying a map of the battle-zone – in particular, he was intrigued by the caption *Great Sand Sea* on an area of the Western Desert.

It was the metaphoric use of the word *sea* that induced his sudden insight. The commandos had been raised as sea-soldiers, trained to make attacks on enemy coasts in ALCs, but what if, instead of landing on the Mediterranean coast, they hit the Axis from the Great Sand Sea, on the unguarded southern flanks? Attacks from this direction on vital lines of communication – supply convoys, petrol, ammunition and water dumps – would be totally unexpected. Seaborne commando ops required large formations, Stirling reasoned – at least two hundred men, half of whom were wasted in securing the beach-head – and they could only attack one target at a time. But broken into smaller groups, patrols of five, for example, they could assault many targets simultaneously. Even if only fifty per cent successful, they would still have achieved far more than a conventional commando raid.

Stirling immediately started pencilling out a proposal for a new parachute unit to go into action during Auchinleck's November offensive. As the Eighth Army rolled forward, his parachute commandos would drop behind enemy lines and knock out Axis aircraft on five airfields around the Cyrenaican towns of Tmimi and Gazala.

The proposal, now considered the founding document of the SAS, shows the degree to which Stirling was out of touch at the time. The idea of striking at enemy lines of communication from the desert was hardly a great revelation: it was the principle on which Wavell had founded the Long Range Desert Group, and that unit had been doing an excellent job since September 1940. The LRDG, itself based on an Italian idea – the Auto-Saharan Companies – had long ago pioneered routes through the Great Sand Sea. It had raided the Italian post of Murzuk, six hundred miles from its home base, and had assisted in the capture of Kufra Oasis by the Free French.

The image of men dropping out of the skies on parachutes might have been appealing, but Stirling was ignorant of desert conditions. He had not yet understood the one key fact that mobility is the key to desert power. LRDG Commanding Officer Lieutenant Colonel Guy Prender-gast, Royal Tank Regiment, said, 'Once on their feet, a party of men in the desert can't get far.'

In fact, even the parachuting aspect was not Stirling's idea; his fellow commando subaltern, Jock Lewes, had come up with the idea first; he had tried to get his boss, Bob Laycock, to consider a parachute operation as early as May. Lewes, who had managed to get hold of some parachutes being sent to India, had proposed the very experiment in which Stirling had been injured — indeed, Lewes hadn't invited Stirling along on that inaugural jump, as he regarded the lanky Scots Guards subaltern with suspicion, one of the frivolous 'Hooray Henries' who abounded in 8 Commando. Stirling had gate-crashed.

Lewes's reservations about Stirling were well-founded. The son of a retired brigadier who was also a wealthy Scottish landowner and MP for Perthshire, Stirling had been educated at Ampleforth and – sporadically – at Trinity College, Cambridge. Even before the war, he had been unable to settle down to anything. His two periods at Cambridge studying archi-tecture had not resulted in a degree; instead, he had run away to Paris to become an artist. When his tutor told him that he would never amount to anything, he at once decided to become the first man to climb Everest, a project interrupted by the war.

At the Guards Depot at Pirbright he had been noted for both falling asleep during lectures and skipping orderly duties. 'He was quite, quite irresponsible,' William Whitelaw, a fellow cadet at Pirbright, said. 'He would simply ignore duties and go off to a party in London or wherever and he would invariably be found out … He was quite incorrigible.'[1]

David Stirling's brother Peter was Second Secretary at the British Embassy in Cairo and had a flat near GHQ in Garden City. Using Peter's place as a pied à terre, Stirling spent most of his nights in Cairo partying, lurching back to his brother's flat in the early hours, waking up with a massive hangover and, inevitably, missing parade. When a nurse acquaintance showed him how to cure a hangover by taking a couple of deep breaths from a cylinder of pure oxygen, Stirling even took to sleeping in an unoccupied room at the hospital itself so as to wake up nearer the cure. He was eventually caught there by an irate matron. At the time of the parachuting accident, he was due to appear before a Court Martial on a charge of malingering.

This is just one of the myths surrounding the man who would go on to found the world-famous SAS Regiment. Like many of them, it is not borne out by any documentary evidence. The fact is that in the British Army of 1941, subalterns of the Scots Guards, whose fathers were landed aristocrats, retired generals and Members of Parliament, simply did not get court-martialled for malingering. Stirling, a deliberate mythogeniser who told countless tall tales about the origin of the SAS, always liked to paint a picture of himself as a rebel and an outsider, but his behaviour was that of a privileged schoolboy who knew he could get away with it because his father was a friend of the headmaster. Brigadier Sir Colin Gubbins, the brilliant officer who virtually created irregular warfare in the Second World War and paved the way for both the commandos and the SOE, was never forgiven by the military Establishment for having sacked a Guards officer for incompetence: Guards officers could not, by definition, be incompetent.

The story of how Stirling discharged himself from the hospital in Alexandria and made his way to GHQ Cairo on crutches, bluffing his way past a sentry without a pass is as well known as the founding myth of the SAS: having eluded the guard, Stirling eventually barged into the office of Auchinleck's Deputy Chief of the General Staff, Major General Neil Ritchie, and persuaded him to read his proposal. Having done so, Ritchie immediately promised the 26-year-old lieutenant – who had just broken every military protocol in the book – that he would have an answer from C-in-C Auchinleck in forty-eight hours.

That no one ever asked how David Stirling managed to hobble the eighty-one miles from his hospital bed in Alexandria to GHQ in Cairo on crutches is of little consequence. More important is that Ritchie knew the Stirling family well; he had shot grouse on the Stirling estate at Keir before the war. It was not so much *Who Dares Wins* as *Who You Know*. In all probability Stirling had deliberately targeted Ritchie when considering whom to approach with his proposal; he knew that he would not be turned away because of their social connections. Keyes and Stirling had this in common: in both cases, social rank was the hidden factor behind their success.

Whatever the reason, it worked.

On 28 July, a cable was sent to London asking for approval for the raising of sixty-six officers and men for the newly promoted Captain Stirling's 'L' Detachment of the Special Air Service Brigade. The name was suggested by Dudley Clarke, the master of deception who had also come up with the term 'commando'. Lieutenant Colonel Clarke thought it expedient to let the Axis believe there were large numbers of airborne troops in the North African theatre. Like the name *Layforce*, though, Special Air Service remained only a paper title. To those who were aware of its existence in the autumn of 1941, it was simply the Parachute Unit or, more commonly, Stirling's Parashots.

10 OPERATION CRUSADER

September 1941

In September German forward interception stations ('Y' Stations) picked up wireless chatter from British lines suggesting that the South African and New Zealand Divisions were being moved from the Nile Delta to the desert front at Mersa Matruh. This information, coupled with the results of interrogation of POWs, indicated that a British offensive was building up. Rommel still didn't believe it, but decided to take the 21st Panzer Division – actually his favourite 5th Light Division, now upgraded – on a reconnaissance in force deep into Egypt south of Sidi Barrani. This operation, designated *Midsummer Night's Dream*, would not only sharpen his spearhead force, but would enable him to see for himself whether the British were stockpiling supplies in a forward dump, which they would undoubtedly have to do if an offensive was really near at hand.

Leading his convoy personally in a Mammoth command vehicle, Rommel was exhilarated to be once more at the head of a mobile force. He had with him his good friend, Major General Johannes von Ravenstein, the commander of 21st Panzer, a First World War veteran who, like Rommel himself, had been awarded the *Pour le Mérite*.

The column found no supply dumps, but the search nearly killed Rommel – twice. The whole convoy ran out of fuel – Rommel often pushed things to the very limit – and on its return, it was carpet-bombed by the RAF. Rommel's driver was hit and mortally wounded, and he himself was sent sprawling into the dust: a huge bomb fragment had sheared off the heel of his shoe, but, like Tom Kelly at the Litani River, the attack left him untouched.

Another bomb fragment had lodged itself in the Mammoth's tyre, unseen, causing a slow puncture that only became apparent hours later, when the vehicle was already separated from the rest of the column. It took hours to change the huge tyre, during which time Rommel was entirely without protection. At any moment the British could have appeared and taken him ... but they did not.

This only added to Rommel's mystique. By 16 September, the Desert Fox was back behind his own lines. He had narrowly escaped death or capture twice, and had himself captured an abandoned South African command vehicle containing papers suggesting that the British would retreat if attacked. These were entirely misleading, but, with the lack of supply dumps, confirmed Rommel's belief that there would be no British offensive, at least before the end of November. Rommel was certain Tobruk was ripe for the plucking. He decided that his only alternative was to fly to Rome at the beginning of November, consult with his nominal bosses, the Italian Supreme Command, and get Hitler's prohibition revoked.

11 OPERATION CRUSADER

August/September 1941

Although 11 Commando had managed to dodge the *Layforce* disband-ment order while in Cyprus, on its return to Egypt, on 7 August, the process of deconstruction finally began. Officers and enlisted men were packing their kitbags daily; some shipped back to their parent units, others to the Far East, or to alternative private armies like the Long Range Desert Group, Stirling's new parachute unit and the Special Boat Section. Eric Garland, MC – now with a second MC for his brave action in crossing the Litani River – transferred to the RAF for pilot training.

Geoffrey Keyes, now also the proud holder of both an MC and a *Croix de Guerre* (from the Litani action), was dismayed to see his unit disinte-grating so soon after he had acquired it. The bullet with Dick Pedder's name on it had landed him a command at the tender age of 24; he wanted to show the world that he was worthy of his promotion to lieutenant colonel. Thanks to his father, he had been given permission to retain a small cadre of 110 volunteers; if these remnants of 11 Commando were also taken away, he would revert back to the rank of major and be obliged to return, as a virtual nobody, to the Scots Greys, or to Staff College in Britain. He would probably never get another chance of glory at the sharp end. What he needed was a major PR coup that would vindicate the very existence of his unit, and push GHQ into giving him both reinforcement and support.[1]

Some time in September, Keyes discovered that Rommel had been spotted by Arab agents at an HQ in Beda Littoria, six hundred feet up the escarpment of the Jebel al-Akhdar, or Green Mountain, in Cyrenaica. Though Beda was some two hundred and fifty miles behind Axis lines, it lay only eighteen miles from the coast, an easy day's march for trained commandos. Landed by sea with the element of surprise, a special forces unit could strike inland, right into the heart of the *Afrika Korps*. They could even snatch Rommel himself – or kill him.

Keyes first heard of Rommel's HQ through the grapevine at GHQ Middle East Forces. It was lucky that an acquaintance – a fellow officer of the Royal Scots Greys, Lieutenant Colonel Henry J. 'Kid' Cator – was Second-in-Command of a secret intelligence cell there known as G(R). Originally the Cairo branch of MI(R), Military Intelligence Research, a War Office department responsible for irregular warfare, G(R) was now part of the Special Operations Executive. It was the cover name for the Directorate of Special Operations, one of SOE's four directorates in Cairo, headed by Lieutenant Colonel Terence Airey (Durham Light Infantry and Egyptian Army).

'Kid' Cator, his understrapper, was a First World War veteran who was awarded the MC serving with the Greys on the Western Front in 1915. Although he had left the army in the 1920s to look after his estate at Sandringham – the Royal Family were his close neighbours – he rejoined his regiment in 1939 as a very senior lieutenant. He was in Palestine, quelling Arab dissidents, when he encountered the 22-year-old Lieutenant Geoffrey Keyes. Cator stayed on in the region to raise a labour company of Palestinian troops, remarkably, of both Jewish and Arab origin. This unit, known as No. 1 Auxiliary Military Pioneer Company, was deployed in France in 1940; Cator had used his connections with his Sandringham neighbours to get permission to covert it into a combat unit – No. 51 (Middle East) Commando – in October 1940. With two other Middle East Commando units – Nos. 50 and 52 – recruited from British regiments stationed in the area, it had been merged with *Layforce* on its arrival in March 1941, leaving Cator without a job until he found a niche with G(R).

Lieutenant General Sir Alan Cunningham, 'The Auk's' new General Officer Commanding, Western Desert Forces, set up his HQ at Maaten Baggush, near Alexandria, on 9 September 1941. In early October he received a visit from Geoffrey Keyes, the army's youngest lieutenant colonel. Keyes, plodding and short-sighted, wearing spectacles that gave him a distinctly studious look, sported tent-like shorts, high socks and a Glengarry with pom-pom and a black hackle on the side. He looked an unlikely special forces officer, and an even more unlikely assassin. Tommy Macpherson summed it up: 'He wasn't everyone's cup of tea.' Not popular with either his officers or his men, he was shy and silent, lacking in warmth and, according to his sister, Elizabeth, was 'never much of a conversationalist. Equipped with the current string of artless clichés, he disguised his not inconsiderable brains in the conventional public-school manner.'[2]

Cunningham was thirty years older than Keyes, and he was very different, both in character and in appearance. A small, blue-eyed, beef-faced pipe-smoker, his amiable manner made him appear more like a successful businessman than a general. He was currently a little overawed by the enormity of his task. Early in 1941 he had fought a glowing campaign in East Africa, smashed a vast Italian army under the command of the Duke of Aosta, and returned the Emperor Haile Selassie to his Ethiopian throne. He was already famous in Britain, but his East African campaign had been a war of pack-animals, foot soldiers and improvisation, and his command had never exceeded four infantry brigades. Now Auchinleck had given him just eleven weeks to plan a campaign with two divisions of infantry and three armoured brigades. Cunningham had won both the MC and the DSO while serving with the Royal Horse Artillery in the First World War, but he knew nothing about tanks. His lack of experience in armoured warfare was causing him sleepless nights.

In such circumstances, the GOC would normally not have spared time for a lad hardly old enough for a captaincy, let alone the crown and pip on his shoulder-straps ... but Geoffrey Keyes' father was both a personal friend of Winston Churchill's and of his own brother, Admiral Sir Andrew Cunningham, Commander of the Mediterranean Fleet. Cunningham took the meeting and Keyes unfolded his plan to decapitate the Axis forces by killing or capturing Rommel. Keyes described the mission as distinctly 'dirty work at the crossroads', but it would also be a tit-for-tat operation: in April, Cunningham's predecessor, Dick O'Connor, the gifted corps commander who had crushed an Italian army five times larger than his own force, had been taken prisoner by one of Rommel's night recce patrols. Though it had happened by chance – O'Connor's staff car had got lost, and the German patrol had itself wandered behind enemy lines – it had been a major setback for the British.

O'Connor, whose plan of attack had been so original that Rommel copied it twice in his own campaign, was probably the only British general who might have outfoxed the Desert Fox, but by that October, O'Connor was languishing in an Italian POW camp. Now Rommel's main opponent was Alan Cunningham, a man who had never commanded armour in the field. Taking Rommel out would not only avenge O'Connor; it might go some way to redress the balance of the war in Africa.

The GOC need not have been surprised by the proposal; certainly Wavell would not have been. As early as 1936, Captain Harry Fox-Davies of the Durham Light Infantry had come up with the idea that troops specially trained in guerrilla techniques could be used to destroy the 'brains' of an enemy force – the commanders and HQ staff – as well as lines of communication. Wavell, then chief of an experimental infantry unit, had been sympathetic, and had allowed Fox-Davies to use his ideas on manoeuvres. So successful were his techniques that the exercise had to be called off.

Cunningham said later that he was impressed by Keyes' apparent enthusiasm at having a real task to perform after a long period of inaction, and by his coolness in the face of what was obviously a highly danger-ous undertaking.[3] He himself understood the risks of sending a commando raiding party behind enemy lines, but he also realized that if Keyes' stormtroopers could eliminate the bogeyman, it would demolish the Rommel cult, solving that problem once and for all. Cunningham's response to the initial proposal was favourable; Keyes' new adjutant, Tommy Macpherson, who celebrated his twenty-first birthday that same day, recalled how, on his return to camp at Amiriyya, Keyes had 'burst radiantly into our orderly room' and declared, 'If we get this job, Tommy, it's one people will remember us by!'[4]

Macpherson never doubted Keyes' courage and determination, but he was astute enough to realize that his CO had a major flaw as a special forces officer: he had something to prove. 'Geoffrey was, I'm quite sure, committed to what he was doing,' Macpherson said later, 'but he [was a] complex character, withdrawn to some degree. I think he was hugely conscious of his heritage and the need to do well in a situation where he was not terribly well equipped ... he was not strong; he was tall and, you might say, weedy in build ... he was slightly more "Bertie Wooster" ... than most of us. But because he was not a natural athlete-soldier, and I think he had a slight chip that he must do well: he was absolutely deter-mined to excel somehow as a soldier.'[5]

Keyes had won the MC in Syria, but in his own mind this hardly put him on the same level as his father, an Admiral of the Fleet and a national hero. What he needed was a mission with such a high profile that no one would ever forget it: the capture or assassination of Rommel would fit the bill perfectly. But it was not simply business on Keyes' part: to be worthwhile, he himself had to play the central part in the drama. Even though Bob Laycock entreated him, right up to the last moment, to delegate leadership of the mission, he adamantly refused.

By the end of October, Cunningham had decided on his strategy for the new offensive, by now codenamed *Operation Crusader*. Ignoring the lesson that German panzers could best be knocked out by artillery – the most excellent but least romantic of the British arms – he was going once again for a face-to-face tank battle. The plan was to lure Rommel into a trap, where his forces would be hacked to bits by superior British numbers. At the same time, he would be knifed in the back by a sortie from besieged Tobruk.

That was the theory. *Crusader* was to be prepared under conditions of the greatest secrecy, and was to get rolling at first light on 18 November. A few hours earlier, at midnight on 17 November, commandos would carry out two operations. One would be an airborne assault involving Stirling's parachute unit of about sixty men. Armed with incendiary bombs, they would drop from Bristol Bombays on five Axis airfields at Gazala and Tmimi in Cyrenaica, disabling as many Axis aircraft as possible. The second, *Operation Flipper*, would be a seaborne mission carried out by Keyes' amphibious commandos, sixty-three in number, who would land by submarine on a beach somewhere in Cyrenaica, play havoc with tele-phone-lines and intelligence centres, and, if possible, take out the enemy commander.

Keyes was delighted at this chance of glory, but his CO, Bob Laycock, was less sanguine: even if the raiding party did manage to take out Rommel, they stood almost no chance of being evacuated from the beach with Axis forces hot on their tail. 'When the plan was submitted to me as Commander of the Middle East Commandos,' Laycock wrote, 'I gave it my considered opinion that ... this attack, even if initially successful, *meant almost certain death* for those who took part in it.'[6] In spite of this view, Laycock had stronger reasons of his own for going along with the plan.

He had never been court-martialled for disobeying orders on Crete, but his reputation among his peers had suffered. After his personal appeal to Winston Churchill in July a commando force of sorts, the Middle East Commando, was reconstituted in Egypt with Laycock as its commander, but he railed against becoming typecast as a 'rear-echelon warrior'. 'I shall be bitterly disappointed,' he wrote in a memo to Auchinleck on 17

October, 'if so little is thought of my powers of leadership and of any experience I have gained of Combined Operations … that my future contribution to the war must be to run a sort of domestic agency whose role clearly will be to dish out small parties of specialists as required by other formations … I should have no prospect of fighting myself and think that such an appointment could be equally well filled by an older and less active officer.'[7]

Operation Flipper did not require an officer of Laycock's level and there was no military justification for his presence on the mission. He clearly went along for his own private purpose, that purpose almost certainly connected with what had happened on Crete six months earlier. To join Keyes as an observer – to hold the beach-head while Keyes did the dirty work at the crossroads – would suit him admirably, and help to remove the blot from his copybook. 'Laycock was, in our eyes a "society cavalry-man",' Tommy Macpherson wrote, 'with a close and exclusive interest in his own career: he was a bullshitter of the highest order. For him the Rommel Raid was a no-lose situation. If it was successful then by going along he would get the credit, and if it wasn't then, by staying on the beach, he would almost certainly be in a position to get out.'[8]

12 OPERATION CRUSADER

September/October 1941

In his 17 October memo to Commander-in-Chief General Auchinleck, Bob Laycock expressed approval for the progress of Stirling's Parashots, who were still officially under his command. 'The parachutists ... are already well advanced in their training,' he wrote, 'and in my opinion, when properly equipped will constitute a unit of some potential.'[1] The satisfactory progress of SAS training was not, as Laycock might have preferred to think, the product of his 'smart set' friend Stirling's new-found management skills, but the gift of Lieutenant Jock Lewes, who had finally been persuaded to join the unit at the end of August.

Though an 8 Commando officer, Lewes was certainly not one of the Silver Circle Club. The son of a chartered accountant, he had been brought up near Sydney, Australia, and had read Modern Greats at Christ Church, Oxford, where he had also been President of the University Rowing Club. He had won a Blue in the 1937 boat-race: his team had beaten Cambridge by three lengths, after a long string of Cambridge wins. Lewes, a thinking man's soldier who looked like someone incessantly trying to solve a chess problem, was, Stirling admitted, the finest leader he had met. Carol Mather wrote that Lewes stood alone in 8 Commando Officers' Mess, among the 'effortless ease and nonchalance, surveying his companions knocking back their pink gins and muttering into his beer that, after the war, "all this would change", meaning that society would change and us with it.'[2]

Tall, slim and classically handsome, Jock Lewes was one exception to the rule. 'He was the very opposite of many in our party,' Mather said. 'He had an inventive and creative mind … It was the combination of single-mindedness, inventive skill, improvisation combined with leadership qualities that marked him as a man apart.'[3]

Lewes's reluctance to join the fledgling SAS was not because of any opposition to Stirling's ideas – which were in part his own – but by the suspicion that Stirling himself lacked commitment. 'I think Jock wanted to be sure that if we got the thing working, I was going to stay with it,' Stirling admitted, 'and also tackle the enormous problems at [GHQ] which he possibly foresaw more clearly than me … Jock was a serious sort of chap, he could be very short on humour and I suppose I'd come across to him in the past as a sort of good-time Charlie. You wouldn't, for instance, find Jock catching a quick drink in Cairo or taking a flutter at the racecourse.'[4]

What Lewes did not realize at first was that Stirling was one of those talented people who go to seed unless they are challenged. He was highly challenged now, and pulling out all the stops with GHQ, finding, just as Geoffrey Keyes was to discover shortly, that the middle-management officers were anything but amenable unless General Ritchie himself was leaning on them. Naturally, in Stirling's case as well as Keyes', they resented young whippersnappers who had obviously been given their head by dint of social connections: Stirling called them *layers of fossilized shit*. However, Lewes and Stirling together complemented each other perfectly: Lewes organized the unit from within and Stirling from without. The SAS probably owed its existence to both in equal measure, and to the third of the triumvirate who was soon to join them.

Training started at the beginning of September. The men were not told the objective of the raid, only that they would get a good crack at the Hun. At first the emphasis was on personal initiative and endurance. The flaw in commando training up to now had been that there was no real objective standard: officers and men had been selected on the *he's a good chap* basis, and they were often RTU'd simply because their faces didn't fit.

In the SAS, though, training was to be a pass/fail affair, with no back doors for favoured officers: all ranks would have to achieve precisely the same standard, and those who fell short would be RTU'd. There were to be no officers' servants to bring them hot water-bottles and bedtime toddies. There would be no passengers in the SAS.

Although Lewes and Stirling initially disagreed over the basic unit – Stirling favoured a five-man sub-section, Lewes a ten or twelve-man unit – they eventually agreed on a four-man formation, which was to be called a patrol. Each man in the patrol was to have a specialized task: medic, driver/mechanic, navigator or demolitions-expert. Even more revolutionary, there would be no leader – the patrol would be mutually dependent on each other's skills. The fact that a four-man patrol broke down into two pairs of 'buddies', with no odd man out, made it ideal.

The belief that small is beautiful as far as military formations are concerned was Stirling's greatest single contribution to the evolution of special forces, and one that was entirely his. He, like many young soldiers of his generation, was repulsed by the mass formations and wasteful slaughter of the First World War; it had troubled Stirling deeply, even during commando training on Arran. Although he admitted that the commandos were as efficient a bunch of fighting men as the British Army then possessed, he had always felt a sense of nagging doubt. 'We plunged around the glens like one of the thundering herds of cattle I'd helped drive in America,' he told his biographer. 'It seemed wrong. There we were, being taught the art of silent killing and the like, signalling our presence to all and sundry as we ground forward in unwieldy groups of twenty or more.'[5]

In a small unit, the emphasis had to be on quality rather than quantity, so only the very best men could be accepted, which in turn implied a stringent selection test and no favouritism. Stirling was convinced that once he had the best men, the sky was the limit: with the right transport and the right weapons they could make an impact out of all proportion to their numbers. In this, Stirling's concept had the clarity of a religious revival; it was a resurrection of the original commando ideal, whose purity had been sundered when *Layforce* was used as cannon-fodder in Syria and on Crete. It was also highly progressive in social terms: men as committed and as well-trained as those Stirling envisaged would not need officers, or even leaders. In the First World War warriors had been reduced to serial numbers; in Stirling's army every man would be a natural aristocrat in his own right. It was revolutionary, and, in a sense it was the point at which Western military thinking finally caught up with a technology that had outstripped it by forty years. On the Western Front in the First World War the frontal attack had been the only tactic; Stirling and his ilk showed that there were more ways than one to skin a cat. For now though, the four-man patrol that was to become a hallmark of the SAS was a thing of the future.

Lewes concentrated on endurance marches of fourteen or fifteen miles across the desert by day and by night, believing – incorrectly – that men could be trained to go without water. All ranks were expected to be highly skilled in the use of map and compass, and were trained in first-aid and demolitions. The men practised weapons training, including the use of enemy weapons, until it became a fine art.

They also began parachute training. No one knew much about it, and enquiries sent to the RAF Parachute Training School at Ringway, Manchester, evoked only terse responses, so Lewes had the men erect their own training equipment in their camp at Kabrit – swings, scaffolding, training towers and gymnastic gear. Lewes had the idea of simulating landings by having the men jump backwards off the tailboard of a fifteen-hundredweight Bedford truck moving at thirty miles per hour. This was another mistake; this practice, rightly frowned on by professional parachute instructors, was highly dangerous and resulted in many unnecessary injuries, wiping valuable personnel off the active list. According to one of the original detachment, Corporal Johnny Cooper, Scots Guards, these injuries were 'treated with scant sympathy and a curt reminder that anyone permanently injured would be returned to their parent unit.'[6]

The men who made up the original SAS detachment were mostly

from 8 Commando and 11 Commando. A small cadre, including Johnny Cooper, Charlie Cattell, Sid Stone and Sid Bolland, had belonged to Stirling's 8 Commando Troop, which had returned to a Scots Guards battalion at Buq-Buq when *Layforce* was disbanded. Cooper was the youngest in the unit, one of the many to lie about his age to get into the army. He had grown up in Leicester; when he left Wyggeston Grammar School he had been apprenticed to a wool-grading firm in Bradford, but had volunteered for the Scots Guards in 1940, on the grounds that both his parents were Scottish. Ernie Bond, a married man with two children, and Jimmy Brough, both Scots Guards, had been NCOs in the same troop, and were also sought out by Stirling for the SAS. Corporal Bob Bennett, a pale-complexioned, thin-faced Grenadier, was an almost stereotype Cockney, with rapier-like repartee, quick wits and a tendency to play the barrack-room lawyer. Corporal Dave Kershaw, Grenadier Guards, had seen service in the Spanish Civil War, where he had fought with the International Brigade, as had an ex-11 Commando private, Chick McCormack.

The 11 Commando men were particularly welcome: unlike the majority of the 8 Commando men, they had all seen combat at the Litani River. Billy Morris, Black Watch, had been with 3 Troop on Keyes's near-suicidal advance to contact south of the Litani. Corporals Bob Tait and the giant Sergeant John Cheyne, were both Gordon Highlanders from 11 Commando who had fought at the Kafr Badda Bridge, where Tait had put an armoured car out of action with an anti-tank rifle. In the same fighting Cheyne had taken over command of a troop from Bill Fraser, whose helmet had been hit by a bullet and who was dizzy with concussion. Private Douglas Keith, aged 21, Sergeant Jeffrey Duvivier and Corporal Jock Byrne were all Gordons from 11 Commando. Privates Kenneth Warburton and Joseph Duffy were both Seaforth Highlanders from Dick Pedder's 6 Troop at the Litani. Reginald Seekings was an ex-8 Commando man, a short, stocky, ex-boxer from East Anglia who had served in the Cambridge Rifles, while Corporal Leslie Brown was an ex-11 Commando trooper originally from the Duke of Cornwall's Light

Infantry. Malvern Nixon, 22, was a Royal Scot who had joined 11 Commando with his mates Denis Coulthread and Adam Archibald.

Stirling had brought along his own henchmen; so had Lewes: Sergeant Jim Almonds, an exceptionally tall Coldstream Guardsman, 26 years old, the son of a Lincolnshire smallholder and a professional soldier who had been in the army since 1932, was one of the so-called Tobruk Four with whom Lewes had already carried out several behind-the-lines capers in besieged Tobruk. The other three were Sergeant Jim Blakeney, Grenadier Guards, an ex-trawlerman from Grimsby, Sergeant Pat Riley, a six-foot Coldstreamer – a great bull of a man, an American from Wisconsin brought up in Britain, and Bob Lilley, a 40-year-old married man, also from the Grenadier Guards.

Lieutenant Bill Fraser, the reserved yet highly capable son of a Gordon Highlander sergeant, was himself with the SAS, together with another 11 Commando officer, Eoin McGonigal, a small, dark-haired solicitor from the Irish Republic.

It was almost certainly Eoin McGonigal who suggested to Stirling that he should take on another officer of 11 Commando, Blair 'Paddy' Mayne – his best friend – who had distinguished himself at the Litani River action in June and been Mentioned in Dispatches. Stirling, who had not yet heard a shot fired in anger himself, was keen to recruit officers who had already experienced battle, and agreed to have a word with Mayne.

Their first meeting was another milestone in the creation of a legend.

Lieutenant Robert Blair Mayne – Paddy – was the same age as Geoffrey Keyes, but his opposite in many ways. His middle-class family came from Newtownards in Northern Ireland; he had studied law at Queens College, Belfast, and was a solicitor by profession. Immensely fit, fast and powerful, Mayne was both an Irish Universities heavyweight boxing champion, and a rugby international – capped six times for Ireland, and once for the British Lions on their South African tour in 1938, when his scrum-work had been called outstanding.

Mayne had done time as a subaltern in the Royal Artillery's 5th Light Anti-Aircraft Battery before transferring to the Royal Ulster Rifles then, later, to the Cameronians en route to 11 (Scottish) Commando. He was superb in action, but he had a dark and irrational side. Shy and introverted, with an ingrained resentment of authority, particularly of the upper classes, he 'instinctively recoiled,' as his biographers have put it, 'from what he regarded as the "snooty" public-school type.'[7]

'Few people got to know him really well,' one comrade wrote. 'He was shy of newcomers and had a strong natural reserve from which, with most people, he rarely emerged. When he did, they found he possessed more than his fair share of wit and charm.'[8]

Mayne also had a habit of erupting into uncontrollable fits of what David Stirling later described as satanic ferocity. This was all very well when he was fighting the enemy, but less appropriate with his fellow officers, at whom he had been known to take pot-shots with a pistol. The only person who seemed to be able to control him in this mood was McGonigal, who would point a revolver at him just as he was about to go off and warn him, 'I'll shoot you, Blair!'

Mayne's irrational bursts of fury were almost certainly a result of repressed sexual drives: he deliberately shunned the society of women and had no recorded relationship with the opposite sex. 'A creative urge within the recesses of his subconscious mind was constantly seeking expression without achieving it,' David Stirling commented cryptically years later. 'It got bottled up to an intolerable level and this led to some of his heavy drinking bouts in an attempt to open the closed door ... this frustration explained some of his violent acts and black moods. Among its positive effects it also explained Paddy's astonishing intuition and inspiration in battle.'[9]

Stirling liked to give a cowboyesque flavour to their first meeting – this encounter of giants – by intimating that Mayne was in jail at the time, and that he had sprung him out in return for Mayne's promise that he would serve with the SAS. Stirling also suggested that though Mayne was suspicious of him at first, he managed to bring him round and extract from him an assurance that he would not do to him what he had apparently done to his previous commanding officer. Rumour had it that Mayne was in clink because, one night in the mess he had knocked out Geoffrey Keyes.

Certainly there was antipathy between Mayne and Keyes. Mayne, who detested the Bertie Wooster type anyway, believed that Keyes had achieved his promotion through nepotism alone; a man of Keyes' obvious physical limitations should not have been in the commandos at all, let alone as a commanding officer. Mayne had been with 11 Commando on that first gruelling march from Galashiels to Ayr in 1940, when Keyes had only completed half the trek. Instead of being RTU'd, he had eventually been promoted to Second-in-Command.

There were two versions of what had happened: the first had it that Mayne and McGonigal were placidly playing chess in the mess tent at Salamis on Cyprus one night shortly after surviving the Litani 'horlicks' – or cock-up – when Keyes had pompously objected, upon which Mayne had simply swung his ham-like fists and knocked him down. The second claimed that it was Keyes who was playing chess when Mayne staggered up drunk and insulted both Keyes and the game of chess itself. When Keyes rose to say something 'commanding officer-like' Mayne 'pushed him down', and he hit his chin on the table. The men also talked of another Mayne/Keyes run-in, when Mayne went berserk in the mess and chased Keyes out at the point of a bayonet.

Stirling was building his own legend; the truth was that Mayne was not kicked out of 11 Commando for assaulting Geoffrey Keyes, nor was he in prison when Stirling met him. According to the 11 Commando War Diary, Mayne left the unit on 23 June – the same day Keyes was visited by Laycock. That was a week after returning from the Litani action. And Geoffrey Keyes' personal diary, kept almost daily between January and September 1941, gives a much clearer picture.

On 20 June, Keyes dined with Sir William Battershill, the Governor of Cyprus, in Nicosia, to fill him in of the details of the Litani action. He stayed the night at the Residence and returned to the 11 Commando officers' mess the next afternoon, where he found an appalling scandal in progress. The previous evening had been guest night in the mess and in Keyes's absence Mayne had got drunk and started throwing his weight around. When he was rocketed by Major Charles Napier and Captain David Blair – both of whom had remained on Cyprus during the Litani action – Mayne had become uncontrollable.

When Napier had gone back to his tent, the big Ulsterman had followed and assaulted him in the dark, either in the tent itself or on the way there; he gave Napier a sound thrashing with his fists. This was not a particularly heroic instalment in Mayne's career.

'Later,' Keyes wrote in his diary, 'Charles [Napier] got beaten up, by a large unknown assailant. Paddy [Mayne] suspected, and Charles sure of it; but no proof.'

Though Napier obviously had been unable to identify his attacker, by the morning of 22 June, Keyes was sufficiently certain that Mayne was responsible to put the case before the Divisional Commander. On the following day, 23 June, he wrote in his diary: 'Produce Paddy before Div Commander, and he is rocketed and removed. Very sorry to lose him, as he did awfully well in the battle [the Litani River action], and is a great fighter. He is, however, an extremely truculent Irishman when he is "drink taken" and is as strong as a bull.'[10]

Both Keyes' personal diary and the War Diary confirm that Mayne left 11 Commando on 23 June 1941, but there is no mention of him being jailed or court-martialled. But Mayne did not join Stirling at this point, as the SAS detachment did not yet exist; it was only a week since Stirling's inaugural parachute jump near Fuka.

Eoin McGonigal was officially posted to the SAS on 15 August, when the Commando was back in Amiriyya. SAS training began at Kabrit twenty-one days later, on 5 September, but according to Jim Almonds, who was with L Detachment from its first day, and who kept a diary, Mayne did not join them until a few days later.

If the stories of Mayne's incarceration were true, this would mean he was kept in jail for an inconceivable eleven weeks without trial. Yet the evidence suggests that he was not in jail at all. In June a nursing sister at 19 General Hospital, Geneifa, in the Canal Zone, wrote to Mayne's sister, also a nurse, telling her that Paddy had been in hospital there for some days, suffering from a bout of malaria. Following this, he was sent to a convalescent hospital for two weeks. That would mean he was recuperating until 27 July or so.

11 Commando returned to Egypt on 7 August, not much more than a week after Mayne left the convalescent hospital. Stirling must have interviewed Eoin McGonigal between 7 August and the date of his transfer, 15 August; McGonigal must have recommended Mayne at the same time. This narrows down the meeting between Mayne and Stirling to one month, between 7 August and 5 September 1941, probably at Geneifa or nearby Kabrit, on the Suez Canal. It was certainly not in a military jail, although it is possible that Mayne still had a charge hanging over him when he encountered Stirling, and that Stirling managed to get it quashed via his connection with Ritchie. But whatever the case, any charge against Mayne cannot have been for knocking out his Commanding Officer, Geoffrey Keyes.

Mayne quickly settled into Lewes's training routine, and – almost to Stirling's consternation – began to emerge as the natural leader of the SAS group. Stirling was still regarded with suspicion by some of his men, who considered him a wastrel, one of the Silver Circle Club; on top of that, he was constantly away, setting things up with GHQ. Mayne's popularity with the rank and file made Stirling realize that he would have to be seen at Kabrit more often. Still, he never regretted his decision to take on the Irishman whom Keyes described as extremely truculent; Mayne was to finish the war as one of its outstanding heroes: a lieutenant colonel, the Commanding Officer of the first SAS Regiment, and one of only eight men in the Second World War to win the DSO four times.

MINUS 39 DAYS
10 October 1941

The wheels were already in motion for *Operation Flipper*. After dark on 10 October, a week after Keyes had met Cunningham at Maaten Baggush, the submarine *Torbay* closed the beach at Khashm al-Kalb in Cyrenaica, a possible landing site for the raiding party. *Torbay*, skippered by Lieutenant Commander Anthony Cecil Miers RN, had put to sea from Alexandria three days earlier. Miers, despite the unfortunate nickname 'Crap', was a submariner with a reputation for bold, determined and decisive action. The submarine had only two passengers aboard: British agent Captain John E. 'Jock' Haselden of G(R) and his assistant, an Arab NCO from the Libyan Arab Force, a British-officered unit made up of Arab exiles from Libya.

All that summer G(R) bosses Terence Airey and Kid Cator had been running a dozen agents behind Axis lines in Libya. They were, almost to a man, European expatriates – cotton brokers, managers, schoolteachers, university professors, bankers – who had worked in Egypt before the war and spoke fluent Arabic; in many ways, they were the most remarkable of all the special forces men deployed in Libya in the Second World War. These 'civilians in uniform' were often shy, retiring, middle-aged family men, whose exploits required not gung-ho, but calculated two o'clock in the morning courage. It is one thing to venture behind enemy lines as part of a strongly armed force; quite another to go it alone, armed with only a pistol, in disguise, knowing that every step might end in betrayal and certain death.

John Haselden, Intelligence Corps, was their kingpin. Born and raised in Egypt of a British father and a Coptic Egyptian mother, Haselden was educated at King's School, Canterbury. He was able to transform himself from English gentleman to Arab tribesman at the drop of a hat. Fluent in Italian and French, as well as a number of Arabic dialects, he appeared 'more British than the most stay-at-home British'[1] to his comrades, while the swarthy looks and dark eyes inherited from his mother allowed him to pass as an Arab – not even T.E. Lawrence could claim that ability in the First World War.

Before the war Haselden had worked for Anderson, Clayton & Company, the Houston–based US cotton-house founded in 1904, and had been manager of their Upper-Egypt Agency at el-Minya. Here he and his Egyptian wife, Nadia, occupied a white villa on the banks of the Nile, set by a huge cotton-hangar among impeccably-cut English lawns, occasionally providing the backdrop for glittering soirees that featured Arab orchestras and midnight dipping in the river. A tall, robust, tanned and hardy-looking pipe-smoker, Haselden was quietly spoken and modest, but impressive in a peculiarly British understated way. His usual means of delivery behind enemy lines was by the 'Libyan Taxi Service' – the Long Range Desert Group – who held him in high esteem. 'Haselden … was the outstanding personality of the dozen odd men who worked with the tribes in Cyrenaica behind the Axis lines,' wrote Bill Kennedy-Shaw, the LRDG's intelligence officer. 'Untiring, strong, courageous, never without some new scheme for outwitting the enemy, yet with a slow and easy-going way of setting about a job which was far more successful with the Arabs than the usual European insistence on precision and punctuality, which they neither like nor understand.'[2] By October 1941, his exploits had already become the stuff of fireside tales: how he would wander into Italian-occupied towns disguised as an Italian officer; how he would sit by the roadside counting vehicles in Italian convoys dressed as a Bedouin with a radio under his blanket; how he once drove a flock of sheep across an Axis airstrip under the eyes of Italian guards to pace out its dimensions.

Tonight, for the first time, Haselden was going in by submarine. *Torbay* and her sister-boat *Talisman* had been withdrawn from the 1st Submarine Flotilla's normal occupation-cycle for five weeks and assigned to *Operation Flipper*. Though her crew had not been briefed about the operation, for security reasons, 'Crap' Miers himself was one of the few officers in the know. A Scotsman from Wick in Inverness-shire, he was a stocky, cool-nerved bulldog of a man, 34 years old, with 13 years' service in the Royal Navy behind him. Much of his service had been in submarines, though he had never yet heard a depth-charge dropped in anger. His thirty-strong crew were similarly inexperienced. Paul Chapman, his first lieutenant – a combination of boat's policeman and housekeeper – was twenty, and had held his commission for just nine months. Miers had been criticized by other skippers for taking on a first lieutenant who was so young, but he felt that in wartime an older first officer would quickly graduate to his own command, while a younger one would remain and 'grow into' the boat. On a submarine it was important that the crew knew and trusted each other. In any case, while Miers had until recently been on assignment with the staff of the C-in-C Home Fleet, Chapman had already won a DSC for his role in the evacuation of Crete: technically, the young first lieutenant had more war service than his boss.

Torbay was a 'T' Class submarine, the largest type under construction in British dockyards, but smaller than some obsolete models – the 'River', 'O', 'P' and 'R' minelayer series. Built at Chatham in 1940, she had been launched on New Year's Day, 1941. She carried formidable armaments: ten 21-inch torpedo tubes, six internal and four external. The external tubes could not be reloaded at sea, but the internal tubes could, so that she was capable of firing a broadside of ten shots, followed quickly by six more. But the tubes all faced forwards and the torpedoes were not 'smart': like the galleons of old the submarine had to be pointed in the right direction to make a strike. On her gun tower she carried a 4-inch quick-firing gun, that could be used to engage other ships as well as land-based targets.

Despite Stirling's parachute aspirations, submarines were more suitable for use by special forces troops than aircraft. They ensured secrecy and surprise, and were capable of a greater range than any aircraft then in existence – *Torbay* could traverse the Mediterranean from Alexandria to Gibraltar and back five times without having to refuel. She was not fast compared with most submarines; she could do 14 knots on the surface and 9 submerged, then she had to surface to recharge her batteries, which in turn ran the compressors charging the boat's air-bottles. Air was needed to fire the torpedoes, to blow the ballast tanks and to replenish the atmosphere, and so prevent the potentially lethal build-up of carbon-dioxide. It was Chapman's job as first lieutenant to judge when the boat could safely surface and submerge.

Torbay also carried a *folbot* (pronounced fol-boat) detachment of the Special Boat Section, two crews of one officer and one NCO each, all of them former commandos. The *folbots* themselves were sixteen-foot, two-man, kayak-style canoes, constructed of canvas on a wooden frame and, theoretically, collapsible. In practice, as the joints were sealed by insulation tape, and it was a tedious job to assemble them for each launching, they were left fully assembled in the racks and manhandled through the fore hatch when required.

The SBS had been founded in 1940 by Roger 'Jumbo' Courtney, King's Royal Rifle Corps, a tough-as-nails 40-year-old canoeing enthusiast then serving with Laycock's 8 Commando. Courtney, who had once paddled the length of the Nile single-handed, had been a gold prospector, an East African big-game hunter, and a sergeant in the Palestine Police. In 1938 he and his wife had spent their honeymoon canoeing down the Danube. While training on Arran, Courtney had put forward his idea for a canoe-borne raiding and reconnaissance unit; the Navy had been highly skeptical – until the night the captain of the commando landing-ship *Glengyle* was dining shoreside at the Argyll Arms Hotel. Courtney had paddled up to *Glengyle*, boarded her unobserved and left his name in bright green paint in the captain's cabin. The captain had not been best pleased, but Courtney had made his point. He was promoted captain and given permission to recruit eleven men for a regular *folbot* troop (the name was taken from the name of the company manufacturing the canoes at the time). The *folbot* unit had accompanied *Layforce* to the Middle East, where Courtney had proved its worth by helping carry out a beach-reconnaissance of the island of Rhodes.

Anthony Miers had not been slow to see the usefulness of *folbots* for the Submarine Flotilla. Submarines traditionally carried no boats of their own, so the *folbots* filled a vacant niche. They were small and light enough to stow in a flooding chamber, and their SBS crews could be the boat's eyes and ears, reconnoitring harbours and beaches, bringing back vital information that a submarine commander had previously been unable to obtain. Though essentially a reconnaissance unit, the SBS also had a limited offensive capability: *folbot* crews were fully trained in demolitions and commando tactics.

Torbay lay three hundred yards off the beach in darkness. A single *folbot* was disgorged from the fore hatch and loaded by its handler, SBS corporal Clive Severn of the Northamptonshire Regiment. The stores were sealed in four-gallon petrol tins. Miers took his place on the gun tower as the canoe was lowered; Paul Chapman took charge of the landing party on the forward casing. The usual drill when landing personnel was for the Special Boat Section team to go in first, check the route to the shoreline for enemy forces or obstacles, then secure the landing-point. Tonight it was different. 'I'll swim,' Haselden said.

A moment later, stripped stark naked, Haselden dived into the sea and struck out strongly for the shore, swimming with one hand and holding in the other a torch sealed in a condom. The night was warm and the sea calm; there was no breeze. Chapman timed him, out of interest: exactly 12 minutes over the three hundred yards. Once out of the surf, Haselden checked the beach methodically. It was a perfect crescent shape, and there was a ruined fort about 250 yards away on the western side. There was no enemy; Haselden grinned to himself, wondering what the Italians would have made of him had they picked him up anyway. Fluent in both Arabic and Italian and without a shred of uniform to betray him, they would have been hard put to prove that he was a British officer. He flashed the OK-signal to Miers on *Torbay's* gun tower. Minutes later Clive Severn paddled the *folbot* out of the swell, carrying the Arab NCO and the petrol tins containing Haselden's Arab clothes and stores. The unloading was done in absolute silence. Then Severn shook hands and headed back into the darkness. Moments later the *folbot* had been recovered, hatches were sealed and *Torbay* was ready to submerge. The entire operation had taken thirty-four minutes.

By the time the *Torbay* was ready to depart, Haselden and his companion, now in Arab robes, were heading west along the rugged coast, looking like any unremarkable pair of Bedouin on a journey to visit relatives. They bypassed el-Hania, where there was a garrison of Italian colonial *carabinieri*, and turned sharply inland, up the escarpment. The weather had been warm and balmy for the past days, though in the Jebel this was the beginning of the rainy season, and already the Mediterranean *maquis*, the brushwood, was starting to blossom: thick brakes of juniper, lentisk, myrtle, ilex, wild olive and arbutus, whose waxy leaves gave a heady scent to the air, and whose density made the hill-terraces impenetrable except where there were narrow paths. Geographically the Jebel was more akin to southern Europe than to the vast reaches of the Sahara to the south. It was a rain-shadow area, trapping the humid winds off the Mediterranean so that the northerly slopes were a series of thickly wooded ridges, clad in Aleppo pine, cypress and wild fig, while the southerly ones were arid steppes of hardy goat-grass giving way to the stony wastes of the pre-Sahara.

A week after they had been dropped by *Torbay*, Haselden and his Arab companion arrived in Slonta, about a day's walk west of Beda Littoria. Without raising any suspicious eyebrows they made their way to the house of an Arab called Hussain Taher, the *Mudir*, or Italian-appointed administrator of the town, who welcomed them inside. A powerfully-built, slightly sardonic-looking man sporting European-style pinstripe lounge-suits with a native skull-cap, Hussain was one of Haselden's most important assets. Hussain had no particular feeling for the Germans. Like most of the Senussi Bedouin of Cyrenaica, he respected their warlike qualities, but he felt no animosity towards them except for the fact that they were allies of the hated Italians. Hussain owed his elevation as *Mudir* of Slonta to his Italian masters, and to them he appeared compliant and submissive, yet, like a true Bedouin, he would never forgive or forget what they had done to his folk.

The Bedouin hill-tribes of the Jebel al-Akhdar differed in their degree of nomadism. Some raised cattle and sheep and inhabited caves among the *maquis* on the northern slopes, while others pitched black tents and raised goats and camels on the more arid southern skirts. Yet they were united in their adherence to the Senussiyya, an Islamic holy order founded in Cyrenaica by an Algerian ascetic, Mohammad bin Ali as-Senussi, in the eighteenth century. The Italians had officially annexed Libya in 1912, and between 1922 and 1931, determined to break Senussi power, they had appropriated Bedouin land, subjected settlements to random bombardments, burned crops and sent eighty thousand men, women and children to concentration camps. Many had died of starvation and disease; many more had fled to Egypt. To prevent their exodus, General Rodolfo 'The Butcher' Graziani, the Italian military supremo, had closed the border by erecting the five-foot-high, fifteen-inch-wide, barbed-wire fence that entered local mythology as The Wire.

Tiny bands of Bedouin partisans – no more than a couple of hundred fighters in each, and no more than seven hundred in all – had kept up the war of the flea against Italian columns in the Green Mountain for years. It had only ended on 11 September 1931, when their leader, septuagenarian guerrilla genius Omar al-Mukhtar, had been captured at Sidi Rafa, the town now called Beda Littoria by the Italians. He had been hanged a week later, in front of a crowd of twenty thousand people.

Graziani's campaign against the Bedouin had amounted to genocide, reducing their population by as much as two-thirds within ten years. 'The

Italians detested the Bedouin,' wrote the anthropologist E.E. Evans-Pritchard. 'Long years of campaigning against guerrilla bands had infuriated them … and made them increasingly … brutal … The Italians spoke of them as barbarians, little better than beasts, and treated them accordingly.'[3]

Broken but not defeated, Senussi resentment simmered on. In 1939, the astute among them saw that war would soon break out in Egypt between the Italians and their colonial rivals, the British. In January that year, the sheikhs of the Senussi tribes met in Alexandria to announce their allegiance to the exiled Senussi leader, Sayid Idriss, who was firmly in the British camp. Hussain Taher had no special love for the British, but he wanted to liberate his country from the Italians, and to be in a position to influence its new masters after liberation. He was also a loyal supporter of the Senussi chief. Now, over Arab stew, griddle-bread and sweet tea, Hussain confirmed to Haselden the previous intelligence reports that the German commander, General Rommel, had been seen using an HQ in Beda Littoria; he slept in a villa not half a mile away. Haselden was delighted with the news. He trusted Hussain enough to tell him that a commando landing was due in Cyrenaica in a few weeks: the *Mudir* must have sensed that something even bigger was in the wind, because he asked Haselden for a certificate of loyalty to the British. The certificate, which later decorated the wall of his house in Beda Littoria, was dated 20 October 1941, and stated:

> HUSSAIN TAHER, the Mudir of Slonta, has been a great help to me and has given me very useful information re enemy camps, etc. He is 100% pro-British and I recommend him for special consideration on our re-occupation of Cyrenaica.
>
> 20-10-41 (Signed) J.E. HASELDEN

MINUS 29 DAYS

20 October 1941

Jock Haselden, concealed in a wadi near Slonta, was woken by a messenger from Hussain Taher. Two Arabs had arrived in the town and were asking for him by name. Haselden was immediately suspicious. He had no illusions about his job; he knew that there were Bedouin in Italian pay who would willingly sell him to their masters. But he also knew this might be important, and so he agreed to meet them. As it turned out, the Arabs were no more Italian spies than he was – they were agents from the Libyan Arab Force in Egypt, carrying an urgent verbal message from Captain Easonsmith of the Long Range Desert Group. The LRDG patrol was in the desert to the south, and had been sent to bring him home.

By 1941 the LRDG had become so useful in ferrying G(R) and other agents in and out of Axis territory that it was referred to affectionately as Libyan Taxis Ltd. In many ways the first real special forces unit ever formed, it had been raised in 1940 under the aegis of Sir Archibald Wavell. It was originally part of a brilliantly executed bluff designed solely to convince the Italians that there were British forces behind them. It was a tribute to Wavell's efficiency that he had managed to perform the trick of putting a square peg in a square hole back in 1939, when he had intervened to prevent a major of the Royal Signals, Ralph Bagnold, from being sent to an inappropriate posting in East Africa.

Bagnold was a genuine desert expert, more of a boffin than a soldier, who had been elected to the Royal Society for his original work on the movement of sand dunes. It was while stationed in Egypt in the 1920s and 30s that he and a group of like-minded men and women – mostly but not exclusively peacetime army officers – had explored the *terra ignota* of the Western Desert, pioneering the use of motor vehicles and light aircraft in desert terrain. Bagnold and his followers, including Guy Prendergast, then a captain in the Royal Tank Regiment, now the LRDG's chief, and Bill Kennedy-Shaw, then a District Officer of the Sudan Political Service, now the LRDG Intelligence Officer, had developed between them almost all the techniques and technologies of desert motoring that had since become universal – including the water-cooled radiator, the sun-compass, the sand-channel, and the petrol and water dump. The LRDG had long since learned the lessons of living and surviving in the desert that Stirling, Lewes and their Parashots had yet to discover for themselves. In the desert anything that does not move is dead. Using stripped-down two-wheel-drive thirty-hundredweight Chevrolet trucks, they could move far and fast, while carry heavier armaments than Stirling's parachutists could ever have dreamed of – including Vickers K and Lewis machine-guns, and even 15-pounder Bofors field guns.

The terrain the LRDG operated in was very different from the hills of Jebel al-Akhdar that were the haunt of G(R) men like Haselden. Extending as far east as the Nile valley, and as far south as the arid savannahs of the Sudan, this territory – the eastern Sahara, or Libyan Desert – was as large as the Indian sub-continent, with only a tiny fraction of India's population – people were so few that one could travel for days and never see another living soul. Throughout the campaign in North Africa, most of the fighting was confined to the Mediterranean coastal plain, a rocky escarpment with characteristics entirely different from those of the true desert. Exposed to heavy and frequent rains in winter, the littoral was fertile enough for the local semi-nomads to raise sheep and cultivate barley, yoking their camels to the plough. Standing on the edge of the escarpment and looking out was like standing on the shore of a vast and uncharted sea: a sea of sand, gravel and rock that everywhere stretched to the limits of one's sight. To the south that sea extended for fifteen hundred miles, while to the west one could drive off into the sunset and never cross a road, a river, or come upon a city until one reached the shores of the Atlantic Ocean, more than three thousand miles away.

The vastness of the region was awesome. In the easternmost part of the Sahara – confusingly called the Western Desert – it was so arid that no one, not even the hardy desert nomads, had lived there since prehistoric times. In the central part of that region, nothing could survive: not a thorn-tree, nor a fly, nor a blade of grass. Watering points were so few that even nomad raiders crossing the area had to leave dumps of water in amphorae for their return journey. There were places a man would count himself fortunate if he had seen it rain more than once in his lifetime, and cloud cover was almost non-existent – the eastern Sahara was two hundred times more arid than California's Death Valley, and exposed to direct sunlight more frequently than any other place on earth: a staggering 97 per cent of the time. In summer the sun stood so high in its zenith that at noon there were virtually no shadows, and in that huge emptiness, sandstorms screeched across the plains like dragons, gathering momentum until they had the power to blind men and scarify metal until not a scrap of paint remained. The eastern Sahara was a formidable obstacle to conventional military forces. Of all the units deployed in the North African theatre in the Second World War, Allied or Axis, only to the Long Range Desert Group was it truly home.

The commander of the patrol sent to pick up Haselden, Jake Easonsmith, was rated as the best patrol leader the LRDG ever had. A Royal Tank Regiment officer, he had been a salesman for a Bristol wine-merchant before the war. He was one of those men despised by the rest of the cavalry, who enjoyed tinkering with carburetors and spark-plugs. He was also one of those Englishmen, a few of whom arise in every generation, who are instinctively at ease in the desert. He seemed to have a feel for it that was noticed by everyone who travelled with him. 'I never knew his equal,' David Lloyd-Owen said. 'He had a guile which was almost uncanny in his ability to foresee how the enemy would react. He was always thinking ahead and asking himself what he would do if the enemy adopted a certain line of action. Thus he was always prepared and I never knew him to be caught on the wrong foot.'[1]

Devoted to his family back in Britain, Easonsmith was a rational, deep-thinking man who would weigh the risks and balance dangers carefully before taking action, but he was bold and decisive once he had chosen a course. He displayed an inner sureness that was just right for a man who had to navigate the vast reaches of the Sahara, whose dimensions alone could cause panic. His directness and simplicity evoked confidence in his patrol, many of whom were New Zealanders: men who had been with the LRDG from its inception, and had little time for the usual stuffy British officer. Like Haselden, Easonsmith was also famous among the Arabs of Cyrenaica, who called him *Batl As-Sahara*, the hero of the desert.

Easonsmith's patrol – fifteen men in five Chevrolet trucks, divided into A and B parties – had been ordered to reconnoitre three areas of desert near Mekili and find out if there were obstacles to the Eighth Army's advance. They were also to drop some booby-trapped Italian ammunition, and to pick up Jock Haselden at one of two possible rendezvous, and 'send him back as soon as possible to Siwa.'[2]

Easonsmith arrived at the first RV, Abd al-Krim, six days after Haselden had been dropped by submarine; the place was deserted. The following day he moved the patrol twelve miles to the south, to ruins called Garet Tecasis, where three British enlisted men were hiding. They had been captured by the Germans in April, but had escaped from a POW camp at Benghazi a week earlier, and had been helped by Haselden's agents among the Senussi tribes.

Easonsmith waited at the RV for two days, his men scouring the area for any sign of Haselden. By 19 October he still had not shown up, so Easonsmith left B party, with two Chevies, at Garet Tecasis, and dispatched two LAF Arabs on foot to Marsua, west of Slonta, to look for him. Easonsmith himself took his remaining three vehicles and eight men to the fallback RV twenty-five miles away. Haselden was still not there either, and Easonsmith began to worry that the man had been bagged. He hid his vehicles and their crews in a wadi and went off alone on foot with a Tommy gun, water and three days' rations in a haversack to look for the elusive British agent.

The going was tough. For hours Jake Easonsmith marched over endless plains of sand and wind-graded serir, the black limestone slag that clinked underfoot. Here, without the folding wadis and rocky bluffs of the escarpment to hide him, a man was a dark comma on the horizon that could be spotted miles away. The vastness of the landscape dwarfed him; it required a very special mentality to feel at home in this loneliness, to keep control of the terror that could be engendered by the lack of landmarks for the mind to grip on. Even one's sense of scale quickly evaporated, so that a stone far off looked as large as a house, and a moving vehicle could be mistaken for a stationary rock. Flashes of light winked inexplicably out of the emptiness – the effect of sunlight on silicon crystals – and in places it seemed that placid lakes of water lay on the surface, an effect the desert people called The Devil's Mirror. There were eerie sounds too: the dull thud of a boulder splintering due to temperature fluctuation, mournful musical notes produced by the wind on the rocks, the crepitation of sand-grains moving against each other, so loud and rhythmic that the desert folk thought of it as the sound of Ra'ul, the Demon Drummer. To travel alone and on foot here required an absolute confidence in one's powers of survival and navigation. The most frightening aspect of the Sahara was the way in which conditions, idyllic one minute, could a moment later explode into a raging maelstrom of choking sand and whirling dust.

Easonsmith continued doggedly, guarding his water ration. He saw no sign of Haselden, but after almost a day's walk, he heard the sound of gunning engines. Creeping silently forward, he observed an Italian camp in a depression below a circular hill and a rocky ridge. On the crest of the hill was a ruined fort, or guard-sangar, manned by lookouts, and on another rise nearby was a camp of bivouac tents. There were an unusual number of motor vehicles moving in and out, and for a moment Easonsmith forgot Haselden and decided to watch the Italians instead. There were four light tanks parked below the hill, and he counted a further thirty or forty soft-skinned vehicles as well. This volume of traffic was abnormal, he decided: these were not routine desert patrols, but part of a regular division on the move. And if a whole Italian division was on the move, that could herald the start of a new Axis offensive.

His curiosity piqued, Easonsmith lay up and observed. After sunset, temperatures plummeted, leaving him quaking with cold under his light blanket. He dozed fitfully, waking occasionally to the sound of Italian voices carried across the void, or to the jagged chorus of engines being fired. He lay up all the next day, baked by the sun, dogged by flies, but not daring to move, observing an almost constant stream of vehicles heading off along the track towards Mekili.

Now satisfied that an Italian division was being redeployed, Easonsmith was determined to find out why. This information could only be obtained from an enemy prisoner, he reasoned, and the best way of snatching one would be to lay an ambush on the Mekili track. Waiting till it was fully dark again, he silently withdrew from his observation point and hiked back to his patrol.

Twenty-four hours later, Easonsmith's three Chevies were lurking by the Mekili road. It was just after dawn, and traffic had not yet started to move so, leaving the trucks concealed in a dip, Easonsmith stalked off again on foot for a shufti. The plan he decided on was audacious but simple: while two of the Chevies were concealed on a nearby ridge with a field of fire commanding the track, his own truck would halt several hundred yards away, its bonnet raised as if it had broken down. Posing as Italians, he and his crew would stop the first Italian vehicle to come along and nab a prisoner for interrogation. As they moved into position, Easonsmith dropped the specially doctored Italian ammunition he had brought from Siwa along the track as an extra bonus for any Italian trusting enough to pick it up.

He chose his position carefully. No sooner had his Chevy stopped than an enemy lorry suddenly popped up out of dead ground only two hundred yards away. Easonsmith's driver and co-driver quickly stuck their heads under the raised bonnet as if inspecting the wrecked engine. Their machine-gunner, New Zealander Ed Spottiswoode, was already hiding under a tarpaulin in the vehicle. Easonsmith, wearing a desert duffle-coat and looking piratically Latin with his unkempt black hair and dark beard, held up a hand for assistance, trying awkwardly to conceal the Tommy gun behind his back. As the enemy truck slowed to a halt, he noticed with consternation that it was being followed by a large convoy, emerging like a string of dark pearls from the morning heat-haze. He had to act quickly.

Not waiting for the Italians to open the door, he walked up to the vehicle and opened it himself. For a split second the driver and his passenger – an officer – stared at him uncertainly. Easonsmith produced his Thompson, but before he could fire, the driver leapt out of the cab on top of him, knocking him down. As they grappled desperately in the sand, the Italian officer drew his Beretta and pumped off rounds, but he was anxious not to hit his own driver, and all his shots went wide, though one hit and punctured the radiator of Easonsmith's Chevrolet. The officer dropped out of the cab and bolted uphill towards safety, but got just a few yards before a burst of drumfire from Ed Spottiswoode brought him down.

The officer was killed or wounded – Easonsmith did not have time to find out which, because the driver had now ripped the Tommy gun from his grasp and was making off with it at a fast sprint. Easonsmith's pockets were full of No. 36 Mills grenades; pulling one out, he yanked the clip and hurled it after the Italian. A few seconds later there was a deafening crump and a mushroom cloud of smoke and dust. The driver was bowled over, probably dead. Easonsmith, amazed by what he later called a fairly lucky shot, suddenly realized that the other vehicles in the convoy – about twenty of them – were pulling up less than a hundred yards away, and their crews debussing.

'Things became quite fast and furious,' he observed later. The convoy was already under fire from the Lewis gun and a .303 rifle on the two reserve vehicles Easonsmith had stationed on high ground to cover the ambush, though their Vickers K had jammed and was silent. Some of the Italian crews were taking cover under their lorries, while others were firing back.

Easonsmith was perturbed: he knew that the sound of the gunshots could be heard at the Italian camp three miles away and it would not be long before an overwhelming force would be sent to investigate. Meanwhile he had two dead or nearly dead Italians on his hands and no prisoner. Ignoring the clatter of rifle-fire, he ambled down the line of enemy vehicles through the smoke and dust, repeating – according to one of his crew – 'I must get a prisoner! I must get a prisoner!' like a mantra, and rolling grenades under the Italian trucks as calmly as if he had been on a bowling green. The leading truck went up with a ripping report in a spectacular ball of orange flame and the Italians began to bolt, quailing under the rat-at-tat-tat of the Lewis gun from the nearby ridge. More than a dozen were hit as they ran. Easonsmith pulled two of them from under one of the trucks and made for his own vehicle, having decided that it was now time to clear off. The Lewis gun and the rifle on the hill were keeping the enemy's heads down, and in a moment the driver was firing the Chevy's engine while Ed Spottiswoode was furiously rattling off drums of .303 tracer at the Italians. Easonsmith and the spare man got the prisoners on board and the Chevy lurched off to RV with the covering vehicles. One of the prisoners was bleeding badly; within two hours he was dead.

By nightfall, though, they had covered one hundred and forty miles without pursuit. The few enemy aircraft they did see didn't appear to have noticed them. Easonsmith was now faced with a hard decision. The day had been critically hot, and the two extra men had helped deplete their water-reserves. To cap it all, the chance shot in the radiator had holed it, which meant that Easonsmith had had to keep topping it up with precious drinking water. The patrol hadn't yet completed its mission – it had neither picked up Haselden nor carried out a recce of the Mekili area. But without sufficient water, to attempt either of those objectives now would be suicide, and the intelligence they had already gathered from the surviving POW – that the Trieste Motorized Division had been ordered to occupy Mekili – might be vital to GHQ. Easonsmith decided to make directly for base.

Driving night and day, they arrived at Siwa Oasis at 0900 hours on 25 October to find good news awaiting them. John Haselden had been found by the two Arab scouts Easonsmith had dispatched to Mersua on 19 October, and had been brought straight back to Siwa by B party, arriving the previous day, 24 October. Though Easonsmith did not know it, Haselden had brought confirmation that Rommel was at his HQ at Beda Littoria, and there were three other targets the commandos could usefully hit in the vicinity: the Italian HQ at Cyrene, the Italian Intelligence Centre at Apollonia, and a cable mast at Cyrene crossroads that carried the Axis telephone and telegraph wires for the whole region.

15 OPERATION CRUSADER

MINUS 33 DAYS
16 October 1941

On the morning of 16 October, while John Haselden was tramping around Cyrenaica in Arab dress, the men of L Detachment, the SAS Brigade – including Blair Mayne and Jock Lewes – lined up at the doors of five Bristol Bombays from 216 Squadron RAF Transport Command, for their third practice parachute jump. The Bombay was a high-wing monoplane, which, though slow and antiquated, was far more suitable than the Valentia Lewes and Stirling had used for their original experimental jumps. Gone were the days of attaching parachute static lines to seat-legs: the Bombays at least had custom-built rails bolted to their floors. The static line was a webbing strap issuing from the parachute-pack, looking like a dog's lead, which had to be attached to these rails with a steel clip, something like the ring-attachment on a carabiner used by mountaineers. When the parachutist threw himself out of the aircraft, the static line yanked the folded parachute-canopy out of the pack. As the parachute caught air and inflated, it would break the strings holding the static line in place until finally the inflated chute broke free of the static line altogether, leaving the line dangling from the aircraft. Every parachutist had a secret terror: that he would exit the aircraft without the static line hooked up properly: with nothing to pull his canopy open, this would mean a very short plummet to certain death. At military parachuting altitudes – usually eight hundred to a thousand feet – even a reserve chute could not be guaranteed to save a life, and in 1941, L Detachment had no reserve chutes.

David Stirling had participated in the first two jumps himself, and they had gone off without casualties. On 16 October he stayed on the ground to observe the landing-patterns and to develop ideas for regrouping on the drop zone (DZ). Stirling watched as the Bombays approached. In the first aircraft the red light was already on, giving the parachutists a few seconds' warning. The Bombay was flying at nine hundred feet, the door was open and the SAS men braced at action stations, ready to go. The RAF dispatcher stood by the door facing the file of parachutists, known in military terminology as a stick. As it happened, the first three men in the stick were all Scotsmen, and all ex-11 Commando. Facing the door with his arm braced against it, but looking straight ahead rather than down, was Private Kenneth Warburton of the Seaforth Highlanders. Behind him was his friend Private Joseph A. Duffy, also of the Seaforths. The third man was Billy Morris of the Black Watch, formerly of 3 Troop, 11 Commando , who had fought beside Jim Gornall at the Litani River, and had been one of the 14 men to cross it with Eric Garland and George Highland.

The green light flashed on. The dispatcher yelled 'GO!' Ken Warburton disappeared through the door. Joe Duffy, a step behind him, hesitated for a fraction of a second, sensing something was wrong. 'What are you waiting for, man?' the dispatcher balled. Duffy stepped out into the sky, and it was only then that the dispatcher noticed what Duffy must have registered subconsciously: the static lines of both parachutists were no longer attached to the clips on the rails welded to the floor: Duffy and Warburton had just jumped to their deaths. The dispatcher, horrified, grabbed Billy Morris just as he was about to go and yanked him back from the door. He pulled the door shut and told the pilot to go down. After that, Billy Morris always considered himself the luckiest man alive.

On the DZ, Stirling watched in helpless horror as Duffy and Warburton smashed into the ground from nine hundred feet. According to legend, their bodies were found lying side by side, as if for a funeral, head to head and foot to foot. Marks on Duffy's parachute-pack suggested that he had tried to pull open his canopy himself.

Stirling was distressed and shaken, but he was astute enough to realize that a calm demeanor was essential if the confidence – and perhaps even the integrity – of L Detachment was to be preserved. When the men assembled later, he told them, 'The trials are cancelled for today. Once we have found out what went wrong we will pick up where we left off. Go away and relax and be ready to start again tomorrow morning.'[1]

That evening he spoke to them again, saying that the problem had been identified: the snap-links on the end of the static lines had been inefficient and had twisted open under pressure. The links had now been replaced by more robust ones, and the accident would not happen again. They would all jump together the following day. Later, every man was issued with fifty Players cigarettes apiece, which convinced them, as Jim Almonds wrote in his diary, 'that the chips were well and truly down.'[2]

Bob Bennett recalled this was the worst twenty-four hours any of the men ever spent. 'We sat in our tents,' he said, 'smoking one fag after another, trying not to think of it. But we did.'[3]

The following morning every man in the detachment jumped, including David Stirling, who was the first out of the aircraft. He later admitted that he had always hated parachuting, but this exit was the hardest he ever made.[4]

The men of the detachment were still in the dark about their objectives on the coming mission that was being organized under the aegis of Cunningham's Eighth Army HQ. The plan was that five groups of 10 or 11 SAS men each, under Stirling, Mayne, Lewes, Bonnington and McGonigal respectively, would attack the aerodromes of Gazala and Tmimi, on the coast of Libya, slightly west of Tobruk. These airfields were bases for the Messerschmitt Bf 109; the German fighters outclassed the Hurricanes and Tomahawks of the RAF Desert Air Force, and putting them out of action would prevent major damage to Cunningham's supply lines as the Eighth Army advanced into Libya. The sticks would be dropped about twenty miles short of their objectives on the night of 16/17 November and would move into LUPs – lying up places – overlooking their targets that same night. They would remain hidden throughout the day of 17 November and go into action on D-1/D1, destroying all the ME 109s, and then withdrawing across the desert on foot to an RV called Rotunda Segnale, on an ancient caravan route known as Trig al-'Abd, or Slaves' Road. Here, they would be picked up by Jake Easonsmith's LRDG patrol.

To bring this off effectively, Lewes had realized early on that they needed a new kind of explosive – one easy and quick to set up, which would both explode and burn at the same time. A Royal Engineers ordnance expert Stirling brought in from GHQ told Lewes that this was impossible: any explosive mixture – gelignite, thermite, ammonal – would either explode *or* burn, but would not do both.

Lewes ignored this disheartening pronouncement and spent three weeks in his makeshift lab at Kabrit trying to invent exactly what he needed. Finally, he came up with the goods: a blend of one pound of plastic explosive to a quarter pound of thermite, stirred with a dash of *Ingredient X* – nothing more than common diesel oil. Thanks to the PE – plastic explosive – the mixture could be moulded into shape and carried in pound blocks that fitted into a ration-bag, together with a primer, a length of cordtex instantaneous fuse and a time pencil. The time pencil was a six-inch-long, pencil-slim cylinder containing differing strengths of acid that would eat its way through a lead wire of a set thickness; the lead wire held a spring back from a detonator. When the operator pressed a ridge on the pencil, the acid was released. When the acid had eaten through the lead, the spring would snap to the detonator, igniting the cordtex and causing a chain reaction through the primer and the main charge itself. Time pencils were useful because they gave the setter a choice of delays varying from ten minutes to a month – the time was pre-set and colour-coded – but in an emergency the charges could be set off using the detonator alone. The charge itself was reasonably stable and was unlikely to explode unless primed, but the detonators were another matter entirely: they were dangerously volatile. They had to be carried separately and activated only just before the charge was set.

Lewes demonstrated his new formula to the unhelpful sapper who had told him it was impossible by attaching it to an old aircraft wing supported by two oil drums half filled with aviation fuel. When Lewes detonated the bomb it went off with an earsplitting *crack!* and cut a hole sheer through the wing and the skin of the oil drums, igniting the aviation fuel with a gush of orange flame. The experts had to concede that Lewes had done the impossible.

The new device was to be called the Lewes Bomb, and each SAS man was to carry eight of them on the operation. Lewes had studied the best position to place the bombs for maximum effect and decided that they should be attached as near to the fuel tank as possible.

By the end of October, Stirling's Parashots were ready for their final test before the Big One. They were to attempt to mount a dummy sabotage raid on the RAF airfield at Heliopolis, a suburb of Cairo, having first crossed the ninety miles or so of desert between there and the SAS camp at Kabrit. The RAF knew they were coming and airborne patrols would be out looking for them by day. Sixty-one men – the entire strength of L Detachment – set out on foot from their camp at night, each man carrying four full water-bottles, three pounds of dates, some glucose sweets and a haversack full of stones weighing the equivalent of eight Lewes Bombs. They moved at night, as they would on a real operation, lying up during the day under lengths of camouflaged sackcloth. Not a single man was spotted. Moving separately, the groups converged on the airfield about midnight on the fourth day, entering from different directions by cutting through the perimeter fence. They ran about the place unobserved, plastering the parked aircraft with sticky labels marked *bomb*. By first light they were safely out of Heliopolis and back at the army barracks at Abbassiyya. They had pulled off a superb coup, to the distress and fury of the RAF. The SAS men had been apprehensive about this exercise, considering it an impossible task, but now they had achieved it, their confidence hit the roof. Stirling knew, and they knew, they were ready for the Gazala/Tmimi raids.

It was now, during a few days' leave in Cairo, that they were issued with their new headgear – snow-white berets – and their distinctive parachute wings, designed by Jock Lewes and based on an ancient Egyptian-style fresco of a sacred ibis he had clocked in Shepheard's Hotel. The white beret did not last; it became the butt of ridicule from other units, and was replaced first by a khaki forage cap, then by the sand-coloured beret the SAS Regiment still wears today. They were also assigned their new cap-badge, usually referred to as the Winged Dagger but actually meant to represent a winged sword: Excalibur, of Arthurian legend. The badge was designed by Sergeant Bob Tait, Gordon Highlanders, ex-11 Commando, the winning entry in a competition organized by Stirling. The *Who Dares Wins* motto was Stirling's own addition; it was, in effect, a slightly more robust version of that adage most favoured by Geoffrey Keyes' father, Sir Roger, the hero of Zeebrugge: *He Most Prevails Who Nobly Dares*.

MINUS 30 DAYS
19 October 1941

Tommy Macpherson, Geoffrey Keyes' adjutant, knew that something big was in the offing because Keyes was continuously up and down from Alexandria to Cairo during early October. 'I knew he was cajoling the army's top brass – to whom he had access through his father's connections – into some bold operation,' Macpherson said, 'but he gave me no clue to his intentions beyond that.'[1] In late September Macpherson had returned from a short mission to Nobariyya, a vital oasis and watering place in the Western Desert, where he had been sent with twenty commandos on what amounted to little more than sentry duty. This was the kind of job he had joined the commandos to get away from, and the boredom had been relieved only when his troop intercepted a gang of Egyptian thieves and a lorry laden with Italian rifles and British Army property.

At Amiriyya, on 19 October, Macpherson came back from a training session at the gym – while Haselden was meeting with Hussain Taher at Slonta – to find a signal waiting for him from GHQ Cairo, in Keyes' name. He was instructed to report immediately to HMS *Medway*, lying in Alexandria harbour, where he was to contact Captain Dewhurst RN. He was to tell nobody where he was going.

Macpherson tried to telephone Keyes in Cairo for confirmation, but the switchboards were jammed. 'I just set off as I was,' he recalled, 'expecting that I would attend a conference and get a brief on moving the Commando to some operational rendezvous. I was wrong.'[2]

Medway was the Depot Ship of the Royal Navy's 1st Submarine Flotilla, and when Macpherson arrived he saw the submarine *Talisman* was moored alongside. *Torbay* was also in the harbour, having returned from delivering Haselden to Khashm al-Kalb only the previous day. Macpherson knew nothing about Haselden's recce, or that *Torbay* and *Talisman* had been assigned exclusively to the Rommel Raid, codenamed *Operation Flipper*. In *Medway's* wardroom, he saluted Captain Dewhurst, nicknamed 'Dogberry', a veteran submariner with three DSOs, whom he already knew well. He was delighted to find with him Lieutenant Commander Michael Willmott RN, skipper of *Talisman*, the youngest submarine commander in the Mediterranean and a close personal friend.

Macpherson was not prepared for what came next. 'You are to embark on *Talisman* forthwith to reconnoitre a beach in Cyrenaica for a commando landing to take place in three weeks' time,' Dewhurst told him. 'In particular, you are to test the feasibility of a night route up the escarpment of the Jebel, which lies about a mile back from the beach. You will have to go carefully because the place is crawling with enemy patrols.'

'How will I be landed, Sir?' Macpherson asked.

'By *folbot*,' Dewhurst said. 'You will be accompanied by two officers and an NCO from the Special Boat Section.'

Macpherson had never been in a *folbot* before, and his confidence was not improved when he met the two SBS officers, Captain Ratcliffe and Lieutenant Ravenscroft. James Ratcliffe, of the Middlesex Regiment, had been a town clerk in civilian life, and had the same sort of mentality as an officer, Macpherson thought, perhaps unfairly. He knew Trevor Ravenscroft, Royal Scots Fusiliers, because he had been an officer of 11 Commando; he was officially along as a trainee. Ravenscroft had only been with the SBS since 13 September and knew even less about canoes and marine navigation than Macpherson did. Macpherson thought he would be better off with the NCO, Corporal Andrew Evans of the Highland Light Infantry, a dour Glasgow Jock, who seemed a solid and reliable man. But the *folbots* were precious: they were irreplaceable in Egypt, and they were lent to the operation only on the understanding that an SBS officer should come along.

As Ratcliffe was a week or two senior to Macpherson, he would be in command. Macpherson was a bit worried by the inadequacy of the briefing, and by the fact that there were no land maps, only nautical charts of the coast. But Dewhurst told him that *Talisman* would not be again available before the date of the actual operation. 'The alternatives were to accept or to abandon the opportunity for good,' Macpherson said.

When *Talisman* put out to sea the same evening, Tommy Macpherson was on board.

On the voyage Macpherson and the SBS team fitted into the normal roster, standing watches with the naval crew, something SBS men were trained to do as a matter of course. There was only one emergency, when what might have been an Italian destroyer was sighted by periscope, and the boat went deep and switched off all instruments. The following night, at midnight, she surfaced in calm seas off Tobruk. While she was recharging her batteries, a *folbot* was launched to give Macpherson his first taste of sea canoeing, to check the canoe for seaworthiness, and to confirm the accuracy of the compass. *Talisman* moved ahead to an RV, and Macpherson and his partner, Evans, located her on a compass bearing. They brought it off with such success that Macpherson's confidence soared.

After moonset on 24 October, five days after leaving Alexandria, *Talisman* surfaced about three miles off Ras Hilal, one of the two possible sites earmarked for Keyes' landing. The weather had been calm throughout the voyage, but suddenly it began to turn. Macpherson and his colleagues checked their equipment, and the cook issued them their rations – three ham sandwiches each. As they clambered out of the fore hatch, the crew manhandled the *folbots* on to the forward casing. While the landing party were making a final check of their Mae West lifejackets, Michael Willmott pointed into the darkness and said, 'The beach is that way, chums. Don't worry, we'll be exactly on this spot until 0400 sharp. If you can't make it by then, we'll be here on the next three mornings, from one minute past midnight till 0400 hours.'

They nodded, and started to get into the *folbots*, held on ropes by the crew. This was the most difficult manoeuvre of the whole action, because the canoes were flimsy and could easily be smashed against the side of the boat, or overturned by a clumsy move. The canoeist who got in first had to hold the craft stable with his paddle while his mate slipped aboard. Luckily the sea was quite calm. Macpherson and Evans pushed off first, with Ratcliffe and Ravenscroft not far behind. Macpherson had the only compass and Ravenscroft the only torch, their sole means of signalling to the submarine. 'That part of the plan went early astray,' Macpherson commented, 'for Ravenscroft somehow lost the torch in the surf during landing, and we weren't able to recover it. At the time this didn't seem a very grievous blow as our rendezvous with the submarine was at a point governed not only by compass bearing but also infallibly recognized by the intersection of lines to clear beach landmarks.'[3]

The surf was not high and the landing was relatively easy. The night was warm and the men wore their standard-issue khaki drill shorts, shirts and sweaters, with woollen cap-comforters and suede desert boots. They carried only pistols. The beach was gravelly shingle and a quick survey was all it took to convince Macpherson that it would be entirely suitable for a commando landing. That done, the team concealed their *folbots* in scrub at the edge of the shingle, covered them with sand and prickly pear, and went off to look at the escarpment.

Between the shingle beach and the escarpment there was a road, and the party stopped to recce it, marking the give-away lights of two enemy patrols, one static, the other mobile. This was not unexpected; in fact, Macpherson had anticipated a much heavier Axis presence. Making a mental note to avoid these patrols on the day, they boxed around and came to the first of the two broken terraces they had to negotiate, steep, rocky and covered in thorny *maquis*. They worked their way up and from the top confirmed their position – the surf was luminous in the darkness and they had no doubts about being able to find their way back. On top the going through the *maquis* was tough, but they moved fast to their objective, the place where the commando landing party would, on the day, be met by Arab agents. It was lying at a low point between two escarpments.

Once they'd got there, they immediately turned back, moving more slowly this time, planning out the route for the main party to use in two weeks. The only time they hesitated was when a salvo of shots rang out over Apollonia, but the shooting was distant, well away from their position. They made good time and were back in the *folbots* by 0335 hours. This was much earlier than Macpherson had anticipated, and gave them time to get back to the submarine before first light.

'But that was where our troubles began,' Macpherson said. 'The sea was smooth and we reached our RV with six or seven minutes to spare, confirmed our position, and found that the cupboard was bare. We couldn't find *Talisman* at all.'[4] This was an unexpected blow, especially as everything had gone so well until now. Willmott had obviously given up waiting for them, they thought, which was surprising as the RV time wasn't up yet, and it was not like the Royal Navy to cut an RV short when lives were at stake. Ratcliffe suggested that the boat's watch might have heard the shooting near Apollonia and thought the patrol had been compromised, but Macpherson didn't buy this: the gunshots had been too far from their area of interest.

All in all, the absence of the *Talisman* was worrying, especially as it was already near first light. This put them in a quandary. The best thing to do would be to return to the beach, find an LUP and lie up there until night fell again. On the other hand, by the time they had paddled the three miles to the beach it would be daylight, and they would run the risk of being spotted by shore patrols. In the end they decided to spend the whole day at sea, staying about five miles out, paddling just enough to counteract the drift. It was a very long day; they had no means of sheltering from the furnace sun, or of hiding from the enemy aircraft that frequently flew over, obliging them to pretend to be native fishermen. To make matters worse, Macpherson had nothing to eat: he had been so certain they would be picked up on time that he had given away his precious ham sandwiches to the others when they had shown signs of fatigue the previous night.

At last light they returned to the RV. Midnight came and there was no sign of *Talisman*. At 0130 hours it suddenly grew very dark, and a swell began. The waves started showing white crests. Then, over the sea-sounds, they suddenly became aware of the throb of an engine. Moments later the pitch darkness was punctured by a red light showing shorewards, not very far away, just as they had agreed with Willmott. It had to be *Talisman*.

They began to paddle towards the light as fast as they could– faster than Macpherson had ever paddled before. But they were just ten yards distant from the vessel when they suddenly realized that what they were approaching was not the *Talisman* but a motorized caique loaded with Italian soldiers. Frantically they turned their *folbots* about, retiring hastily into the folds of the night.

They paddled for another half hour, but the waves were still high, forcing them to bail continuously. Macpherson knew they had to head back to the beach now, or be caught once again by daylight. They had been paddling almost continuously for twenty-four hours, virtually without food, and immediately before that they had hiked several miles across the escarpment. If they had to spend another day at sea, Macpherson thought, they would almost certainly be unable to keep up the bailing, and would be swamped. To cap it all, Macpherson's *folbot* had become unseaworthy; it was unlikely to stand up to another day at sea.

Macpherson and his men headed for a beach about six miles from their original landing place – in case that beach had been compromised –

and were lucky enough to find an ideal LUP: a cave with a concealed entrance, where they hid the *folbots* just as the skies opened and a torrential downpour began. This was also fortuitous, as they had finished what water they'd brought with them, and they managed to catch rainwater in a tin can they found in the cave. The downpour stopped after an hour and they ventured out, finding some wild broccoli from the nearby scrub. They lit a fire in the cave and made wild broccoli soup in the tin can – it turned out to be thoroughly unpleasant, Macpherson remembered.

At least they were out of sight, and they dozed until night fell on their third day. As one of the canoes was unserviceable, they decided that the two SBS officers would make for the RV in the one good *folbot*, and, if they found *Talisman*, one of them would return for the others. While they were away, Macpherson and Evans went foraging for water; Ratcliffe had left his water-bottle. The only spring they had come across was near the road they'd spotted the previous night, and that was being guarded by the static patrol whose tents were pitched close by. However, they were thirsty and there was nothing for it but to chance a foray. 'Fortunately it was not unduly difficult to approach,' Macpherson said, 'and, while Evans kept watch, I crept up to fill the flask and slake my own thirst. Evans then drank the flask on his own account, and filled it again to bring water back for the other pair. Sure enough, we found them unsuccessfully returned.'[5]

Not only had the two SBS officers not encountered *Talisman*, but their *folbot* had been badly damaged in the heavy swell and, while trying to keep it off the rocks, the compass had been smashed into the bargain. This really was a disaster, as it meant that they had no chance of finding the RV again. Now they had no choice but to make for Tobruk on foot through enemy territory. The worst of it was that, without the compass, they would have to hug the coast, where there was certain to be considerable enemy activity.

They hid the *folbots*, covering them in sand and scrub, but kept their

Mae Wests – water was hard to come by on the Libyan coast, and the lifejackets could double as very effective water-bags.

At last light they set out, making first for the spring where Macpherson and Evans had filled their water-bottle earlier. Macpherson crawled in just as he had the previous day and filled the water-bags successfully, but as he withdrew, the enemy patrol's dog woke up and, smelling the intruder, made a beeline for him. Macpherson whipped out the knife he was carrying and as the dog sprang, embedded it very neatly in the animal's throat. It went down without a whelp. 'We heard as we departed a considerable inquest round him,' Macpherson said. 'But as far as I know, no pursuit was attempted.'[6]

This was the escaping party's first mistake, for it alerted the Italians at once to the presence of enemy forces in the area. If Macpherson had had the chance to think carefully, he probably would not have killed the dog, but he had been obliged to act quickly and his action had been natural and instinctive.

It was too late for self-reproach, so they pressed on quickly eastwards along the line of the first escarpment. 'Constant ups and downs in to the steep wadis meant that mileage was great but progress distressingly small,' Macpherson said. 'If we were able to find a secluded route under the shadow of the cliff-line, we made a certain amount of progress during the day as well as by night. Periodically there were odd groups of soldiery to be avoided, but for the main it was only a question of keeping out of sight of the beach-road camps and of the movement on the second escarpment.'[7]

They carried their Mae Wests slung over their shoulders like bandoliers and were able to refill them periodically from rain-pools in the cliffs, but by 1 November, two days into the escape and evasion phase, hunger had become an acute problem. It had been four days since their unpleasant broccoli soup, and six since the ham sandwiches, and Macpherson knew that if they didn't find something to eat pretty soon they would be in trouble. Trevor Ravenscroft, the trainee SBS officer, was in a particularly bad way.

There were no Senussi camps or even Italian settlers' farms in the region, but that night they came across the camp of a German transport unit and decided to raid it for food. While the two SBS officers remained in hiding with the group's water-supply, Macpherson and Evans approached the place. Close up, Macpherson saw that it was a mobile workshop, 'full of the most delightful machinery but wholly devoid of stores or cookhouses.'[8] Unlike British soldiers, who cooked communally, German troops were issued with their rations individually. There was no alternative but to step right into the lion's den: they would have to raid the tents of the sleeping troops.

'There was the usual guard at the entry,' Macpherson said, 'but a very easy perimeter fence to get through, and the tents were big ones – I left Evans outside and went into one of the big tents – the trouble is when you get in the tent you don't even have the stars – I tried to accustom myself for a time, and began to see the shadows of the bunk beds they were in – three-tiered bunks which I'd never seen before – it was absolutely black. Each bunk bed had a sort of locker tray at the end of it so the only thing I could sensibly do was feel in those locker trays and you got the happy feeling of long bread rolls in one, and some cheese in the next one which I could smell – I took what I thought was easy and quick – I beetled out for the door but going out maybe I wasn't as careful, or maybe my hands were rather full, but the tent flap hit with the noise of a gunshot, and there were immediate shouts of alarm … and turnout and this and that and as far as I could see the two sentries were shooting each other – but I dived through the hole in the fence and we got away.'[9]

The noise of the gunshots had awakened every German soldier in the area. Macpherson and Evans had to move sharply to evade the pursuit, but when they got back to the RV with Ravenscroft and Ratcliffe, they found that the two SBS officers had already vanished, probably thinking the others had been bagged. They pressed on through the darkness for hours until the hullabaloo was far behind them, then settled down to devour the bread and cheese. Ravenscroft and Ratcliffe had gone off with the water and they had to force the bread and cheese down their dry throats. In spite of the discomfort, the food made them feel like new men, and gave them the energy to press on. It was a further twelve hours before they found an Arab water-hole and were able to slake their almost overwhelming thirst.

The following night – 2/3 November – Macpherson made his second and last mistake. They came across an unguarded automatic military telephone exchange at the top of a cliff, and couldn't resist the temptation to play the commando. They worked off their frustrations, smashing everything that could be smashed, tearing out wires and hurling parts over the cliff. Macpherson realized too late that this was a bad move, as it would pinpoint their exact position to the enemy. The reaction was slow in coming, but it was decisive when it did. The next night, just as they were approaching Derna along an apparently deserted road, a platoon of thirty Italian regulars on bicycles suddenly appeared out of nowhere and surrounded them. They just had time to throw their pistols and ammunition away before being captured. ' There was no point trying to fight it out as there were too many,' Macpherson said. 'I felt bloody irritated because I realized that destroying the telephone exchange was a stupid mistake. Evans made absolutely no comment – he was a stolid reliable individual and he took life as it came.'[10]

Macpherson was now grimly aware that in drawing the enemy's attention he and Evans also ran the risk of compromising the 11 Commando landing due here in only two weeks' time. They were taken to Derna and separated. Macpherson was immediately subjected to harsh tactical questioning, but as he and his interrogators had no common language, it was easy for him to ignore their questions – asked in broken English, French and even, to his amusement, Latin – giving only his name, rank, serial number and date of birth. Meanwhile, Evans was getting the *good cop* treatment – food, wine and a comfortable bed. The Italians probably reckoned that, because he was an enlisted man, he would show his gratitude by spilling the beans. 'But Evans was one of the dourest lads that ever came from Glasgow,' Macpherson said, 'and he accepted everything with politeness and without repayment.'[11]

After eight hours solid of interrogation, Macpherson was taken to a washroom for a drink. The washroom had a window and without a second thought he plunged through it, finding a motorcycle outside. It started on his first kick and, hardly believing his luck, Macpherson roared off into what he hoped would be the wild blue yonder. Unfortunately, the machine conked out after only twenty yards – the petrol feeder had been switched off, and before he could find the valve, he had been grabbed by the Italians.

Two days later Ravenscroft and Ratcliffe were brought in to join them. They had split up the night Macpherson and Evans had raided the mobile workshop; Ravenscroft had given himself up to their pursuers the next day. Ratcliffe had been caught and captured the following night. The four of them were bundled into a closed van and taken to Benghazi, where they were interrogated again; this time the tactical questioning was less rough, but more cunning. It amused Macpherson later to find that in his POW dossier there was a report of what he called a purely fictitious interview, which his interrogators must simply have made up as he was completely unable to communicate with them. The Italians did find the *folbots* concealed in the cave and must have worked out that Macpherson's patrol had come in by sea. They must also have realized this was a recce party, and that suggested a landing in the near future. They were on the alert for a British offensive anyway – a G(R) sabotage team they had captured recently near Derna had revealed that a push was imminent. On 15 November, *Ultra* intercepted an Italian report via army Enigma that they had 'learned from various reliable sources that the British were planning a landing near Apollonia.'[12]

The opening gambit of the Rommel Raid had, as Macpherson later admitted, displayed the woeful amateurism of special forces in 1941. 'When, in the professionalism of the Montgomery era, and after,' he wrote, 'one looked back on those days, one could not but shudder and wonder at our survival.'[13] Yet the main culprit in this particular case was, as it turned out, once again the Royal Navy: a navigation error had put *Talisman* in the wrong bay, though why Willmott had not been able to correct the error on subsequent nights has never been explained.

For Macpherson it was the beginning of two years as a POW in both Italian and German camps, but it was not the end of the war. For the Rommel Raid, though, it meant that a possible landing by 11 Commando at Ras Hilal was now irrevocably compromised.

17 OPERATION CRUSADER

1–9 NOVEMBER 1941

When *Talisman* came back to Alexandria without Tommy Macpherson and the SBS team, Geoffrey Keyes realized that Bob Laycock had been correct; he had predicted that although it might be easy enough to reach the objectives, it was going to be a different kettle of fish getting back on the boats. Mike Willmott could not tell him what had happened to the recce party, but it had to be assumed they were dead or in the bag. On 1 November they were officially posted Missing.

The Ras Hilal landing site was no longer viable, but instead of calling off the operation, Keyes decided to go for Haselden's beach at Khashm al-Kalb. He must have known by this point, if not earlier, that there was no way they would be able to snatch Rommel alive. Since the chances of getting back on the submarines were only about fifty-fifty anyway, the enemy Commander-in-Chief was going to have to be bumped off before they got back to the beach-head. It was looking more and more like a kamikaze operation, but Keyes refused to be put off. When Laycock voiced his reservations, Keyes begged him not to repeat them in front of Eighth Army commander General Cunningham in case he decided to put the kibosh on the mission. Cunningham himself said later that he would not have hesitated to cancel the operation 'had Keyes shown the slightest apprehension or doubt as to its feasibility.'[1]

Three days later, on 3 November, Keyes' men were issued with infantry reconnaissance boats and bussed to Alexandria harbour to practise with them. These boats were quite new to the commandos: they were two-man inflatables, with black rubber skins, about eight feet long and weighing about sixty pounds. They came in yard-long packets, each with a pair of bellows, and had to be inflated by foot on the submarine's forward casing – the noise the bellows made was astonishingly loud, and was likely to alert any shore-watchers miles away. When the dinghies were inflated and the commandos in position, the idea was that the submarine would gently trim down and the dinghies would float off. The commandos would then paddle furiously for the shore.

Their kit, apart from what they carried in their webbing, would be secured in the dinghies, waterproofed by oilskins, sealed in petrol-cans or simply tied up in the ever-trusty condom. This included their weapons, so if they were fired on from the beach, they could not immediately return fire; they would have to rely on the SBS *folbot* crews and the blue-jackets with their 4-inch gun. The two-man landing boats were stable enough in glassy seas, but easily rolled in a swell; they were at their most vulnerable when the commandos were actually getting aboard – if a dinghy were washed off the casing then, the men might easily be drowned, especially those who couldn't swim. They would be issued with Mae West lifejackets, but in view of the weight of their equipment, it was generally agreed they needed two each.

Once the men had landed on shore, the dinghies would be towed back to the submarine on a floating line – a grass line – by the SBS teams. The handling of the grass line proved a problem even in Alexandria harbour. This was the only time the commandos were able to practise landing with the boats before the operation, and to make matters worse, the actual submarines were not available for training: they had to rehearse inflating and launching the dinghies from a single motor-torpedo boat. The weather was very calm, and Keyes was pleased to note that after a little practise they had the landing-time down to an hour. Some of the men were distinctly unimpressed by their new transport, though: 'Can't say I have much faith in the rubber boats,' Corporal Charles Lock wrote in his diary that night. 'I feel depressed about this "stunt" and life in general. Shall I ever see Ruth [Lock's fiancée] again?'[2]

On 5 November the raiding party was mustered for a trial night march. They had been told that they would probably be behind enemy lines for ten days, and though no date had yet been given for the stunt, most of them guessed it was near. Lock, who had developed a fever after the night in Alexandria harbour, did not take part in the march. 'I don't like the look of this stunt a bit,' he wrote, 'and I think they are trying to do too much.'[3]

The actual objectives remained a secret, even to the other officers, though parties were sent out into the desert to practise placing demolition charges on lengths of disused rail. Haselden had arrived back at HQ Western Desert Forces from Siwa on 27 October, bringing an update on Rommel's presence at Beda Littoria and promising two Senussi guides from the Libyan Arab Force who would be landed from the submarines; they knew the way to his HQ. The promised Senussis arrived at the commandos' base at Amiriyya on 7 November. Their appearance convinced the men that the stunt was about to take off. That day, the Senussis showed the commandos how to wear the Arab *jurd* – a thick woollen robe used as both a cloak and a blanket, similar to a Moroccan *djellaba*. This caused some consternation as the commandos had not been trained to operate in disguise as G(R) did: it would be a breach of the Geneva Convention, meaning that if captured, they could be shot as spies. There were even more ominous rumblings ahead – all the Bren-gunners but one were dropped from the Orbat – the Order of Battle – meaning that the commandos now had virtually no infantry support weapons at all. The tension became palpable. The following day, a Saturday, they were allowed to attend the NAAFI concert at the YMCA, but their minds were on other things. 'Waiting for this stunt is rotten,' Charles Lock wrote in his diary. 'Everyone makes jokes but the strain is showing.'[4]

It had been decided that Haselden and a group of G(R) agents and Arab NCOs would go in early with the LRDG. Haselden and one of the Arabs would complete the journey on foot disguised as Bedouin tribesmen, secure the beach and vector in the submarines on a pre-arranged signal – a set of four dashes given three times. Haselden also sent along a corporal from the Middle East Commando, a Palestinian Jew named Avishalom Drori, who spoke both Arabic and Italian. He would be Keyes' Arabic interpreter.

Drori had been called by Colonel Airey at the beginning of November and told to take a letter to Keyes at Amariyya. The G(R) chief had told him nothing about the nature of the mission, though Drori realized he was involved in something hush-hush, which excited him and made him, in his own words, 'feel very important'. Drori, an unassuming man, who nevertheless had all his wits about him, had expected a beef-faced Colonel type, but was pleasantly surprised to find that Keyes was a tall young man, without formality, who asked him to sit down and quizzed him about his languages.

One thing that bothered Keyes was the fact that he had only one officer he knew well, and more importantly, knew he could rely on: Captain Ian Glennie of the Gordon Highlanders, who had fought with 11 Commando at the Litani River. For the rest, he had to depend on untried strangers. Lieutenant Roy Royston Cooke, of the Royal West Kent Regiment, had arrived at the Commando HQ a few weeks earlier, just as everyone else was leaving, and asked to be taken on. He was a few years older than Keyes, and highly enthusiastic, though he had no commando training and was certainly not *one of them*. He had one great asset, though: he spoke fluent Italian.

The other officers were also new to 11 Commando. Captain Robin Francis Campbell, General List, had come out with Laycock's 8 Commando as liaison officer. He was a friend of Randolph Churchill, with whom he had been working since its disbandment at a desk in Cairo, turning out information broadsheets. Campbell was 29, a journalist by trade. He came from London, had attended Wellington School and had read history for a year at New College, Oxford. The son of a baronet, he had slipped easily into Laycock's White's Club set, even though, unlike most of his fellows, he was married with two sons. He had also had a proper career before the war: he had spent eighteen months as Reuter's correspondent in Warsaw and another eighteen months as their man in Berlin, then he joined the BBC and worked as a sub-editor on their Polish/Czechoslovakian Desk from 1939–40. He spoke French and German fluently, was a fair shot with a rifle, could swim, sail, drive a truck and fly an aeroplane, and on recruitment to 8 Commando had just completed the SOE Irregular Warfare course at Inverailot in Scotland: altogether, as the commandos interviewer wrote on his application form, a very good type.

Keyes thought Campbell's German would probably come in useful, and took him along as his detachment Second-in-Command. The third newcomer, Lieutenant David G. Sutherland of the Black Watch, had actually been training with 11 Commando since 26 September. An Old Etonian who had been in the same house as Keyes at school, he was only on loan to Keyes' detachment: he belonged to 51 Middle East Commando and had been brought in to beef up demolition drills. Sutherland had brought with him several men, including Sergeant Fred Birch and Corporal John Kerr of the Liverpool Scottish, a TA battalion of the Cameron Highlanders. Birch, a one-time meat-porter at Liverpool Abbatoir, had served with No. 7 Commando on Crete. He and scores of other fugitives had escaped from the island after Laycock's departure by jumping on an ALC. They had pointed the landing craft towards Egypt and hoped for the best. Halfway across the Mediterranean, the engine had conked out and they had jerry-rigged a sail. Almost miraculously they had hit the North African coast near Buq-Buq, behind their own lines. In spite of the total lack of food and water, they had not suffered a single casualty.

Since 7 Commando had virtually ceased to exist on Crete, Birch and Kerr had been attached to 51 Middle East Commando, where they had trained in special demolitions. Keyes had imported them simply to help bring his men up to speed in sabotage. Then, only days before *Operation*

Flipper, an entire tent of six men had been wiped off the Orbat, put into quarantine when one man was found infected with scabies. Birch, Kerr and others had agreed to join the mission as replacements.

There was also a Frenchman, Lieutenant H.G. Chevalier, a cotton-company man like Haselden, and one of the dozen Arabic-speaking G(R) agents who had been working in Cyrenaica, but whom Keyes didn't know at all. He would also take part in the operation as a saboteur. As for Laycock, Keyes was ambivalent about his presence and his role. Even though they had both attended the same school, there was little mutual admiration. Although *Operation Flipper* had been Keyes' idea from the outset, Laycock was the senior rank, and OC commandos, and would obviously have the final say. According to Macpherson, Laycock's 'equivocal stance, continued presence and interference ... muddied the waters considerably for Keyes'.[5]

On Sunday 9 November, the commandos were issued with rations and Arab *jurds* and told to pack for a full dress-rehearsal that afternoon. Some thought the rehearsal was a ruse and that the real operation was at last underway. At 1400 hours they were bussed back to Alexandria harbour and taken aboard *Medway*; from her deck they scrambled on to the casings of *Torbay* and *Talisman* – the first time they had encountered the submarines. After a familiarization tour of the boats, they waited until it was dark, then practised inflating and launching their dinghies from the forward casings – the only practice they were to get before the real thing. Though they were shipped back to Amiriyya at 2100 hours, most of them were pretty sure that this was to be their last night of peace before the op. 'I will do my duty, with God's help, on this job,' Charles Lock wrote in his diary. 'But I am not looking forward to it much.'[6]

While his commandos were being shown around the submarines that afternoon, Keyes had been at Maaten Baggush collecting Operational Order No. 1 for *Operation Flipper* from the Senior Naval Officer attached to Cunningham's HQ. *Operation Flipper* came under the command of Western Desert Forces, but until the commandos got ashore at Khashm al-Kalb, it was a naval operation.

The orders, dated 9 November and signed by Laycock, were marked *Most Secret* and *Not to Be Taken Ashore*. They consisted of three badly typed sheets and were terse to the point of brevity. There was almost no information about the dispositions of enemy troops, except that the area was 'many miles in the rear of enemy main defences' and that 'a few coast watchers might be encountered'. There would be no back-up from friendly forces: 'Our main forces are making a large-scale attack on LYBIA (sic),' the instruction read, 'but are not expected to enter the area until later.' The RAF would be bombing roads in Cyrenaica on 19 November, but no close air-support could be expected.

The aim of the raid was 'to inflict maximum damage on enemy HQs, comms and installations,' and the orders broke down the operation into four primary tasks. Detachment 4, commanded by Jock Haselden and consisting of G(R) agents and NCOs from the Libyan Arab Force, having gone in overland with the LRDG and after meeting the landing party, would sabotage the HQ of the Trieste Division spotted by Jake Easonsmith on his previous journey. They would blow up motor transport and then cut the telephone line near Slonta. Detachment 2 – eleven commandos commanded by Lieutenant Chevalier – would sabotage the wireless station and the Italian Intelligence Centre at Apollonia. The third detachment – twelve commandos under David Sutherland – would go for the Italian HQ at Cyrene and destroy the communications-cable mast Haselden had spotted at the Cyrene crossroads. Detachment 1, under Geoffrey Keyes himself, and consisting of Roy Cooke, Robin Campbell and twenty-two commandos, would hike the eighteen miles over the escarpment to Beda Littoria and assault both the *Afrika Korps* HQ and the villa where Rommel slept, about half a mile to the west.

The landing would be in the bay at Khashm al-Kalb, designated Bay 1; there were five other bays specified in case Bay 1 was compromised. Curiously, no date was mentioned for the actual landing and no precise time for the assaults, although Keyes was told verbally that he must operate if possible on the night of 17/18 November, which was designated D-1/D1. Detachment leaders were to carry out daylight recces of the targets on 17 November and to hit their objectives at precisely 2359 hours that night.

The orders specified that the landing would be carried out 'on the first night considered suitable by the Royal Navy', but in practice, Keyes was told, the navy would aim to get the submarines lying off the beach before last light on D-4 – 14 November – so they could carry out a daylight recce of the area by periscope before the landing. Keyes was also warned that the landing might have to be postponed because of the weather, especially as the beach at Khashm al-Kalb was exposed to the prevailing wind, but that he was to continue attempts to land until he and Laycock judged that the condition of the commandos had deteriorated too far. No landing would be attempted after the night of 21/22 November.

An RV and supply dump would be set up at the beach-head on the night of the landing and would remain open for six nights. The submarines would be available from the fourth to the sixth nights, with *Torbay* lying off Bay 1 and *Talisman* off Bay 6 – about three miles to the west. This meant in practice that all personnel would have to be back at the RV by at least two hours before dawn on 20 November. If re-embarkation was impossible, the instructions read, 'Dets [detachments] will restock from reserve dump at RV and will take to the hills and lie up and subsist as best they can on local resources until such time as they can join our own forces.' In his report later, Laycock wrote, 'The chances of a successful re-embarkation on the open beach were … considered questionable.'[7]

Apart from its primary tasks, the force would also hit opportunity targets such as telephone lines, supply dumps, convoys and aircraft, but only after the primary tasks had been completed. An SBS *folbot* detachment of two officers and two men would secure the route in before the landing, and would rake over footprints and traces of the landing after the departure of the raiding-parties to their objectives. In practice, four SBS teams came along.

The one thing the orders did not mention was the assassination or kidnapping of the German Commander-in-Chief, in case they fell into enemy hands. Nor did they provide any solutions to the problems that exercised Geoffrey Keyes most of all: how was Rommel to be recognized, and how was he to be dealt with, assuming he did not wish to be taken prisoner? Deep down, Keyes must have realized that he did not have enough men for the job. One entire troop – almost half of his men – had to be left behind at Amariyya simply because there wasn't room in the submarines and no third boat was available. This was essentially a sabotage mission; each raiding unit should have been divided into a demolition party and a covering party. The covering party would be responsible for defence, both at the objective and while moving to the objective. But Keyes didn't have the personnel to provide covering parties for all the detachments: the demolitions men would have to cover themselves.

The other thing he didn't have was detailed intelligence on the target. He did not know the obstacles he was going to be faced with: fences to cut, dogs to silence, walls to scale, spotlights to deal with, mobile patrols, how to get into the houses, how many sentries he would have to deal with, and where they would be. The idea of successfully assaulting not one but two houses was a logistical nightmare – to be effective, this would have to be done simultaneously and again, he simply didn't have the manpower. He had no aerial photographs of Beda Littoria, no detailed plan, no hard information at all. There would be no rehearsal – they would just have to improvise on the day.

To make matters even worse, Keyes had no signallers. Once landed by the submarines, the commandos would be totally out of communication with friendly forces. The only means they would have of signalling to the boats would be by electric torch.

The orders made it painfully clear that once they were on the beach at Khashm al-Kalb, they were on their own.

18 OPERATION CRUSADER

MINUS 11 DAYS
7 November 1941

Two days before Geoffrey Keyes had received his orders, Jock Haselden had once again disappeared into the blue with an LRDG patrol. The patrol, designated T2, was commanded by Captain Tony Hunter, who had been instructed to drop Haselden near Slonta. Hunter, an officer of the Royal Scots Fusiliers, had only been with the LRDG a few weeks and this was his first operation. His patrol of five Chevrolet trucks and eighteen men was carrying enough food for twenty-one days; each thirty-hundredweight truck carried thirty cases of petrol. He had to be at Haselden's drop-off point by 10 November and find a place to lie up with the vehicles until the night before *Operation Crusader* started. Then he would put a covert road-watch observation post on the Mekili-Benghazi road, and report back to HQ on the movement of all enemy traffic. He was to maintain complete radio silence until 17 November. Hunter would keep up the road-watch until 29 November, then pull out and make for the RV with Haselden near Slonta. If Haselden and his men weren't there by 0600 hours on 1 December, Hunter was to return without them.

Haselden had with him three other G(R) agents: Bob Melot, Bill Chapman and a trainee, Westall, as well as two Senussi Arabs, Mohammad Khaufer and Hussain bin Jadallah, both of the 3rd Battalion the Libyan Arab Force. Captain Melot, a Belgian cotton-merchant from Alexandria, had been a fighter ace in the First World War. Before the war he had been an enthusiastic desert motorist and had frequently taken part in desert expeditions with his wife. Later Melot would do superb work in Cyrenaica, living for weeks in a cave, collecting intelligence and transmitting it to GHQ, and later still would serve with distinction in the SAS. Captain Chapman was a quiet, self-effacing Englishman, a Cairo schoolmaster before the war. Married with three children, studious and intellectual, without any delusions of glamour, Chapman was hardly the stereotypical dashing secret agent, yet, like Melot he was to do sterling work among the Senussi later. Second Lieutenant Westall was a newcomer to G(R), a military draftee still in training, whose Arabic was not yet up to scratch. Haselden and his three comrades wore Arab robes with British Army battledress underneath. The LRDG patrol usually wore Arab *shamaghs* on operations, but this time they'd been told to leave them behind so as to look as much like the enemy as possible.

The patrol left Siwa Oasis on the afternoon of 7 November, heading past the dunes of the Great Sand Sea that rose above the oasis like frozen waves, some of them hundreds of feet high. Cyrenaica, their destination, lay north-west of the sand-sea, beyond endless plains of black limestone reg. In the sands, progress was relatively slow. Though the LRDG had perfected a technique of driving across the dunes, racing at high speed up the hard slopes on the windward side and cruising down the steep but soft slip-slopes on the leeward side, the desert was full of surprises. It was dotted with patches of soft sand like tank-traps, where the LRDG crews had to dig the wheels out with shovels and insert their steel sand-channels beneath the tyres, then pull, push or winch the vehicle out.

On this trip, though, the patrol avoided the sand-sea, heading across the plains of limestone and rippled sheets of peach-coloured sand, through areas of blasted rock and shattered hills, across gently undulating stony downs. The colours changed continuously, from black to grey to chocolate brown, to sulphur yellow and red ochre. Here and there the eye sought out a *hattia*, a tiny island of coarse halfa grass and spiky desert sedge raised by the occasional rains. There were almost no trees. Occasionally they spotted troupes of Dorcas gazelles springing away into the heat haze at forty miles an hour. November was the cool period in the Sahara, but daytime temperatures were still in the 30s centigrade as the sun blazed down from a cloudless sky. Travelling at high speed, the crews didn't notice the heat; they stripped off their shirts as the day wore on and drove wearing only shorts and chaplis, the Indian-style sandals favoured by the LRDG. As the sun rose higher, dust devils whirled mysteriously in the distance; along the horizons a heat haze quaked and trembled. Sometimes they spotted recent vehicle tracks, but they met no enemy patrols: Axis forces rarely ventured out here. The thing they feared the most was being spotted from the air – on these open plains there was no hiding place, and if an Axis pilot got a fix on them, they were sitting ducks. Fortunately this happened rarely – LRDG Chevrolets were painted a curious blend of rose-pink and olive drab that made them almost invisible against the desert's hues. On this trip Hunter noticed a lot of air activity – mostly German aircraft flying east to west – but though some of the aircraft were flying as low as three thousand feet, there was no sign that they had been noticed at all.

The patrol used a sun-compass for navigation: a steel rod welded on to the Chevy's bonnet, efficient but tedious to set. The navigator took a bearing with a magnetic compass while the vehicle was stationary, then the driver angled the vehicle until the rod on his bonnet cast a shadow on precisely the same bearing. The driver set off, taking care to keep the shadow at this angle. The sun-compass was a simple but ingenious solution to the problem of using a magnetic compass in a vehicle, where the presence of large amounts of steel constantly threw it out. Invented by Bagnold and his club before the war, its use had been pioneered and perfected by the LRDG.

At noon, the patrol would halt for a cold lunch – tinned sardines or salmon and tinned fruit salad, eaten out of their mess-tins – while the signaller got comms with Siwa, and the navigator fixed their position

General Erwin Rommel seen wearing the Knight's Cross awarded him by Hitler and the Pour le Mérite he won in 1917. Since his arrival in North Africa in February 1941, he had inflicted a succession of defeats on the British and Commonwealth forces. By October, he was aware the British were planning another attack on his positions: what he did not know was that he, himself, was the target of a commando attack planned by British special forces. *akg-images, London*

RIGHT General Sir Claude Auchinleck was dispatched to North Africa by Churchill in July 1941, replacing General Wavell, who had failed to deal with Rommel. Despite the Prime Minister's badgering, Auchinleck refused to be stampeded into premature action and scheduled his offensive – *Operation Crusader* – for November. *Imperial War Museum*

BELOW The vital port of Tobruk was still held by the British and Commonwealth forces, but now lay 80 miles behind enemy lines. The garrison was to attack the forces surrounding it at the same time as the British advanced from the east. Here, tank crews are briefed on the forthcoming battle. *IWM*

LEFT David Stirling, founder of the SAS, wove many of the creation myths surrounding its establishment. His social connections were the key: a case of who you know, rather than *Who Dares Wins*. IWM

BELOW German Junkers Ju-87 Stuka dive-bombers over Tobruk. The first ever SAS combat mission involved 60 officers and men, parachuting behind enemy lines to blow up the German aircraft on their airfields. If the British plans worked, *Operation Crusader* would begin with the German air force grounded and the German commander-in-chief captured or dead. *Hulton Archive*

RIGHT Lieutenant-General Neil Ritchie (left), Auchinleck's Deputy Chief of Staff, knew the Stirling family well; he had shot grouse on the Stirling estate at Keir before the war. He gave his blessing to Stirling's idea of an airborne raiding force. *IWM*

LEFT Battle is opened: a Bren gun carrier of the Indian army passes a knocked out Panzer III as the British forces advance on Tobruk. *IWM*

ABOVE *Luftwaffe* ground-crew beside a Messerschmitt Bf-110 fighter-bomber. Desert airfields were temporary bases, often lightly defended. It was hoped that the small SAS teams could get among the parked aircraft without detection and destroy them with explosive charges. *akg-images, London*

ABOVE British Matilda tanks on the move outside the Tobruk perimeter on the second day of *Operation Crusader*. *IWM*

BELOW LEFT Men of a South African armoured car squadron celebrate Christmas on the Cathedral Mole at Benghazi at the end of *Operation Crusader*. Although defeated, Rommel broke contact and withdrew to regroup. His reputation among both British and German forces was, if anything, even higher after *Operation Crusader*, and his men chalked defiant messages on the walls of Benghazi. They would be back. *IWM*

BELOW RIGHT A British Vickers Mk. VI light tank crosses an anti-tank ditch on its way to the front, late November 1941. *IWM*

ABOVE Rommel's friend, General Johannes Ravenstein, commander of the 21st Panzer Division was captured on 29 November. The driver of his staff car thought he was heading towards a German unit, when he stopped next to an outpost of the 21st New Zealand Battalion. *IWM*

LEFT David Stirling seen in 1942, by which time the SAS had absorbed the hard lessons of its first mission and replaced the casualties. *IWM*

ABOVE Lieutenant-Colonel Geoffrey Keyes was awarded a posthumous Victoria Cross for the attack on Rommel's HQ. The raid was born of one man's ambition to achieve glory and, as so many times in British history, it was rescued from ignominy by the valour and determination of the ordinary enlisted men. *IWM*

BELOW Rommel's real headquarters was in the field, with his famous half-track, packed with radios. Here, he addresses some of his *Afrika Korps* soldiers outside Tobruk. © *Hulton-Deutsch Collection/Corbis*

from dead reckoning calculations. Then they would press on until darkness fell. As soon as the sun had vanished, the heat dissipated quickly and the temperature plunged. Shirts and pullovers went back on first, then greatcoats or desert duffle-coats. Someone would make a fire by pouring petrol into a tin filled with sand, then they would cook bully-beef stew and brew strong tea laced with army-issue rum – a special prerogative of the LRDG. After the crews had eaten, they would fill their water-bottles from the tanks on the trucks and sit round the fire talking until the flames burned out. When the signaller had finished his messages the wireless would be tuned to the BBC for the news at 2000 hours, or to a music station such as the Axis-held Radio Belgrade. Afterwards each man would look for his own soft patch of sand and curl up in his sleeping-bag or blanket. No sentries were posted: the chances of being discovered by the enemy at night in the Sahara were virtually nil.

In the morning the crews would be up as the first crimson flares of dawn crept over the desert sky. Breakfast was porridge, tinned bacon, sausage, oatmeal biscuits and tea, and afterwards they cleaned their mess-tins and mugs with handfuls of sand – it was efficient, and anyway, water was far too valuable to spare for washing utensils. By the time the men were packed up the drivers were already warming the engines, and as the sun burst across the dark shelf of the desert in its full glory, the patrol would be on its way.

On 10 November the landscape changed abruptly. The smooth gravel plains merged into brown undulating moorland dotted with stunted acacias and beds of sun-bleached goat-grass. Here at last were signs of life: goat tracks, camel tracks, cairns of stones marking ancient burials or showing the direction of some long-lost camel-path. Now the going became so rough that the drivers were no longer able to keep to the bearing; they had to resort to the more hallowed faculty of the mark one human eyeball. Haselden and one of the Arabs were particularly good at this, and piloted the patrol safely to their destination in the deep system of wadis created by the run-off from the Jebel al-Akhdar hills. In the Wadi

Heleighma, about twenty-five miles west of Mekili, they hid the vehicles in a patch of spindly acacias a mile from the main track. The trucks were strategically arranged to make best use of the available cover, then the crews went about making them invisible, covering them in camouflage nets and twigs. After dark that evening Haselden and Mohammad Khaufer set off towards Slonta, leaving the remaining four G(R) men with the LRDG.

There was little for the crews to do now but sleep and wait, but sleeping in the desert by day was a real penance. There was no shelter from the sun and the heat and flies pursued them relentlessly wherever they moved. It was a relief when the blessed cool of sunset came. The patrol had endured three days of this purgatory when Haselden's LAF man, Mohammad Khaufer, suddenly materialized like a djinn out of the desert, carrying some urgent news: the Trieste Division, the unit Jake Easonsmith had seen moving into place three weeks earlier, had now left Slonta; it had been seen heading east. This suggested a move against Tobruk: it was priceless intelligence.

Hunter had been instructed to maintain radio silence until 17 November; he pondered whether he ought to break it. In the end he decided that GHQ had to know, despite the risk of compromising the current op, and had his signaller send the message in cipher to Cairo. The remainder of Haselden's party left that night, and Hunter's patrol moved off with some relief to carry out the second part of their mission.

Haselden had spent his time wandering through Bedouin camps and villages, eliciting the latest intelligence on the movement of enemy forces. At midnight on 13 November, the day before 11 Commando was due to land, he knocked on the door of his old friend, Hussain Taher, at Slonta. The *Mudir* welcomed him; Haselden was exhausted, having walked the best part of a hundred miles in just three days. After they had eaten and drunk sweet tea, Haselden said, 'I need two men to go with me to Marsa al-Hammama [the local name for Khashm al-Kalb] on a very important mission – good, trustworthy men – and a horse.'

Hussain promised he would do his best, and while Haselden rested in his house, he set out to find a guide, returning a little later with a venerable old Senussi tribesman called Mikhael Hamad, saying that he could only get the one man. He agreed to lend Haselden his own horse, provided he returned it within three days.

At first light on 14 November, Haselden and his companion set off for the last time towards Khashm al-Kalb.

19 OPERATION CRUSADER

MINUS 8 DAYS

10 November 1941

For 'Crap' Miers, meanwhile, there was a new problem: *Torbay* and *Talisman* had never carried soldiers before. With fifty-nine commandos and four SBS *folbot* crews, he had sixty-seven men with full kit to accommodate. There were also the four *folbots* and twenty-eight rubber dinghies to be stowed away. Paul Chapman, first lieutenant on *Torbay*, who had to find a place for everyone without interfering with the smooth running of the boat, was acutely aware that 'these chaps had to be landed well fed, in the peak of condition and with their morale high.'[1] His solution was drastic: the six torpedo reloads for the internal tubes had to be sacrificed and their racks converted into bunks. There still wouldn't be enough space for everyone, but the commandos would just have to follow the naval practice of hot bunking, occupying the bunks of the bluejackets who were on watch. Similar arrangements were made on *Talisman*.

Originally, Laycock maintained, he was to have travelled on *Torbay* with Keyes, but swapped to *Talisman* at the last moment when Ian Glennie reported sick, since there was no other officer on *Talisman* who knew the plan. Laycock devoted a full paragraph to this in his official report, which is significant, because Operational Order No. 1, dated 9 November, the day before the operation kicked off, stated unequivocably that 'in the event of non-arrival of *Talisman*, Lieutenant Colonel Keyes to take command.' This clearly indicated that Laycock had always intended to go with *Talisman*. Laycock was evidently making a *scusatio non petita* – an unasked-for excuse – in his report, because separating himself from the senior naval officer – Miers – was a major *faux-pas*. Paul Chapman said, 'The whole, sometimes unhappy, history of Combined Operations has pointed to the importance of co-location of the officer commanding troops and the senior officer afloat. Unfortunately, in this case, personalities may have led to disregard of military prudence.'[2] Though Chapman didn't go any further, he had said enough to indicate that Laycock had problems with either Miers or Keyes – or perhaps both. Miers was senior to Laycock in length of service, and was his superior until the commandos were on shore.

Miers must also have heard about Laycock's shabby behaviour on Crete: to a Navy man, the idea of a captain abandoning ship before his men would have been absolute anathema; he could never approve such behaviour. There was little love lost between Keyes and Laycock and Miers was an old friend of the Keyes family. He had served under Admiral Sir Roger Keyes years ago on Malta and remembered Geoffrey as a boy.

On the other hand, Laycock knew and admired *Talisman's* skipper, Michael Willmott, whom he had recommended to Auchinleck in his 17 October memo as 'a really bold young naval officer'. Whatever the case, Laycock should have travelled on *Torbay* with Keyes and Miers, and he clearly knew it.

Torbay and *Talisman* were still moored alongside *Medway* in Alexandria Harbour on 10 November when the commandos came aboard at 1500 hours and settled in. Keyes, bunking with Robin Campbell and Roy Cooke on *Torbay*, felt a little alone; Ian Glennie, the one officer he knew well, had been left behind. Still, he was excited: his big chance had at last arrived. To him, the raid was an inspired mission.[3] During the voyage, he wrote to Pamela, a long-term friend with whom he corresponded regularly, saying that he had finally got his wish: 'I am on my way to do more dirty work at the crossroads,' he went on. 'It is by no means an easy task, it is my show, my men, and my responsibility. The chances of getting away are moderately good, but if you get this letter, it means I have made a bit of a bog, and not got back ... Even if you do get this letter it may only mean that I am languishing in an Eyetie clink, or trekking through darkest Africa … if all goes well … I should be one more rung up the ladder.'[4]

In her biography of Keyes, his sister Elizabeth turned this – Geoffrey's last letter to anyone outside the family – into a tragic expression of unre-quited love. In fact, the main object of his message was to congratulate Pamela on having become engaged in September to one of his best friends. According to Geoffrey's younger brother, Roger (Lord Roger Keyes of Zeebrugge), Geoffrey and Pamela had never been close; there had never been any question of their ever getting married.[5] Elizabeth herself mentions, earlier in her biography, that Geoffrey once told his brother, 'We stayed friends because I never tried to kiss her.'[6]

'He was quite content,' Elizabeth wrote, 'that their friendship should remain "absolutely platonic".'[7] It is unlikely that Geoffrey ever had a serious girlfriend; he had an overwhelming ambition to distinguish himself and climb to the top of the ladder.

The submarines cast off from *Medway* at 1622 hours and put out into the blue. The standard submarine procedure was to remain surfaced in darkness and to submerge during daylight hours. At 1832 hours *Talisman* challenged another submarine heading for Alexandria; it turned out to be *Thorn*, a sister-boat of the flotilla. A little later they put up identification grenades as they neared three destroyers of the Mediterranean Fleet practising night-shooting. By 2000 hours they had cleared the fleet exercise and were on their own.

At first light the next day, with *Talisman* now trailing twenty-odd miles behind, Miers took *Torbay* down for a routine trim check. For 21-year-old ex-Royal Artilleryman Jim Gornall, it was an exciting and eerie experience to be suddenly so far below the waves; it reminded him of the time his father had first taken him to sea, when he was only six years old. His dad, a Fleetwood trawler skipper in civilian life, had been a 'Wavy Navy' minesweeper captain in the First World War; he had had two ships blown from under him.

His father had taken Gornall to sea four times between the ages of six and ten; they'd travelled as far as Iceland, St Kilda and Bear Island. Gornall had loved it. 'Nobody bothered in those days,' he said. 'If anyone complained about you being off school [you said] it was for reasons of health.' He often used to tell his commando mates the story of the time his father had been taking him to the boat early one morning with a school friend called Billy Fiddler, who lived round the corner. 'So we're walking down Church Street in Preston,' he said, 'with our things in pillowcases over each shoulder – Dad behind – and a copper stopped us – said, "Where are you going with these two?"

'"I'm taking them to sea with me," Dad said, "so off you go!"'[8]

Though Gornall often felt he should have gone for the navy, instead, in 1937, he enlisted in the 4th Battalion the Royal North Lancashire Regiment, as the Number Two on a Vickers anti-aircraft gun. 'I finished up in Orkney in the 62nd Searchlight Regiment, Royal Artillery,' he said, 'as Number Four on a 19-centimetre searchlight – on a long arm, controlling a bloody searchlight, and I didn't like it at all, I can assure you. You had no means of fighting back – talk about "fighting your light". It just wasn't on. There were three of us from the Regiment that volunteered for the commandos.'[9]

Now Gornall stood watching the needle on the big fathometer going round and round, wondering when it was going to stop and listening to the hull of the submarine creaking ominously as the boat went down to seventy feet. Suddenly, to everyone's alarm, the strident voice of the Engineer Officer, Lieutenant H.A. 'Tonno' Kidd, could be heard reporting by telephone to Captain Miers, 'Yes sir, we have a hole in the hull under the port muffler tanks.'

The muffler tanks were water-baths designed to suppress the noise of the boat's diesel exhausts, which were passed through them. The leak was a clear round hole in the hull plate over the port main engine, between the 108th and 109th frames, where the bottom of the muffler tank was unjacketed. The commandos didn't fully appreciate how serious this was; Captain Miers, however, was extremely worried. What had probably happened, he thought, was that the tank had been burned through, allowing hot and corrosive exhaust fumes to impinge on the hull. He already knew that the design of these tanks was unsatisfactory, but that didn't solve the immediate problem.

Miers had Kidd and his men hammer a wooden bung into the hole. The plug held for the moment, but he did not know if it would hold if the boat went deeper, or for how long. He didn't know if the plug would pop out, or whether the hole would get bigger, nor if the plating on either side of the hole was also corroded. Cautiously, Miers took the boat down to eighty feet. The plug continued to hold, and Kidd saw no sign of other perforations, but the captain was still unhappy. He knew he should report the defect immediately to *Medway*, but he also knew that when he did so, Captain Dewhurst would almost certainly recall *Torbay*, and that would be the end of *Operation Flipper* – or at the very least, the commandos would be landed with only half their force.

On the other hand, if he didn't call in the defect, he would be expected to go into operation against enemy shipping off Benghazi immediately after landing the raiding party, an extremely hazardous operation with *Torbay* in her present condition.

Miers did not share this problem with Keyes, but mulled it over carefully by himself. After a while he came up with a cunning solution. He instructed his radio operator to send a signal that was deliberately corrupt: 'Will be unable to patrol after landing commandos because of defective *bananas*'. By the time *Medway* had asked for clarification, and he had explained that *bananas* should have read *hull*, the commandos would be off.

He never regretted his hoax. 'There was no way *Operation Crusader* could be held up because a few commandos weren't in position,' Paul Chapman said. 'They knew it; we knew it; the attempt had to be made.'[10]

The boats spent most of the next two days cruising at periscope depth, but they sighted nothing. The commandos found the submarines far more comfortable than they had expected, and were pleasantly surprised at how well the navy looked after them. They spent most of their time sleeping, eating, writing letters home and playing cards.

On 12 November Keyes called the commandos on *Torbay* together and revealed the previously unknown part of their mission: their job was to kill or capture Rommel. In the stunned silence that followed, he added, 'If he comes quietly, we'll bring him along. If he doesn't, we'll knock him off.'

'I thought, *Jesus wept!*,' Jim Gornall said. 'How far are we going? I thought, we'll never get him – not alive anyway. Rommel was no halfwit. He was a bloke like Paddy Mayne – really on the ball.'[11] Rommel was as big an icon to the British as he was to his own troops, and the idea of a weedy young society officer like Keyes, whose experience of battle amounted to precisely one action, taking on Rommel – one of the most brilliant and experienced soldiers of his time – was almost amusing.

Afterwards, there was some controversy as to whether Rommel had in fact been the target at all. In his book on the Rommel Raid, *Das Rommel Unternehmen*, Austrian writer Hans Edelmaier has suggested that since Rommel is not mentioned in the Operational Orders, the idea that they were after the Desert Fox was added later as a propaganda stunt. The testimony of the survivors disproves this. As for the idea of snatching Rommel, Elizabeth Keyes said Keyes himself knew that they were unlikely to take him alive: 'In the official communiqué it was announced that the object of the raid was "to capture Rommel,"' she wrote in her biography of her brother, 'but Geoffrey was far too realistic to suppose that a man of General Rommel's type could be captured and marched across country to be embarked in a submarine. He ... told his men they were going to "get Rommel" – a very different story ... He can have been under no illusions as to the possibility of taking prisoners under such conditions. He himself never expected to get back.'[12]

Miers thought Keyes did an excellent job of keeping his men's spirits up, and was delighted when he gave a lecture to the crew on the forthcoming operation just to keep them in the picture. Meanwhile, he and Willmott occupied themselves practising W/T drills. Signals was always the submariners' Achilles heel: though they could converse with infrared Morse lamps while surfaced, submerged, they were not in direct contact. If *Torbay* had a message for *Talisman*, she had to transmit it on high-frequency radio to the nearest shore wireless station, which relayed it in turn to *Rugby* – a powerful high-frequency transmitter on 16 kilohertz – for re-transmission to the other boat. The submarines could pick up *Rugby* even when submerged, but the process, with the necessary encryption and decryption, usually took hours, and every time it was used it ran the risk of alerting the enemy to the fact that there were British submarines in the area.

At 1840 hours on Thursday 13 November, *Torbay* surfaced off Ras Aamer, a headland about five miles west of the landing beach at Khashm al-Kalb, and stood out to sea while *Talisman* came in for a periscope run. Miers thought the weather was ideal for a landing, but it might not hold till the following day, so he suggested to Keyes that they should go for the beach that night. Keyes countered that they could not land until Haselden's shore party had cleared the beach-head, and Haselden would not be in position until the following night.

'Owing to overriding military considerations,' Miers wrote in his report, 'the opportunity was not accepted.'[13]

Word was passed around the commandos that the landing was to go ahead as planned the following evening. That night, Keyes penned a last letter to his parents: 'If this thing is a success,' he wrote, 'whether I get bagged or not, it will raise our stock a bit and help the cause. So don't worry about me, even if this does arrive ... I'm certain I will roll up all right even if I'm spare for a week or two. This is a hell of a chance.'[14]

MINUS 4 DAYS
14 November 1941

At 1025 hours on the morning of Friday 14 November, *Torbay's* W/T operator was receiving an *immediate* message from HQ when the watch sighted an Italian Caproni CA 309 Ghibli aircraft cruising down the coast. Miers gave the order to dive deep, in case the pilot had spotted them. This meant that the *immediate* message was broken off, which caused Miers considerable anxiety: it could have been an order to abort the mission. The message wasn't repeated, and when Miers finally managed to contact *Talisman*, an hour and a half later, by infrared signal, he found that Mike Willmott had missed it too. The thing that bothered Miers more than the missed signal was the weather. It had been calm since leaving Alexandria, with a north-westerly blowing Force 1–2, good visibility, and the barometer steady. Now, true to form, the weather was beginning to deteriorate, with the wind backing to south Force 2–3, as well as the continued north-easterly. Miers judged the conditions far from satisfactory, but carried out the first part of the disembarkation programme anyway.

At noon the commandos were mustered and given a cold lunch. Then their weapons were broken out from the boats' armouries: rifles, Thompson sub-machine-guns, Bren guns and pistols. They checked, cleaned and oiled their weapons methodically, stripping them, cleaning them with the folded rectangles of cotton wadding known as four-by-two dragged through the barrels with a pull-through, then assembling and rechecking them. Jim Gornall's weapon was a Lee-Enfield .303 Mark

IV, a rifle he had had since 1939. He had grown used to its feel; it was almost an extension of himself – and in his hands, it was the tool of a skilled craftsman. He could give you a four-inch group at 300 yards any day of the week. The .303 wasn't semi-automatic like the American equivalent, the M1, but a bolt-action rifle carrying a ten-round magazine. The rate of fire was incredibly fast for a bolt-action rifle: it was beautifully crafted and not prone to stoppages; it was probably the most accurate and reliable rifle ever made.

Four out of five of the commandos carried .303s, and each rifleman had 30 clips of five rounds – 150 rounds in all – carried in two canvas bandoliers in his side-pouches. When the magazine was empty, the rifleman had to release it with a catch, then feed in the rounds one by one. The commandos were trained to refill the magazine with one round in the chamber so that they could bring the weapon into action as soon as the magazine was on – or if they were interrupted while reloading. In theory you counted the rounds you fired so that you were never caught with an empty chamber, but in combat it usually didn't work out like that.

The commandos had practised application-shooting, rapid fire, and snap-shooting at pop-up targets, by day and by night, until it was second nature, but mostly at short ranges of not more than 300 yards. A marksman of Jim Gornall's calibre could hit a static target a mile and a half away using his Lee-Enfield Mark IV. The rifle was as solid as a rock.

George Dunn, Royal Artillery – the ex-sign writer from London – felt the same way about his Bren. One of the best automatic rifles in the world, the Bren had been designed at the famous Brno works in Czechoslovakia, but it was now produced by the British Royal Ordnance factory. Firing the same .303 rimmed ammunition as the Lee-Enfield, it was capable of churning out 500 rounds per minute. It weighed 23 pounds, could be fired from a bipod or from the hip, and was accurate up to 800 yards. Its ammunition came in box magazines of 30 rounds apiece, and the gun-section – Dunn and Codd – carried twenty-five magazines filled and ready for action.

One in five of the men carried a Thompson – the .45 calibre, US-designed sub-machine carbine that was ideal for close-quarter fighting. The commandos loved the Tommy gun: it was accurate and reliable and fired 700 rounds per minute. The cartridges were blunt-nosed, pistol-type rounds, low-velocity, but with high stopping-power at short range. The commandos were trained to fire from the hip at twelve yards, and from the shoulder at fifty yards. Though the maximum effective range was 175 yards, to hit anything at that distance you had to be lying down. The only thing they didn't like about the Tommy gun was its weight – 10 pounds – and the bulky drum magazines they were issued, which added pounds more. The drums carried fifty rounds, but they were clumsy and awkward. They rattled around when you walked, they were difficult and noisy to fill, and they wouldn't fit into side-pouches. They also tended to drop off at exactly the wrong moment. The Tommy-gunners were issued with one drum magazine and six box-type magazines holding thirty rounds apiece: but despite the Thompson's formidable rate of fire, they were instructed to fire single shots where possible, to save ammunition. The officers carried pistols – some had .45 calibre Colt automatics, and others the standard army-issue Webley .38 revolver. Some of the enlisted men had their own personal pistols, and almost all had their own knives. The famous double-bladed fighting knife that was to become the commandos' symbol hadn't yet been issued to 11 Commando; as Gornall said, 'You just got yourself a knife and learned how to use it.'[1] The riflemen all had standard bayonets carried in a scabbard.

The commandos filled their water-bottles – steel flasks covered in felt that held about pint of liquid – and checked their personal clothing and equipment. They had no special tropical kit, but were wearing the standard British Army battledress: short tunics with trousers of rough worsted, with khaki-drill shirts underneath. The officers wore suede-type desert boots nicknamed brothel creepers; the enlisted men had standard army boots with short felt puttees. They hadn't brought their steel helmets on this mission, but instead wore woollen cap comforters, or the 11 Commando Glengarry bonnet with the black hackle. Their equipment was the '38 pattern webbing, that in essence hadn't changed much since the First World War. However, they had no rucksacks for their explosives and heavy gear; apart from their side-pouches, they carried only a haversack over the right shoulder which contained their water-bottles, grenades, spare socks, gym-shoes, mess-tin, emergency rations, and 1st field dressing. Clasp knives and whistles were carried on lanyards in the breast pockets of the battledress 'blouse'. All of them had been issued with dust-coloured lightweight Arab-style blankets, which doubled up as bivouacking and camouflage. Most had morphine tablets, some had Benzedrine for staying awake, or hip-flasks of whisky. All carried toggle-ropes with a bight at one end and a wooden peg at the other; these could be used for night marching or river crossing. Some NCOs had heavy prismatic compasses and maps; they were under strict instructions not to mark them. A few were issued with wire-cutters.

When every man had checked his kit, Keyes told the commandos to get some final rest. While they were lying down, the bluejackets stacked tins of gelignite, crates of compo-rations in cans, and tins of water below the gun tower hatch.

At noon, Mike Willmott, in *Talisman's* control room, completed a periscope reconnaissance of the beach at Khashm al-Kalb. He identified the old fort, but saw no one but an Arab with three horses and a flock of sheep tracking along the beach. *Talisman* retired to the north-east and an hour later Miers eased *Torbay* into the cove and began his own periscope-scan. The place was quiet, with no movement at all. At 1530 hours Keyes got the commandos up. Nobody had slept much. Now almost everyone had pre-landing jitters at the thought of leaving this cozy, friendly environment and casting themselves into the wilderness. They stowed away their bedding while the bluejackets prepared the heaving-lines and grass-lines that would be used for manhandling the dinghies and coiled them in the control room. The SBS teams rigged their *folbots* and placed them in the racks, and the packets containing the rubber boats were stacked under the fore hatch. At 1600 hours the commandos were served a last hot supper; few of them ate heartily.

When the remnants of the meal had been cleared away, they were mustered in the control room and engine room and issued with their ammunition. The grenades were brought up in tins, chalked by the NCOs as primed and ready for use. They were No. 36 Mills 'pineapple' grenades, with a handle and a clip attached to a ring. When you wanted to throw the grenade, you grasped it with the handle depressed and pulled the ring. It wouldn't explode until you released the handle, and then you had a delay of either four or seven seconds, depending on how it was primed. The grenade was packed with high explosive; when it went off the 'pineapple' segments on its skin fragmented into shards of shrapnel. It could be a deadly weapon at close quarters but you had to be expert to use it right: numerous soldiers had killed themselves by pulling the clip before they were completely ready to throw, and then stumbled or dropped the grenade. The commandos had been instructed never to pull the pin unless they were actually going to use the weapon there and then.

The grenades were laid out on the control room table and every commando took two. When they had all been snaffled, Jim Gornall noticed there was a short cylindrical bomb left over, of a type he didn't recognize. A sergeant told him it was a Brasso-Tin Incendiary Bomb; Gornall immediately bagged it, on the principle that 'anything that went "bang" might be useful on the mission.'[2]

Finally, at 1730 hours, the commandos were given their packs and ordered to the wardroom, where Keyes inspected them. He had no Churchillian speeches to inspire his men. 'The last thing he said to the boys,' Jim Gornall reported, 'was "the first person to light up a cigarette when we get ashore, I'll shoot him!" He was a great one for shooting people, was Geoffrey Keyes. The very last thing he said to me, personally, was "Gornall, when we get back, get a haircut!"'[3]

It didn't come across well, but Keyes was a man who had been brought up by his mother to believe that showing emotion was a weakness; this was the nearest he could get to telling young Jim Gornall not to worry, and reassuring him that he was going to make it back all right.

At 1800 hours they synchronized watches on a signal from the W/T office and lined up on deck ready to go. The crew stood to diving stations. Miers had the electric lights switched off to help their night-vision. In darkness the submarine breached the surface, three miles off the target.

In the control room, Crap Miers was still unhappy about the weather. The tide had a strong easterly set of one knot together with a long westerly swell; that hadn't been the case when he'd dropped Haselden here on 10 October. He knew this was going to cause problems with the disembarkation, and that there would be no chance of getting out a grass-line to tow the dinghies back once they reached the shore. To make things worse, the sounding machine had broken down, so he could not approach the beach as closely as he would have liked for fear of running aground.

In any other circumstances, Miers would have cancelled the operation there and then. Three factors stopped him. First, there might not be another opportunity to land, since he couldn't see any prospect of the weather improving over the next few days. Second, the landing had to be made tonight if the timing of the rest of the operation was to go smoothly. Third, Keyes was obviously raring to go.

Miers asked Keyes if the rubber dinghies could be held on shore, and Keyes assured him that his men could deflate them, carry them to the HQ dump Laycock was to set up and hide them pending their return. Miers was still unhappy, but decided to let the operation go ahead. At precisely 1852 hours he ordered the fore and gun tower hatches opened.

Twenty-six men of 11 Commando and four SBS men ascended into the night.

21 OPERATION CRUSADER

MINUS 4 DAYS
14 November 1941   1900 hours

As *Torbay* made her final approach to the beach, Lieutenant Tommy 'Tubby' Langton of the Irish Guards, in charge of the SBS *folbot* detachment, was perched on the forward casing peering into the night. Behind him, two of his four-strong SBS party, Lieutenant Bob Ingles of the Argyll & Sutherland Highlanders – a former 11 Commando officer – and Corporal Clive Severn, Northamptonshire Regiment, were stowing kit into a *folbot*. There was a great deal of huffing and puffing as the commandos, hanging on to the jackstay – the safety-line stretching from the bow to the gun tower – blew up their dinghies with the foot bellows. Luckily, the noise was cloaked by the swell. Langton, an 8 Commando officer who had transferred to the SBS, was quite at home on the water. A Cambridge Rowing Blue, he had been one of the team that had taken part in that disastrous 1937 boat-race, when Jock Lewes's Oxford crew had beaten them by three lengths, in the slowest time for years, and ended the years-long Cambridge winning streak.

Langton could just make out the ghost of the shoreline ahead; it remained in utter darkness until, with heart-stopping abruptness, a torch beam stabbed out of the night: a green light, *dash-dash-dash-dash*, pause, *dash-dash-dash-dash*, pause, *dash-dash-dash-dash*, then a longer pause, and then the same thing again. Langton gasped in amazement: it had to be Haselden out there. It was a moment neither he nor the commandos ever forgot.

'We had been told that Haselden would be there to meet us,' he wrote later, 'but I think no one really believed that he would. He had left Cairo quite three weeks before [in fact it was a week], and during the interval there had been several changes of plan.'[1] A ripple of excitement ran round the men standing on the casing. 'In other circumstances,' Langton continued, '[there] would undoubtedly have been a spontaneous cheer.'[2]

Paul Chapman, the boat's young first lieutenant, in charge of the casing party, was supervising the launch of the recce *folbot*. He pointed out the direction of the beach to Ingles and Severn, who paddled off hastily into the swell. Their first job was to check that it really was Haselden sending the recognition signal, and that the beach had not been compromised. Severn had done this run before, when Haselden had swum ashore here back in October, but tonight the conditions were dramatically different. The SBS men were also tasked to make sure there were no enemy craft lurking in the darkness, and no hidden obstacles – rocks, sea-defences or mines – on the approach. Miers had given instructions that if all was well, the *folbot* men should wait on the beach for an hour. If the commandos hadn't started to land by then, they were to come back to *Torbay*.

After they had gone, Miers tried to manoeuvre the submarine nearer to the beach. On the casing, the commandos had stowed the stores and weapons in the dinghies, and some were already sitting on them, waiting for the submarine to trim down for launching. Paul Chapman had advised them: 'Grind your arses into the bottom of the boat when the sea comes over and bear up with your arms against the jackstay.'

Then, at that moment, things started to go wrong. In Jim Gornall's words: 'As we were lying there and the submarine started blowing her tanks or what have you, there was a ruddy great wave came over the casing and some of the dinghies were swept off.' Spike Hughes, the 40-year-old ex-London postman, was in one of them. Langton made a dive for him, but too late: Hughes had vanished into the night, yelling 'I can't swim!' Lance Corporal Denis Coulthread of the Royal Scots, from Glasgow – Keyes' batman – almost followed him. He made a grab for the jackstay at the last moment, while still trying to hold on to his dinghy at the same time, and dislocated his shoulder. In just a few minutes, four dinghies had been taken by the heavy easterly swell, and Gornall and his mates doubted if they'd see Spike Hughes again.

Down in the control room, Crap Miers grimly ordered the motors put astern and, calculating the drift, headed the submarine in the direction he thought the boats had gone. His calculations proved accurate, but it still took just under an hour to find the first two. As the casing party peered into the darkness, they suddenly heard a plaintive voice, calling out for help. It was Spike Hughes, resolutely paddling one of the two dinghies he had managed to tie together, and highly relieved to see them all.

Hughes said he had been saved from drowning by his two Mae Wests, which had kept him afloat despite the forty pounds of ammunition he'd been carrying when he was swept overboard. When the big wave came, he'd had the presence of mind to grab two of the dinghies, clambering into one and lashing the second to it. He could see *Torbay* and had paddled frantically towards her, but the current had beaten him, carrying him further and further away. It was only when the submarine had changed position that the current had brought him near.

'Colonel Keyes praised me for saving the dinghies, when I had only been thinking of my own safety,' he admitted later. 'The rest of the party had been saying, "Poor old Spike. Fancy getting wiped out like that!"'[3]

Luckily for the commandos, the two other dinghies were nearby and as soon as they were spotted one of the casing party, Able Seaman James S. 'Ginger' Vine, a red-haired market gardener from Kent, plunged into the sea to retrieve them, quickly followed by another able seaman, Bill Hammond. Langton and his *folbot* partner, Corporal Cyril Feeberry of the Grenadier Guards – a fourteen-stone former boxing champion – also dived in to help. They attached lines to the boats, so that the casing party could heave them aboard, but it took tremendous effort because they were now heavily waterlogged and weighed a ton. Fortunately, most of the gear had been lashed in securely and was still there.

Torbay had drifted two miles off course, so once the men were all safely aboard, Miers nosed the submarine back towards the beach, only to be met by Ingles and Severn in the recce *folbot*. Their hour of waiting was up and they had come to investigate the delay. Tubby Langton sent them back straight away, with orders to flash a light to vector in the rubber dinghies.

Paul Chapman now had to resort to Plan B, which entailed launching the dinghies one by one, and hauling them on lines to the forward hydroplanes, where the pair of commandos would get in and paddle off. They'd been training for this eventuality, but doing it in the calm of Alexandria Harbour was one thing, and doing it in these wild conditions quite another. Keyes and his batman, Denis Coulthread – his shoulder still painful, but now firmly back in its correct place – were the first to go. They were closely followed by Roy Cooke and his partner, who, instead of slipping into their dinghy from the casing, took flying jumps at it and managed to land without capsizing.

It took forty minutes to launch the first seven dinghies, and they got away with only a couple of spills.

By 2216 hours Miers, who had come up from the control room and was standing on the gun tower, realized that the submarine was off course again. He had to halt the operation while he corrected the drift. This took another thirty-five precious minutes, and by the time the manoeuvre was complete, Chapman was dismayed to see that the weather had got worse and the swell increased.

The casing party – Leading Seaman Armishaw, Able Seamen Vine, Hammond and Gavin, Stoker Conaty, Engineer Officer Lieutenant Tonno Kidd, and Chapman, began lowering the next batch of dinghies, but what up to then had been simply hard work became agony as boat after boat rolled over in the roiling waters. One man would get in all right, then his partner would overbalance and both would end up in the briny. The night was pitch-dark and the heaving and roaring of the sea strange and fearsome to those who had never seen such conditions before – which meant most of the commandos. Yet Miers was impressed with the quiet determination they showed. As many couldn't swim, they had to hold on desperately to the dinghy's rope stay until Able Seaman Vine or Hammond – or both – jumped in to rescue them. If the dinghy was water-logged, it meant another excruciating haul for the casing party, and the process would have to be repeated from the beginning. By now the blue-jackets were exhausted from dragging the boats along the casing, where it was almost impossible to keep balanced without grabbing the jackstay, even for the most experienced seaman. All of them were battered and bruised. Ginger Vine's back had been cut by the wet boat-ropes; he had also been injured in the head, but when Paul Chapman told him to go below for medical treatment he refused, declaring that he would stay on the casing till the last boat was off.

That was beginning to look as if it might be a long time coming, as more dinghies rolled and lost their gear – blankets, shirts, boots and rations wrapped in oilskin capes all disappeared beneath the hungry waters. The SBS men, Ingles and Severn, appeared yet again to find out what was going on. They brought with them a message from John Haselden – it was the same news of the Trieste Division's redeployment he had sent to Anthony Hunter, but he knew the LRDG were instructed to keep radio silence and wasn't sure it had got through.

Now Chapman had to turn his attention to retrieving the *folbot* – Ingles, Severn and the gear were taken aboard successfully, then they hoisted the canoe onto the casing. What Chapman didn't realize was that the *folbot* had taken on a lot of water; as she came up the side she tilted. Ingles shouted just too late as the water shifted to one end and broke the precious craft's back. The *folbot* was a total write-off.

Miers, watching from the bridge, was wondering whether something like the copper punt used in home waters wouldn't be better in bad weather than these flimsy canoes. The *folbot* was, admittedly, much lighter, but he thought perhaps a skilled shipwright might be able to strengthen the design. By now Miers had managed to get the submarine into a slight lee off the spit at the west side of the bay, and conditions improved slightly. Spike Hughes, having survived his first ordeal by water, was relieved to find that his new dinghy was as solid as a whale-boat. By midnight, all the dinghies but three were away. Jim Gornall was supposed to be in the last dinghy, and before him were a lance corporal and Tom Kelly, the Scouser whose boot-heel had been shot off at the Litani. They had already rolled three times, so Miers tried to help by trimming down – *Torbay* actually touched bottom in the process. This was a risky business because of the heavy swell, so Miers ordered the main ballast blown and took the boat into deeper water. On his third attempt to get into the dinghy, Kelly smashed his leg in a recess on the side of the casing, re-activating an old cartilage injury. The pain was excruciating. Kelly told Chapman he couldn't go any further, which meant there was a vacant seat in his dinghy. Jim Gornall was next in line, but all his own gear was already stowed on the dinghy behind.

'Out of the way, Tom,' Gornall told Kelly, and took his place beside the lance corporal while Kelly was sent below for medical attention. Anxious at the delay, Miers sent Gornall and his new partner a personal message: 'Do not delay (and therefore jeopardize) the operation any further.'[4]

Not to be outdone by the Royal Navy, the lance corporal sent a reply: 'Sir, we will do our utmost.'

Finally the pair managed to balance the boat and paddle off into the darkness, in splendid style, drenched but in good spirits, as Miers put it. 'The grit of the final pair deserves special mention,' he wrote in his log. 'They had had several spills during the earlier stages of the operation … yet they never lost heart.'[5]

It was 0030 hours on 15 November. Thirteen of the fourteen dinghies had been launched, but what had taken an hour in Alexandria Harbour had turned into a six-hour ordeal. The six-man casing party was on their last legs with fatigue. Chapman had kept going only by taking four tablets of Benzedrine, but it had left him so shattered that he took several days to recover. 'So little did he spare himself,' Miers wrote, 'that he was, at the end, reduced to a state of physical exhaustion.'[6]

Leading Seaman Armishaw, who already held the DSM, had carried out the duties of a Petty Officer; he was recommended for promotion for his outstanding leadership on the casing. Vine and Hammond, who had spent six hours in and out of the sea, were both recommended for the DSM.

At 0035 hours, Miers sent an 'Operation Completed' signal to *Talisman* and put out to sea.

MINUS 3 DAYS

15 November 1941   0040 hours

For Jim Gornall and the lance corporal, the last two men off *Torbay*, the ordeal wasn't yet over. By the time they had got off the casing, the submarine was out of the shelter of the headland, and the waves were rough. 'We were paddling away like hell,' Gornall said, 'and these ruddy great waves were rolling in, and eventually they turned us over. I grabbed the rope round the dinghy and clung on for dear life, but unfortunately [the lance corporal] didn't react quick enough and he was loose in the water. The surf was pounding us, and he shouted, "Give us a hand, Jim!" Just as he shouted my feet touched the deck, and I thought, "You're all right now, the next wave will wash you up," and it did. It washed him up and it washed me up, still clinging on to the ruddy boat. He was pretty shattered after floundering about in the sea, so I dragged him to a safe place, and went about collecting the kit.'[1]

Gornall deflated the dinghy as they had been instructed, but then realized he couldn't find the foot bellows needed to blow it up again; it must have been lost when the dinghy rolled. That was bad, but the thought that niggled him most was that he'd left his trusty .303 stowed in the other dinghy. Now he would have to go into action without it. As he was packing the dinghy up, he noticed something that struck him as odd. 'Keyes had warned us that he'd shoot anyone who lit a cigarette on shore,' he said. 'Now I was the last man off *Torbay*, and as soon as I got [ashore], what should I see but a bloody great fire on the beach! I thought, stone the crows, they're in trouble! But I couldn't hear any shooting. It was a bloody great fire, and they'd lit it in an old fort on the beach, after Keyes had said he'd shoot anyone who lit a cigarette!'

It was about four hundred yards to the fire, and Gornall struggled towards it with the sixty pounds of folded dinghy on his back. The lance corporal staggered along beside him, coughing and spluttering from the sea-water he'd swallowed. 'Anyway, I'm carting this ruddy thing on my back and bits of kit under my arms that didn't belong to me,' he continued, 'and Keyes is stood on the beach watching for who was coming in. I said, "Look, we're the last ones." He had a flask in his hand and it was full of rum and he said, "Have a swig of this," so I had a good swig, and he said, "Off you go then."'

They soon joined the others round the fire in the fort, which had been lit by Haselden and his guide, Mikhael Hamad; it was cleverly shielded from the landward side. Gornall had to step over Haselden, who was in Arab dress and asleep by the fire when he arrived. 'Actually,' Gornall said, 'I thought it was a bundle of rags.'[2]

Everyone was soaked and exhausted – there wasn't a single man who hadn't taken a dunking in the sea at some stage. But there were no major casualties. George Dunn, the Bren-gunner, had blistered his feet badly during the landing and would have to stay with the beach-head RV. Private Bob Fowler of the Cameron Highlanders had taken a rusty nail through his boot just after he'd got ashore, and it had penetrated his foot, but he seemed all right: he was ready to go on.

The fire on the beach had also been spotted by Mike Willmott, *Talisman*'s captain, as she closed on the beach. 'A large fire just lit in the Fort,' he wrote in his log at 0040 hours, 'seemed to indicate that some of the first party had had a rough landing.'[3] Minutes earlier, Willmott had dispatched two of his own SBS men – Lieutenant John M. 'Farmer' Pryor of the Bedfordshire & Hertfordshire Regiment, a Territorial Army officer who had only held his commission since January, and Bombardier John Brittlebank of the Royal Artillery – to vector in the submarine from the landing site. Pryor and Brittlebank had already had a hard time of it.

At 2100 hours, Willmott had sent them to contact *Torbay* to see what the delay was about, but their *folbot* had turned over four times on launching and had to be emptied out by the casing party each time. When they had finally got away, Pryor had discovered that the cross-strut he normally braced himself against had been broken, making the craft difficult to paddle. Worst of all, though *Torbay* had been visible from *Talisman*'s gun tower, Pryor and his partner couldn't see her from sea level because of the swell, and within ten minutes had to return to *Talisman*. When they reported back, Willmott manoeuvred the submarine so that her bows pointed directly at *Torbay* and told Pryor, 'Go straight down that line and you'll find her.' But find her they couldn't. Instead, they almost collided with Jim Gornall and the lance corporal in their dinghy, who told them that thirteen dinghies had now got away from *Torbay* and that they were the last.

Pryor reported this to back to Willmott, who, with Bob Laycock, had already decided to postpone their own landing till the following night. When *Torbay*'s 'Operation Completed' signal appeared, confirming Pryor's report, Willmott changed his mind and decided to go through with it after all, knowing he was in a perilous situation. It had taken *Torbay* almost six hours to land her commandos, but he had only three and a half hours to land his own complement of men because he needed at least two hours of darkness after the landing to recharge his batteries before diving; dawn would break around 0600 hours. To make things worse, the moon was about to come up. In compensation, though the swell had moderated: the breeze was slight and there was no 'sea'. Willmott opted for the original plan of submerging and letting the dinghies float off the casing in order to save time. The little craft were now inflated and ready, with the troops standing by for launch, bracing themselves on the jackstay.

Meanwhile, Pryor and Brittlebank were in trouble again. Pryor had made the mistake of navigating on the bonfire in the fort – the only available light – and it had taken them too far to the east, into the same wild surf that had rolled Jim Gornall's dinghy. Before they knew it, their *folbot* had turned turtle and was being hurled against the shoals. The two SBS men clung to the craft, not wanting to lose her, and managed to struggle on to the rocks, only to be dragged off again and again by the undertow, and bowled over by the surf. Pryor started to think they were going to drown. 'I don't think this canoe is much more use, sir,' Brittlebank gasped.

'No,' Pryor agreed, 'damn the thing!'⁴

They let the *folbot* go and struggled ashore, running into Keyes and Roy Cooke patrolling the beach as they made for the fire in the fort. Pryor left Brittlebank with the *Torbay* men near the fire and went back to the beach to signal to *Talisman*. He was soaked to the skin and shaking with cold, and thought he might be better off without his sopping shirt. He took it off and stood, still shivering and half naked, flashing *dash-dot-dash-dot* to *Talisman*. Keyes and Cooke couldn't help laughing at him.

At 0145 hours, Willmott decided to stabilize the submarine by putting her bows on the seabed – a manoeuvre Miers had carried out success-fully off Crete. But Willmott was less experienced than Miers, and in these conditions it turned out to be a fatal mistake. When they neared the beach the ground swell had increased suddenly; as *Talisman*'s bows dipped, her stern rose with the incoming sea and the waves rushed across the forward casing.

'There was a heavy thud as the ship grounded and started to roll over on her side,' Charles Lock said. 'The next instant a solid sea came thun-dering over us, submerging everyone in a welter of water black and furious. A moment and it was gone, the bows lifting like a cork over the sea, but what a shambles.'⁵

The sea had swept away seven of the eight dinghies, and eleven men. The commandos not washed overboard in the first rush tried desper-ately to hold on to the jackstay, but it suddenly came loose and sent them skittering off the casing. Lock and his companion were the only two left standing. 'Boats and their crews as well were missing,' he recalled, 'others punctured, their stores gone, while the men were half stunned, either by the force of the water or by being flung against the deck.'⁶

To Willmott, it was as if all hell had let rip. 'This sudden transformation of an orderly scene on the casing to one of confusion,' he wrote in his log, 'was most demoralizing.'⁷ He had only two options: either to open the boat's main vents and sit on the bottom as planned, or to blow the main tanks, go astern and get clear of the confusion of men and dinghies in the sea. If he bottomed, he reasoned, then more water would ship over the casing and take the rest of the commandos and dinghies with it. There was also the risk that *Talisman* might broach and run aground. 'I decided to go astern,' Willmott reported in his log, 'and let the men in the water fend for themselves, sending a *folbot* to assist.'

The scene in the water was desperate, with commandos thrashing about and going down. Bob Laycock, who was among them, had the presence of mind to swim for the dinghies, but many of the commandos started to swim back to *Talisman* instead. The *folbot* Willmott had sent to help, manned by Lieutenant Allot of the Middlesex Regiment and an SBS non-com, was wrecked during launching and became another write-off: three of the four *folbots* assigned to the operation were now out of action.

Willmott's time-saving tactic had failed, and the clock was ticking. If he didn't get *Talisman* away in time to recharge her batteries, then she would be caught in daylight and Axis aircraft would be on her like wasps on honey. The moon was almost up. Willmott called the detachment commander David Sutherland over. 'Throw the rest of the boats in,' he told him. 'Then tell your chaps to jump in after them!'⁸

Sutherland did as he'd been ordered and the commandos jumped in gamely, but by this time all but one of the dinghies had rolled.

'Over we went,' Charles Lock said, 'forgetting the hand-grenades and ammo in our pockets, which pulled us down and down. When I surfaced I was quite near the boat – there it was, obviously upside down.

I struck out for it, grabbing the nearest hand-hold and tried to right it. I tried again and again, using all the weight of my sodden clothes and loaded pockets, but to no avail.'[9] Lock was desperate. He could no longer see *Talisman* in the darkness, but dared not shout out, in case there were enemy soldiers on shore. He made a final effort, and this time the dinghy righted herself, revealing on the other side the wryly grinning face of Jimmy Bogle, Lock's mate from the Gordon Highlanders.

'Somehow we pulled each other on,' Lock explained, 'from opposite sides sitting back to back. For a moment we just sat looking at the white line of breakers on the beach, clearly visible as we rose on the swell, and then, feeling in the darkness for the lines with which our paddles were attached, we began to work our way slowly towards the shore.'[10] The breakers became higher as they neared the beach, and they struggled to keep themselves off the rocks. 'We ... were beginning to look for possible landings,' Lock went on, 'when ... a surging roar announced the arrival of a wave far bigger than the rest, foaming with white spray ... the boat seemed to rush into the air, as though we had exploded a mine, and disappeared from sight. I went head-first into the murky water and down and down, a piece of jetsam in the whirling torrent ... the next instant ... I was thrown flat on to the rocks.'[11]

Lock and Bogle managed somehow to drag themselves ashore, but many of the others were carried off by the current. One of them, Lance Corporal Peter Barrand of the London Rifles, Tommy Macpherson's runner from 10 Troop on the Litani, was never seen alive again. His body was washed ashore a few days later. Frank Varney, his close friend – also from 10 Troop – could never understand how Barrand had drowned, since he was a strong swimmer, and all the commandos had been wearing two Mae Wests. Laycock, whose report, mysteriously, makes no mention of Barrand's death, also insists that all ranks were wearing two Mae Wests.

But Paul Chapman wrote later that this was not the case. While the men on *Torbay* were wearing two lifejackets apiece and floated, those on

Talisman were wearing only one each, and sank. He blamed himself for this, saying that he should have made sure *Talisman*'s crew knew that two Mae Wests per man were needed before the submarines left Alexandria. Chapman also claimed that the jackstay on *Talisman*'s casing had never been properly inspected.

Peter Barrand paid the price for these omissions, and so did the Rommel Raid, for Laycock and seven enlisted men were all that got off *Talisman*, and that meant Geoffrey Keyes now had only a little more than half the required number of troops for the job.

23 OPERATION CRUSADER

MINUS 3 DAYS
15 November 1941   0500–0600 hours

Sergeant Jack Terry, Royal Artillery, from Bulwell near Nottingham, woke up shivering. He had been soaked to the skin when his dinghy overturned just before they had made the beach. Terry was only twenty, but he was the most senior sergeant in the group: with four years in the army behind him, he had almost as much service as Keyes, four years his senior. He had never known his father, who had been killed in a Nottinghamshire mining accident when he was a year old. While still at school, Terry had started work with Chambers Brothers, Butchers, in Bulwell, but his ambition had been to join the police. He had taken up boxing as a boy, and had been trained by a local tough-nut named Luther Walker, who paid boys like Terry a penny to go a round with another boxer, and tuppence if they won. But Luther Walker was not entirely above brawling and ended up jailed for manslaughter after a street-fight in which his opponent died. Jack Terry went on boxing until he was a heavyweight. In his teens he came increasingly into conflict with his stepfather, whom he believed was mistreating his mother.

Even at sixteen, Terry was not someone to mess with, and after several altercations that had ended with him pursuing his stepfather round the house with a poker, he had opted for the army – 'Otherwise I'll kill him,' he had told his mum. With a few years as a gunner under his belt, he was certain the police would take him. You weren't allowed to join the army until you were eighteen, but Terry was a big lad and looked older than his sixteen years. He wasn't the only lad to lie about his age.

Charles Lock, the lanky rugby-playing corporal of the London Scottish, also awoke in the old fort, some ninety minutes after falling asleep, because the fire had burned out. A big man like Terry, whom he didn't know, Lock owed his survival, he thought, to the fact that he was a very strong swimmer, but fighting the undertow had been so exhausting that he had virtually passed out once he'd got ashore. Most of the *Talisman* party hadn't made it with him, and it looked unlikely that the rest would now.

The sky was still dark, but a luminous strip across the horizon towards Egypt heralded first light. Geoffrey Keyes and Bob Laycock were waking the men, ordering them to assemble the stores. Lock was a good ten years older than Jack Terry – older than most, though not all, of the men in the raiding party; both Charlie Bruce and Spike Hughes were older. He came from a middle-class background. His father, whose family was originally from Devon, kept a shop called *Goulden & Wind*, which sold musical instruments, in Canterbury High Street, and Lock himself was a gifted pianist as well as a first-class rugby player. He had attended a private school, St Roger Manwood's in Sandwich, where he had joined the army cadets. While training with the Commando on Arran, Lock had met a Glasgow girl called Ruth Pridham Black, a teacher of domestic science, whose family was also originally from Devon, and who had volunteered, with her mother, to work in the officers' mess at the White House. Lock met Ruth at a dance in Lamlash Village Hall, and a few days later, having narrowly escaped death when a consignment of gelignite exploded at the docks, he had vowed to marry her when the war was over. Now, still stiff from last night's unexpected swim, he put thoughts of Ruth aside and got on his feet to start helping the others shift the four-gallon petrol tins of water, compo rations, explosives and spare ammunition.

Fred Birch was even more bleary-eyed than Lock – he hadn't got to sleep until 0400 hours. One of the first men off *Torbay*, he had been on stag – sentry duty – for a solid eight hours before Keyes finally relieved him. Birch was the same age as Jack Terry and like him a full sergeant. Born in West Derby, a small village on the outskirts of Liverpool, in 1921, the son of a bicycle-shop manager, he had won a scholarship to the local grammar school, but like many children of his generation he had been unable to attend because his parents couldn't afford to buy the books and uniform. Instead, Birch had left school at fourteen to work first as a milkman for the Co-op, then as a meat porter at Liverpool Abattoir. He had been a cadet with the Liverpool Scottish from the age of sixteen, and at eighteen had joined the Territorial Battalion just as they were being mobilized at the outbreak of war. In 1940 he had volunteered for 7 Commando, and after training at Newmarket and Girvan, had ended up with his Commando on Arran.

Malcolm 'Spike' Hughes awakened to find that his body had recovered from the ordeal he'd suffered when he'd been washed off *Torbay's* casing. Twenty years older than Terry and Birch, and ten years Lock's senior, Hughes was the old man of the team – at forty he looked to 21-year-old Jim Gornall as old as Methuselah and twice as tough. Hughes was the son of a Surrey thatcher and a domestic servant; his father's drunkenness resulted in an unhappy childhood. Both of his brothers had emigrated; he left home in 1917 to serve in the Royal Flying Corps, at the tail end of the First World War, and after that he had had no further contact with his own family. An enthusiastic greyhound-fancier who rolled his own cigarettes but was only an occasional beer-drinker, Spike had always found it hard to make ends meet: he was known to his wife's family as 'Stoney Broke', or simply, 'Stone'. Spike owed his fitness partly to his job as a postie before the war – plodding the streets with a heavy mail-sack was better than a gym workout any day – and to the constant manual work in the allotment he kept, where he grew his own vegetables to supplement his income. Now he joined Jack Terry, Fred Birch, Charles Lock, Jim Gornall and the others in shifting the equipment. With one section covering and another carrying, they began to move about half a mile away, to a wadi concealed by the *maquis* meandering at right angles to the beach, under the steep face of the first escarpment, where in daylight there would be cover from prying eyes.

It was only when Lock got himself going that he remembered it was his thirtieth birthday. Though he didn't realize it at the time, it was also Rommel's birthday – his fiftieth: there were exactly twenty years between Corporal Charles Lock and Lieutenant General Erwin Rommel, the Desert Fox.

By sunrise the raiding party was hidden in the wadi that Keyes had chosen previously from aerial photos as a daytime LUP. Here, they were issued with a further three days' rations: each man got a tin of bully-beef, a packet of hard tack biscuits, two bars of chocolate, four ounces of raisins, twenty ounces of boiled sweets, cheese, cocoa, sugar and dried milk. John Pryor and John Brittlebank, the two SBS men, were unable to get back to *Talisman* now their *folbot* was lost, so they were detailed to rake over signs of the landing on the beach and pick up bits of kit that had been left behind.

As Pryor and Brittlebank removed all signs of the commando landing, a Bedouin wearing a lounge suit over his robe and a Libyan pill-box cap, suddenly arrived, as if out of nowhere. Pryor's first instinct was to hide, but it was too late for that; his second was to shoot the man, but the Arab seemed friendly and murdering him out of hand might turn the local populace against them. The SBS men muttered a few words of Arabic and the Bedouin asked if they were Italians. When they didn't answer, he smiled and said, 'Ah, English!' and started to hug them embarrassingly. In true Bedouin style he then invited them to his camp for something to eat. Pryor considered the invitation carefully. His main object here was to prevent the raiding party being compromised, and if they refused, the Bedouin might hang around. If they went back with him to his home, it would at least keep him away from the landing area.

The Bedouin's camp turned out to be over two miles away, and Pryor, who had lost his desert boots when his *folbot* had broached, was barefoot and soon footsore. Seeing his difficulty, the Bedouin actually lent him his own rubber sandals, that had been cut from an old tyre. They were no improvement, but Pryor put on a show of gratitude. Eventually they reached the camp, where the Bedouin sat them down and brought them food.

'We were given what looked like linseed poultice,' Pryor described, 'with very underdone goat in it, and what looked like tea but turned out to be muddy water.'[1]

A few minutes after sunrise, the commandos lying up in the wadi saw an Axis aircraft drone into view, flying at about 800 feet. 'It was a biplane with two crew in it,' Jim Gornall said. 'You could see the pilot and the observer. It flew along, and I thought, well, it was very crafty of Keyes to move us here, because if they'd seen us wandering around there'd be hell to pay. Finally, it just flew off.'[2]

There was still a strong wind, and a swell at sea, but the sun was out and the commandos were able to dry their soaked uniforms and equipment, including their Arab blankets, while Bombardier George Dunn, the Bren-gunner, and his Number Two, Larry Codd, cooked a meal for everyone: tinned bacon and beans from the compo rations, hard tack biscuits and hot tea.

Keyes had been up all night, waiting doggedly on the beach with his torch until all the men had come in. Robin Campbell, his Second-in-Command – the ex-Reuter's correspondent from 8 Commando – had arrived at about 0030 hours, and Keyes had put him in charge of hiding the dinghies. When Campbell had completed this task, he volunteered to relieve Keyes' lonely vigil on the beach, but Keyes had turned the offer down.

Now he and Bob Laycock sat down under a bush to discuss the situation. It looked grim. Sutherland and Chevalier, the two demolitions men, had failed to get ashore from *Talisman*; so had the two Senussi guides, and twenty-six commandos. Two others had been left on *Torbay*. They had only a little more than half of a raiding party that had been too small for the job in the first place. Under normal conditions, Laycock should have cancelled the mission and ordered the men to re-embark, but Keyes resisted, unwilling to lose his chance. They considered waiting here another night to see if the rest of the commandos on *Talisman* could be landed, and then proceed as planned.

But this plan had two drawbacks. First, the longer they stayed here, the more likely they were to be spotted – by enemy aircraft, by locals who would betray them to the Italians, or by Axis patrols. Second, it would completely throw out the timing of the operation – Rommel had to be bumped at midnight on 17 November: no sooner and, preferably, no later. The other alternative was to go ahead with the depleted raiding party on a revised plan, and if the *Talisman* commandos were landed eventually, they could be held in reserve to cover the re-embarkation. A decisive factor was the weather. The wind had dropped at first light but was now backing powerfully, and there was a sea running which would almost certainly stop the remaining men getting off *Talisman* that night.

Laycock decided to go ahead on the original timing, but with a modified plan. It was obvious they would have to cut out some of the objectives. Dave Sutherland's task – to hit the Axis HQ at Cyrene – was scrapped, so was Chevalier's job of bumping the HQ at Apollonia. Haselden's plan hadn't been affected, since his G(R) cell was still out in the desert awaiting his return. The main objective was Rommel's HQ and his villa at Beda Littoria. Luckily most of the original Number One Detachment earmarked for these jobs had been on *Torbay*, and the detachment was still intact. Keyes finally conceded, that the idea of hitting two buildings at once was opening his mouth a bit wide. He settled for bumping only one of them, but would reserve the choice until he'd done his final recce on 17 November. The raiding party would make the trek to Beda Littoria as a single unit, and if the Rommel job went off as planned, six men under Roy Cooke would beetle down the road to Cyrene and sabotage the cable mast at the crossroads. If everything went well and these bits of the mission were successful, the two parties might possibly combine to hit the Cyrene HQ later.

The most pressing concern now was for guides across the escarpment – the two Senussis from the LAF had been on *Talisman* and hadn't made it ashore. Lock and the others thought they'd been drowned. Some time during the morning, Keyes consulted with Haselden and Mikhael Hamad, who shot off and arranged for a local shepherd to guide them, then disappeared in the direction of Slonta.

Laycock started to set up his beach-head RV in the wadi: a reserve supply dump of ammunition, food and water, manned by Sergeant John Nicholl, who had fought with Fraser's 8 Troop at the Litani River, George Dunn and Larry Codd on the Bren gun, and the medical orderly Ed Atkins, from the Beds & Herts Regiment, a former circus strongman of whom the commandos stood in awe. Finally there were the two SBS men, Pryor and Brittlebank. Keyes started penning a list, allocating men to various tasks: the entry party who would do the deed on Rommel, the covering party, the demolitions party, and Cooke's detachment.

Keyes knew that the operation had only a slim chance of success because it was so seriously hampered by the lack of manpower, but with all the skill in masking emotions he had learned from his family and at Eton, he put on a poker face when, that afternoon, he briefed his men on the new plan.

'We were to move off that night at last light,' Jim Gornall said, 'and approach Beda Littoria. It was only about 20 miles and it was to be done in two stages, travelling both stages at night, so we wouldn't be spotted by aircraft or anything else … Originally I was part and parcel of the party raiding Rommel's HQ, but when they rehashed it, I was with the people that were to go and do the Cyrene crossroads with Roy Cooke.'[3]

When the briefing was finished, Keyes ordered the ammunition and explosives to be opened and distributed. Miraculously, the stores had survived their many dousings in the sea. Each man was given six sticks of gelignite, long, thin sausages of explosives that they carried in canvas bandoliers designed for .303 ammunition. Keyes also supervised the handing out of detonators, primers, fuse and time-pencils to the demolitions men. During the briefing the sky had become unexpectedly overcast, and now rain began to fall. No one in the raiding party had seen rain for months; it was an ominous portent, especially as they had been told to expect dry North African weather and had no ponchos or wet-weather gear. The atmosphere quickly grew cold and miserable, but Keyes maintained his stiff upper lip. Just after sunset, the commandos blackened their faces with charcoal from the fire and checked their pockets and equipment, making sure they were 'clean' of anything personal – letters, photos or documents – that might be used against them by the enemy if captured. Anything that rattled – loose change, faulty fastenings on their webbing, the sling of a rifle – had to be removed, tied or taped. Finally, they jumped up and down to make certain they had nothing on them that was likely to give them away.

When they said goodbye that night, Laycock told Keyes to send back information by runner at the earliest opportunity. 'If necessary, you can return to the RV after the primary tasks are completed,' he added, 'and stock up before taking on secondary tasks, but in any case no one is, under any circumstances, to make directly for the beach.'

Once again Laycock advised Keyes to delegate the job of leading the raid to a junior officer. Once again, Keyes refused.

'Whatever he may have felt like inside himself,' Robin Campbell wrote, 'Geoffrey certainly appeared confident and cheerful as we set off at about 8 pm.'[4]

Between Khashm al-Kalb and Beda Littoria – Sidi Rafa, as it was known to the Arabs – there lay two steep terraces, varying in height from six hundred to twelve hundred feet. The first terrace, Lusaita, could only be climbed by way of ancient sheep-tracks known only to the Bedouin, which was why a local guide was essential. The commandos travelled in single file, Keyes in the lead behind the Bedouin guide, with his interpreter, Avishalom Drori, close at hand. Though there were no reports of enemy patrols, they moved in tactical mode, with weapons ready. They advanced silently and slowly in the way they had been trained, picking their feet up high in a mark time movement to avoid constantly tripping over stones invisible in the dark, taking short steps to avoid brushing through foliage, testing the ground lightly as they went to avoid breaking twigs or falling into holes. Heavily laden, with their rations, water, explosives and ammunition, they could cover no more than fifty yards a minute – it took an hour and a quarter to reach the top of Lusaita, followed by a further two and three quarter hours of navigating the meandering, rocky, sheep-tracks through the *maquis*. It was, Robin Campbell reported, 'extremely difficult going'.[5]

At 0030 hours Keyes halted the party. The men immediately got down in all-round defence mode. They had kept well closed up on the march, and now each man studied the angle he'd been allotted. Meanwhile, the Bedouin guide was telling Keyes that he could go no further. This was a serious blow, because it meant that from now on Keyes would have to navigate himself, relying on his compass and an inaccurate Italian map. Keyes thought the Bedouin was afraid to go on in case they ran into the Italians, but other than forcing him on by gunpoint – or bumping him off – there wasn't much he could do. The worst of it, though, was the fear that the Bedouin might sell them to the Italians for money: they might, even at that moment, be walking into a trap.

Keyes dismissed these thoughts from his mind as he watched the Bedouin disappear into the brush. The guide was a man recommended by Haselden himself. When he had gone, he, Cooke and Campbell got the men up and they moved on. At about 0200 hours Keyes called a halt on a scrub-covered low hill called Umm Girba and told the commandos this would be the next day's LUP. It wasn't ideal, but there was some cover from the *maquis*, and there seemed to be nowhere better in the vicinity.

Keyes detailed a roster of sentries, with two men awake for each man asleep so that they could fight off an enemy attack even if they were taken by surprise. Those who weren't on stag settled down in their Arab blankets for a welcome rest.

MINUS 2 DAYS

16 November 1941   0600–1800 hours

Robin Campbell awoke at first light to the sound of shouting. Avishalom Drori, the Jewish-Palestinian interpreter, was crying out that they were surrounded by armed Arabs. Campbell crawled over to where Geoffrey Keyes sat, wrapped in his blanket. It was cold and already raining. A moment later, Drori joined them, reporting that they had been spotted by three armed Bedouin, who were hiding in the *maquis* nearby. Keyes and Campbell peered over the *maquis* cautiously to see 'a few rascally-looking Arabs, one or two brandishing short Italian rifles.'[1] The sentries were watching them closely, and Keyes decided he could not run the risk of letting them get away, in case they informed the Italians of his party's presence. He sent Drori back to bring one of them to him.

Awad Mohammad, a herdsman of the Masamir, his father, and a cousin, had been tracking Awad's cows in the neighbourhood of Umm Girba since first light. Their clan, a subsection of the 19,000-strong Dursa tribe, was one of those that stayed put on the plateau all year round, living mainly in caves and under rock-overhangs, herding sheep, goats and cattle among the rich *maquis*. Although they would have considered it presumptuous to predict the weather, the high winds off the sea yesterday and the dampness in the air suggested that there might be a big storm later in the day. That was good, because their people lived not only by trading the products of their animals – butter, milk, wool, skins, hoof and horn – to the townsfolk of Sidi Rafa and Cyrene and other large villages, but also by planting barley in the wadis after the rains. They would return to the crop for harvesting; in a good year there would be enough grain to store until the following year, with a little left over to sell. One drought year they could take, but a succession of them spelled famine and disaster.

The Bedouin women wove the wool from their own goats into tents and rugs using traditional flat looms, but there was still much that had to be bought in the market – tea, sugar, rice, cloth, metal goods, knives, rifles and ammunition. Although the Dursa were not really nomads like the tribes on the southern side of the Jebel al-Akhdar, they still considered themselves a cut above the townsmen and villagers. They prided themselves on having qualities the townsmen lacked: courage, endurance, hospitality, generosity and loyalty to their tribe. And the Dursa knew how to live in the Jebel, how to read tracks and signs, how to hunt and trap, the names and uses of the plants and animals. The Bedouin also prided themselves on having what they called *guwwat al-mulahaza*, the power of observation. No Bedouin child could have missed the distinctive boot-tracks of these soldiers – quite different from those of the Italians or Germans – or the fact that they were trying to conceal themselves in the *maquis*.

Awad, carrying his old Italian rifle, and wearing a *jurd* and rubber sandals, ducked behind a rock when he saw Avishalom Drori coming towards him, a rifle slung over his shoulder. Drori smiled and held out his hand, addressing Awad in fluent Arabic. Judging him friendly, Awad shook hands and answered his greeting. Drori asked if he belonged to the Senussiyya, and when Awad said that he did, Drori handed him an open letter from Sayid Idriss as-Senussi, the hereditary leader of the order, now exiled in Egypt, which urged all Libyan citizens to assist British forces. Awad looked at the paper, but he couldn't read it, so he passed it to his father, who knew Classical Arabic.

Drori asked Awad to accompany him; although suspicious, Awad followed him to where Keyes and Campbell were sitting. Campbell later described Awad as 'a villainous-looking Arab with a red cloth wound round his head at a raffish angle.'[2]

Through Drori, Keyes asked if he could guide them to the *Prefettura* in Beda Littoria. Awad thought about it for a moment, then said he could do so for a thousand lire, and, on the way, could show them a cave where they could rest. For another thousand lire, he said, he would bring them a goat and some Italian cigarettes.

Keyes wondered how trustworthy the Bedouin would be; he reckoned that as long as they were profiting from his party's presence, they would have little incentive to assist the Italians. He also knew that without a guide across the escarpment, his party would find the assault next to impossible to bring off. After considering the offer carefully, he decided to take a chance. He allowed Awad to return to his band.

The gamble paid off. At about noon, Awad returned with a youth called Idriss Musa; they brought cooked goat meat, soup and cigarettes. Jim Gornall was on stag when the hot meal was served. 'I got detailed to man the highest point,' he said, 'to keep an eye on any movement that was going on. While I was up there an Arab approached the party, obviously looking for what he could make out of it. The man who spoke Arabic interrogated him, and it turned out that he was a local bloke that kept a flock of goats and sheep. Anyway, it finished up that Keyes bought a goat from him, which they killed and cooked, and finally, when I got down off duty, I got a cold issue of goat meat – it was bloody horrible!'[3]

Campbell described the hot meal as excellent, but the commandos fell about laughing when Keyes asked Drori to pass this on to young Idriss; the men were more of Jim Gornall's opinion on the culinary merits of cooked goat. Still, it was the first hot food they had had since leaving the RV the previous night, and it was very welcome, no matter the rank taste. The cold drizzle that had continued all morning worsened in the afternoon.

When the light faded and the commandos finally got going, they were almost relieved.

MINUS 2 DAYS

16 November 1941 1830 hours

Three hundred miles to the east, Geoffrey Keyes' sister unit, L Detachment, of the non-existent SAS Brigade, was about to set off on its inaugural mission. The same bad weather that had hampered the commandos' landing came very close to bringing about the cancellation of the Gazala/Tmimi raid too. At the airfield at Maaten Baggush, where the Parashots had mustered that morning, there were forecasts of thunderstorms approaching the central Mediterranean, with winds gusting at 30 knots.

David Stirling, who had arrived there directly from General Cunningham's HQ, knew that this was the worst possible weather for parachuting. The wind in the desert would raise a pall of dust so thick the RAF pilots would be unable to navigate, and the wind-speed would cause the parachutists to scatter in flight, to hit the deck with dangerous force, and to be dragged along by their canopies. Cunningham's Brigadier General Staff, responsible for both *Operation Flipper* and the Gazala/Tmimi mission, had advised him strongly to call it off, but had left the final decision to him. Stirling had agreed to announce his decision within an hour.

Although he knew he should abort, Stirling was reluctant to do so, for a number of reasons. One of the promises he had made his new unit was that they would not be messed around as they had been in the commandos, continually getting geared up for operations that never materialized. If he were to back out now, it would ruin morale. It could also mean the end of all his own plans. The SAS had a lot of detractors at GHQ who would delight in using this excuse to break the detachment up; they were just awaiting the opportunity.

At the airfield, Stirling greeted the officers who were to lead the operation: Jock Lewes, Charles Bonnington, Paddy Mayne and Eoin McGonigal, and asked for their opinions, adding only, 'It seems to me we should take the risk.' Lewes and Mayne agreed at once. After a moment's thought, so did McGonigal and Bonnington. Stirling went away for a while to think it over himself.

He didn't linger long; he returned shortly to his officers and announced simply, 'It's on!'

At 1930 hours, ninety minutes after Keyes and his men had started out with their Bedouin guides to cross the Jebel, L Detachment took off from Maaten Baggush in their five Bristol Bombays from 216 Squadron RAF. Powered by twin Bristol Pegasus engines, these aircraft could theoretically cruise at 160 miles per hour, at an altitude of 10,000 feet. Even though they had only been in service since 1939, the Bombays were already obsolete. The Bombay's normal range was 880 miles. These had extra tanks fitted, extending their coverage to 2,230 miles, but that cut down on space for the human cargo. The aircraft's doors had been taken off to accommodate the extra tanks, and as the aeroplane gained altitude the discomfort levels soared: the troops shivered with cold, were deafened by the noise of the engines and sickened by the stink of aviation fuel.

Despite the forecasts, the weather at take-off was clear and calm, and they began to think – to *hope* – the met boys had got it wrong. But as they headed west towards Cyrenaica the conditions quickly deteriorated and soon the Bombays were plunging into thick cloudbanks, where a savage electric storm was raging. The SAS, shaken about mercilessly, could see the lightning through the windows and could hear the noise of the thunder even over the drone of the aircraft's engines.

In Charles Bonnington's plane, bound for Tmimi, Warrant Officer

Pilot Charlie West couldn't make out the Libyan coast: the Mediterranean was an ocean of darkness. There was nothing to get a fix on, nothing to indicate the direction or force of the wind. West dropped a sea-marker flare and discovered that he was way off course. If he dropped his sticks on schedule – at 2230 hours – he calculated that they would overshoot the drop zone by forty miles at least. The only alternative was to break cloud-cover earlier. He took the Bombay down from 5,000 to 200 feet, desperate to eyeball the landscape, when suddenly an Italian triple-A battery opened up.

'We knew we were losing altitude,' Sergeant Ernie Bond, on board the aircraft, recalled, 'but we didn't realize how much until suddenly tracers from the anti-aircraft guns began flicking past the windows. There was a great shudder and then we were groaning upwards again.'[1]

West's port engine had been hit and the port fuel tank on the wing punctured, and a shell had wrecked his instrument panel, putting it out of action. The engine was losing power, the tank leaking aviation fuel, and the only instrument that still appeared to be serviceable was the magnetic compass. West set a bearing due east for Alexandria and pulled the Bombay's nose around, heading back to base. He flew due east for fifty minutes until he was certain he was back behind British lines, then went down for an emergency landing, 'A bumpy, bouncing, slithering landing,' he wrote, 'on a black, moonless night in the midst of torrential rain and high wind.'[2]

Jock Lewes's aircraft, bound for Gazala, had run into similar trouble, but Lewes's stick had been more fortunate. Ninety minutes out of Maaten Baggush, the pilot had told Lewes he was turning inland for the final run to the drop zone.

'As this information filtered down to the rear of the aircraft,' Johnny Cooper said, 'we were caught in a searchlight beam. At the same instant a firework display comparable with the fifth of November came up from the Italian ground-defences, their streams of tracer seemingly converging on the Bombay.'[3]

The pilot took evasive action, wrestling with the thirteen-ton metal bird, overweight from her extra fuel tanks, throwing her into dives, weaving to port and starboard, trying to duck the probing Italian searchlights.

'All of us were terrified,' Cooper said, 'imagining that we would plunge to the ground. Bits of kit broke loose and flew about, adding to the confusion.' The attack lasted only a matter of seconds, and almost at once they were cowled in the darkness again, but as they skimmed the second line of defences, they were caught in searchlight beams once more. The *ack-ack* fire resumed and this time their Bombay took a hit.

Over the roaring of the engines, Lewes yelled at his eleven men to hook up the static lines of their parachutes for an emergency jump. They waited for the aircraft to lose height, but she had been hit in the fuselage only, and wasn't seriously damaged.

'With a final dive we cleared the coastal strip,' Cooper said, 'to the immense relief of all of us.'[4]

In Stirling's aircraft, also headed for Gazala, the triple-A guns had started the moment the pilot had banked into his final run, but luckily they had taken no hits. As soon as they had hopped the coast defences, the pilot gave them a six-minute warning and the men stood up in action stations. Each parachutist checked the kit of the man in front of him, and tapped him on the shoulder to let him know all was fine. The RAF dispatcher checked them all. Then everyone checked their static lines, making sure they were linked properly.

Now they were ready, their bodies tensed for the jump, bent under the weight of the parachutes.

'Red On!' the dispatcher shouted as the red light by the open door flashed on.

There were two minutes before the green light, and everything but the door went blank. Time seemed to stand still.

Green on.

'GOOOO!'

David Stirling stepped out into the night: the first man out on the first operational jump ever made by the SAS, the first and last parachute drop made in Libya in the Second World War.

This time there were no snags on the tailplane and Stirling's canopy developed properly. He was amazed how calm and quiet it was after the noise and buffeting in the aircraft. The only thing he didn't like was the length of time it was taking to land – at 500 feet the flight should have been no more than twenty seconds. He realized suddenly that the wind was blowing him along sideways like a kite. He could not see the ground in the darkness, but he tensed himself instinctively. For the second time in his parachuting career he hit the deck like a ton of bricks, and was instantly knocked out.

Not far away, Jock Lewes's stick was also in the air, among them Johnny Cooper. 'I felt a terrific tug as my parachute opened,' he said, 'and then I was swinging in comparative quietness ... I could see two other parachutes which both seemed to be drifting away at a vast speed. As it was impossible to see the ground I kept my legs braced, but when I hit the desert I received a tremendous jolt through my body. Before I could gather myself properly I found myself being dragged across the desert at more than thirty miles per hour by the wind'.[5]

Meanwhile, not far away to the east, the Bombay piloted by Charlie West had landed safely, but was being pushed backwards by the same Force 9 wind that was dragging Cooper across the ground. Bonnington and his stick had to clear the ice off their equipment containers and brace them behind the wheels as chocks to stop it moving.

They remained with the aircraft until just before first light, when they noticed a road nearby with traffic on it, and Bonnington took out a patrol to make contact with what he thought were friendly forces. Instead they ran smack into an Italian position.

There was a short firefight that ended with the SAS capturing its first prisoner, an Italian private they dragged back to the Bombay.

At first West found it hard to believe they were still behind enemy lines – they had flown due east for fifty minutes before landing, which should have taken them well into Egypt. He examined the magnetic compass he had been using, and discovered that a shard of shrapnel, lodged under the pivot, had been affecting the readings. Instead of flying due east as he had thought, they had been going round in circles the whole time.

Clearly they had to take off again. West thought this feasible despite the loss of fuel and the damaged starboard engine, but they would have to be quick about it, before the Axis traffic on the road realized there was a British aircraft nearby. The aircrew primed the engines, both of which stuttered to life – the starboard one made wheezing sounds from its holed cylinders, but somehow, it still ran. West opened the throttles and the plane advanced, bouncing across the sand, and took off, just barely clearing the road. The pilot banked to the right along the coast, setting the Bombay's nose towards Tobruk, the nearest British territory, skimming the ground to avoid triple-A fire.

By now the German troops on the road had recognized the Bombay as an enemy aircraft, and they opened fire with small arms and machine-guns. West was more concerned about whether the engines would keep going, and whether the fuel would hold out till Tobruk. Suddenly the aircraft shuddered, then shuddered again.

'I felt something hit me hard,' Ernie Bond said, 'and almost at the same time the Eyetie [prisoner] took off and it seemed that he flew right through the opposite side of the aircraft. The plane was wobbling all over the place.'[6]

In the cockpit, Charlie West heard the AA shells explode in the fuselage, then the calm voice of the second pilot saying, 'Long range petrol tank's blown up and is on fire. The Eyetie's got a scorched backside, and half the skin's blown off the fuselage.'[7]

Incredibly, West got the old kite to climb to seven hundred feet, but by now a Messerschmitt 109F was on her tail. The German aircraft opened up with her machine-guns, and West felt the control column go dead.

The Bombay's nose turned down almost 90 degrees. The last thing West remembered was telling the second pilot to close the flaps fully to try and reduce the speed of impact.

Ernie Bond recovered consciousness to find himself lying in the sand some yards away from the remains of the Bombay. West was still alive, but had suffered a fractured skull, fractured ribs and shoulder and a ruptured diaphragm. The second pilot and the W/T operator were both dead. The aircraft had broken up on impact, with part of the fuselage sliding across the surface like a sledge. All the SAS men had survived, with injuries – one of them later died. They were soon captured by the Germans and taken to a field hospital where they were treated well. Charlie West remained in a coma for twelve days.

David Stirling had been out for just two minutes; he came round to find himself being dragged by his inflated canopy over an abrasive surface of sharp stones. By the time he had managed to press the release-catch on his harness, he was bleeding, but otherwise not seriously hurt. Fortunately, most of his stick were within contact distance, and they managed to regroup within two hours by shouting and flashing torches – throwing tactical caution to the wind.

It was a sorry group of SAS men who gathered in the raging wind in the early hours of 17 November, though. Of the nine enlisted men who had jumped with Stirling, one had a broken wrist and another a fractured arm; two had sprained their ankles so badly they could hardly walk. Everyone was bleeding from cuts and lacerations. One man had vanished entirely – this was 25-year-old Sergeant John Cheyne. They spent a long time searching for him in vain; the giant Gordon Highlander who had served with 11 Commando, and had assumed command of Bill Fraser's troop at the Litani River was never again seen alive. Stirling guessed that Cheyne had been knocked unconscious on landing, as he himself had, and had been dragged miles away into the desert before he'd come round – if he ever had regained consciousness.

Only two of the stick were in reasonable condition: Sergeant Bob

Tait, the 11 Commando designer of the SAS cap-badge, and Stirling himself. The worst blow of all was the destruction of their kit: eight of the ten containers carrying their equipment, rations, Tommy guns and .303s, spare ammunition, and the all-important Lewes Bombs, had gone for a burton. The only two containers they recovered were found to be carrying blankets, full water-bottles, food for twenty-four hours, and a dozen Lewes Bombs with no fuses. The men were armed with a Colt .45 automatic apiece and two grenades, but without the Lewes Bombs, the raid was a non-starter.

Stirling was livid – with himself as much as anyone, for not having considered the possibility that some containers might not be recovered. It was a simple and obvious mistake. Today, paratroopers jump with all their equipment – weapons, ammunition, food, water, radio kit, explosives – in a single container clipped to their parachute harness. Where they go, their kit goes. Stirling was angry because, despite the poor state of the men, if their weapons, explosives and supplies had been intact, they might still have had a crack at the enemy in one way or another.

'As it was we were impotent,' Stirling told his biographer. 'There was no action we could take.'[8] All he could hope was that Paddy Mayne and Jock Lewes had fared better than he had.

Mayne had been destined for Tmimi, but though his aircraft had survived the triple-A batteries, his eleven-man stick had had an even worse landing than Stirling's. Two of his men were so badly injured they had to be left behind, and Mayne himself had suffered a broken toe. A three-hour search for their containers produced only four of them; the sum total of their supplies was two Thompsons, 14 water-bottles, rations for four men, four blankets and sixteen Lewes Bombs – at least the bombs had their fuses.

They still had the means to carry out the job they were being paid for, and Mayne was determined to do it. The stick shook hands solemnly with the two injured, and leaving them with three bottles of water and rations, headed into the darkness towards their target. They marched for three and a half hours, then lay up in a wadi, while Sergeant E. MacDonald, of the Cameron Highlanders – another 11 Commando man – went off to recce the airfield and coast, about six miles to the north. While MacDonald was away a torrential rainstorm began. With startling speed the wadi turned into a river. Before the SAS men could make it to higher ground, vital gear had been damaged or carried away by the torrent, and the detonators and fuses for the Lewes Bombs ruined.

Their last chance of carrying out the operation had gone, but Mayne was still up for it. He vowed he would go in on his own and blow the Messerschmitts up with grenades. According to Reg Seekings, who had been virtually skinned alive by a thorn-bush when he landed, the rest of the group had to talk him out of it. Finally Mayne accepted that his unit was now non-operational, and set a course for the RV with Jake Easonsmith's LRDG patrol at Rotunda Segnale, a fifty-mile march to the east.

Johnny Cooper, with Lewes's stick, had finally managed to get out of his parachute harness, only to see the chute carried off by the terrible wind. Before jumping, Jock had instructed the whole stick to set their compasses on a back-bearing – the reverse of the aircraft's flight-path – so that by walking back on it on the ground they would be certain to find the rest of the stick in the darkness. It was good advice.

'Climbing stiffly to my feet,' Cooper said, 'I felt for broken bones and realized that apart from bruises, scratches and slight dizziness I was still intact. Finding my compass I started to walk back along the bearing given by the navigator and almost immediately bumped into a another member of my stick. Miraculously, after about an hour, the entire stick was assembled and without injury.'[9]

Although, like Stirling's stick, they recovered only two of their ten containers, they had enough Lewes Bombs to make an attempt on the target. But where the target was exactly was another matter entirely: Lewes confessed that he had no idea where they were.

'We can only carry out the operation assuming that we may be within five to ten miles of the DZ,' he told them.

After burying their supplies, they began to march towards the escarpment, where they intended to lie up all day on 17 November, overlooking the airfield at Gazala and attacking it during the following night.

'We set off and walked through the remainder of the night,' Cooper said. 'As dawn broke we were greeted with a torrential downpour of tropical scale … the desert was transformed into a sea of mud. The rain continued to pour down and the thunder in the background played havoc with our compasses, making navigation very difficult.'[10]

D-1

17 November 1941 0600 hours

That same downpour hit Keyes' commandos as they watched the bleary dawn come, lying in the *maquis* on rolling downs, about a hundred miles further west. They had spent most of the night in a cave Awad Mohammad and Idriss Musa, their Bedouin guides, had led them to the previous evening, after several hours' march.

'We set off just after dusk,' Jim Gornall said, 'being led by this Arab type, and we finished up in a cave which stank to the high heaven of goats … he'd obviously used it before.'[1]

Robin Campbell said the night march had been interrupted when they heard the sound of raised voices away on their flank. Keyes got the raiding party into all-round defence and sent two scouts to investigate, but they returned reporting having seen nothing. They arrived at the cave, known as Karm al-Hassan, two and a half hours later. Hidden in a dense wood of juniper and lentisk, the cave lay in a hill called Jebel Zaydan, from which, by day, you could see the Mediterranean in the distance. Karm al-Hassan had a narrow entrance, but was roomy and dry inside, and apart from the raw goat smell, was a comfortable enough place to spend the rest of the night in, if tactically unsound. It was the ideal base for the following night's attack, since Beda Littoria (Sidi Rafa was the locals' name) was now only five or six miles away. As it was still cold, the men lit a fire, and soon Awad and Idriss left them, saying they would be back at first light. When they returned they told Keyes that it would be better to leave the place by day because it looked like bad weather, and other shepherds bent on using the place for sheltering their flocks might spot the commandos and compromise their operation.

Keyes saw the sense in this; just before sunrise he moved the troop to the juniper and lentisk woods nearby. The woods were full of cyclamen and wild arbutus bushes. Awad told Keyes the arbutus berries were considered a delicacy by his people, so the commandos had some for breakfast: a real treat, as the fruits of the bushes tasted like strawberries. These woods were Keyes' reconnaissance point, the place from which he would make his final recce of the target, as planned and detailed in his orders. He told Robin Campbell to take charge of the men and selected Roy Cooke and Jack Terry to go with him and the Bedouin guides.

Shortly after the recce party had gone off, the skies opened and the rain hammered down. When Keyes got back several hours later, soaked to the skin, he told Campbell that he'd decided to move the men back into the cave to keep them as dry as possible for the night's operation, even though there was a risk of compromise. It was only once they were back under cover that he admitted to Campbell that the recce had been unsuccessful. He had managed to get far enough to see the top of the second escarpment, about a mile short of Beda Littoria, but even with his binos he had not been able to make out the town itself. His idea had been to walk right in there with Awad, dressed in Arab garb, but the Bedouin had refused even to consider it – there were too many spies and agents about, he'd said.

Keyes knew he couldn't make his final plan until he had more detailed knowledge. He had decided to send Idriss, the Bedouin youth, into the town to report on the lay-out of the buildings and the number and dispositions of local troops. He called Idriss over and, with Drori translating, gave him careful and detailed instructions about what he wanted to know. He also promised him a big bonus if he got it right.

Idriss hurried off in his rubber sandals towards Beda Littoria and Keyes and his party sat down to wait, glad at least to be sheltered from the foul weather.

'During the Arab boy's absence the thunderstorm continued,' Campbell said. 'Every now and then the clouds seemed to open and a deluge of rain fell. The country we had to march over turned to mud before our eyes. Little torrents of muddy water sprang up all over the countryside we could see from the mouth of the cave, and a rivulet ran into the cave, which sloped down from the opening. The roof began to drip. Spirits were sinking – at least I know mine were – at the prospect of a long, cold, wet and muddy march before we even arrived at the starting point of this hazardous operation.'[2]

Further east, David Stirling and Bob Tait had also run into the wall of rain. They had calculated that the coast was about ten miles from the drop zone, but by first light on 17 November they had walked thirteen miles and there was still no sign of the escarpment.

'This means they dropped us well outside the drop zone,' Tait said.

'There's nothing to do but keep going,' Stirling replied. 'We'll have to hit the coast some time.'[3]

By about 1000 hours there was a change in the texture of the skyline and, peering through his binos, Stirling could make out what appeared to be a rough, uneven line about four miles away. It had to be the escarpment.

'Looks like we're nearly there,' he said. They decided to halt where they were until dark to conserve their water supply – they had only one water-bottle each – and, finding a dip in the sand, settled down under Hessian sacks and a single blanket, to wait for nightfall. For lunch they ate hard tack biscuits and chocolate, but there was no sun, and Stirling was suffering badly from the cold. By mid-afternoon, dark clouds were again lowering in the sky, so Stirling decided to move on. They reached the escarpment by about 1630 hours and soon saw the Via Balbia – the coast road – below them. It was choc-a-bloc with Axis traffic, and all along its shoulder there were tents and huts. Stirling was unable to make out any features he could recognize on the map, but he ventured a guess that they were east of Gazala and a little west of Tobruk.

They lay in the cover of rocks, watching the traffic, while above them the storm clouds gathered. An hour after dark the clouds burst and the rain came lashing down. Within minutes the dry washes on the top of the escarpment were raging rivers and waterfalls. Tait and Stirling were soon sodden once again and to Stirling's chagrin his precious Cuban cigars were ruined. His intention had been to climb down from the escarpment and carry out a close reconnaissance of the enemy traffic, but with this final downpour he had to admit that a descent of the escarpment was impossible: the weather had defeated them. The mission they had been training for all these months had been a costly failure.

It was poor compensation to know that the same weather that had ruined their operation had done their job for them – in such bucketing rain the airfields would be unusable, and the Messerschmitt squadrons unable to take to the skies. Whatever the case, there was no choice now but to turn about and head for the RV.

In the cave of Karm al-Hassan, the commandos brewed tea, dozed or collected water from the dripping roof in bully-beef cans. Geoffrey Keyes called Roy Cooke over and read off the names of the six men who were to go with him to demolish the cable mast at the Cyrene crossroads.

Jim Gornall, who was one of them, was introduced to Fred Birch and John Kerr, who were strangers to him; they had been assigned only the previous day. 'They would do the sabotage,' Gornall said. 'Cooke would be in charge, and the support would be a rifle party consisting of Lance Bombardier Terry O'Hagen and Gunner P. Macrae, Royal Artillery, Private Charlie Paxton of the Cameron Highlanders, and myself. We were to do the Cyrene crossroads job, but after we'd arrived at Beda Littoria. If we were required we would have taken part in that attack. If it was deemed that we were not required we would shoot off down the road.'[4]

After briefing them on their task and telling them that they would hijack a vehicle if possible, Cooke handed each of his party a Benzedrine tablet. He told them the drug would keep the spirits up, and keep them going under extreme conditions.

Idriss had been away for hours, and Keyes began to worry about him. Then, just as he'd begun to give up hope, the youth re-appeared at the mouth of the cave. He had used that famous Bedouin power of observation to its most brilliant extent, and Keyes was stunned with the detail and accuracy of the data he had brought back in his head. He started to draw a sketch-map from the youth's description; Idriss was able to put in even outbuildings and the car park. Keyes was delighted. Idriss's perfect description made up for the lack of a close reconnaissance and allowed the commandos to get a pretty good picture of what they were up against.

Idriss also told Keyes that Rommel was more likely to be found in the HQ building than the villa half a mile away – and this solved the problem of which building to attack.

Keyes completed his sketch of the target buildings and gathered the men together to explain the final plan. His group would consist of seventeen men, and it was to be divided into four sections – an assault party of six, a close covering party of four, an external covering party of four, and a party of three who would cut the telephone wires. The assault party would consist of Keyes, Campbell, Terry, Coulthread and Lance Bombardier A. Brodie of the Royal Artillery. Avishalom Drori would be on hand in case his Arabic was required. For points of entry, they had the option of using the front door, the back door, or the ground-floor windows. The roof was a non-starter as the place was six storeys high. The windows offered a number of choices, but the assault party would be vulnerable while climbing through, possibly silhouetted against the outside and therefore likely to present an easy target to the enemy. The front door offered them immediate control of the hallway, but was almost certain to be covered by a sentry or reception party of some kind. The back door was unlikely to open into a hall, and would therefore give them less of an advantage immediately, but it was also likely to be less well guarded than the front, and offer better cover for the approach. All in all it was decided the back door would be their best bet.

The objective was no more than six miles away, but the trek – six hundred feet up the escarpment, at night, in driving rain – would be a harrowing one, and Keyes wisely allowed six hours from the RV to the target, which was to be hit at precisely one minute to midnight.

There was only one hitch as the party prepared to move out: Awad, their guide, didn't want to accompany them to Beda Littoria.

'The Arab had got cold feet by this time,' Jim Gornall said, 'and he wanted out. Keyes said, "Tell him, if he makes a move, I'll shoot him!" He was a great one for shooting people was Keyes. Anyway, the bloke finished up leading us on the next step.'[5]

The men formed up at 1755 hours with military precision, their faces freshly blackened with burnt cork, ready for the final leg – the big one, the one they had trained for, the one that would be remembered for ever. The cave, Karm al-Hassan, was to be their RV and rallying-point after the attack; it would be guarded by Bob Fowler of the Cameron Highlanders; the man had stepped on a rusty nail on landing, and his leg was now badly bloated. Fowler was to remain here and watch their excess kit – rations, water-bottles, blankets and – most importantly – their boots.

'Whilst we were in the cave,' Gornall said, 'we changed from our boots into plimsolls. Now, all the time we'd been travelling it had been pouring with rain – the worst storm they'd seen in about twenty years. And we changed into bloody plimsolls!'[6]

At 1800 hours precisely, clad in plimsolls, twenty-four men of 11 (Scottish) Commando marched off to a blast from Lieutenant Colonel Geoffrey Keyes' whistle, into the teeming rain and the gathering dusk.

27 OPERATION CRUSADER

D-1

17 November 1941 1800 hours

It was the worst rainstorm Cyrenaica had seen for almost *forty* years. First came a chilling wind, raking up a dustcloud that gathered energy as it raced across the void of the Sahara without hindrance, then the darkness was torn asunder by ragged forks of lightning that dashed to the ground with heart-stopping savagery, heralding the deep boom of thunder that seemed to shake the very earth itself.

The rain, when it came, was merciless, slashing down in torrents and cascades, flooding every wadi and rivulet on the escarpment, washing away boulders, bushes and clumps of earth, turning the goat-tracks to streams of liquid mud.

War correspondent Alan Moorehead, then with the British mobile columns lumbering secretly westwards through the desert, wrote, 'It rained in squalls of bitter sleet that night. Like artillery, the lightning came rushing from the Mediterranean and, as we lay awake and watching in the open, the water seeped through bedding, blankets, groundsheets – everything. Men crouched against the sides of tanks and guns in the futile struggle to stay dry. The infantry sat numbly in their trucks with their greatcoat collars turned up over their ears. No aircraft could take off from the sodden, sticky sand. It was a cold, miserable, disheartening start for the battle.'[1]

Far in advance of the Eighth Army's mobile front, the twenty-four commandos and their two Arab guides moved inexorably and invisibly towards their deadly target. Most of the way they were tramping through ankle-deep mud, stumbling and slipping in their inappropriate plimsolls. One man, Lance Corporal Terry O'Hagen, had a shoe sucked off by the mud and was obliged to walk barefoot, unable to find and retrieve it in the darkness. It was so dark they could only just make out the man in front; they had to form a human chain, each hanging on to the bayonet-frog of the next man like a caravan of elephants moving trunk to tail.

The rain coursed down, soaking their heavy battledress, making it even heavier, seeping into their haversacks, into their ammunition and explosives, even getting into the oilskin packets containing their match-head primers. When one man fell, the entire column would come to a stop while he picked himself up. Occasionally the file would split as a man lost contact with the one in front, and would have to halt while the chain formed once more. It took four and a half hours to reach the bottom of Lusaita, the first escarpment, where they halted for a brief – and much needed – rest.

Then they began their six-hundred-foot assault on the second escarpment, scrambling over turf turned glue-like by the downpour and wet outcrops of rock.

'It was a hazardous climb,' Gornall said, 'with all the rain and the water flooding down. You were pretty much left to manage on your own and you did. If you saw one of the lads struggling you'd give him a hand, and nobody fell by the wayside. We'd been trained in night climbing anyway.'[2]

'It was a terrible journey,' Fred Birch agreed. 'Six miles as the crow flies, but following the winding path over the escarpment, knee-deep in rushing water, it was nearer nine miles. The night was moonless and pitch-black, making it necessary to hold on to the bayonet scabbard of the man in front to keep in contact, the whole party being in single file.'[3]

There were several Arab huts made of flattened-out tins on the escarpment, and as the column passed one of them, about a hundred yards away, someone slipped and dropped his Tommy gun. At once a dog started barking. The commandos froze. The door of the hut creaked open and a bar of light streaked out. They heard a voice shouting at the dog. Finally, when the door closed, Keyes gave the signal to move on.

At the top of the escarpment they came to a muddy track which the guides said led directly to Rommel's HQ. It was 2320 hours.

'As we climbed over the top,' Gornall said, 'through the flashes of lightning you could see what looked like a small village and at the far side you could see the outline of this big building which was the German HQ.'[4]

When the party halted for a breather, Keyes surveyed the scene. In the low ground between them and the high building lay an Arab market, made up of more shacks of flattened tins. The HQ was surrounded by a low hedge and a barbed-wire fence, and lay in a copse of pencil cedars and patches of *maquis*. There was another administrative building to its left, with a block-shaped tower, which Awad and Idriss told Keyes was the town hall; behind that was the *carabinieri* barracks. To the east lay a tower used for drying and storing grain, and to the south there was a block of trim Italian villas, mostly single-storeyed, whitewashed rectangles. The original idea had been for Cooke and his party to split from the main party at this point, box round the town and hit the road to Cyrene, but Keyes now decided to keep them with him a little longer in case his assault party wasn't large enough for the job.

They cocked their rain-sodden weapons and began to move stealthily down the track. Here the Bedouin cried off; Awad told Keyes that he didn't need them any longer, as the track they were on led directly to the back door of Rommel's house. Keyes reluctantly agreed to let them go, but he ordered Awad and Idriss to stay quiet under a stone pine tree about five hundred yards from the HQ and wait for his return.

The commandos moved on again, passing a few buildings, but they encountered no one until they were among Arab shacks about a hundred yards from Rommel's house.

'We got to the outskirts of the huts,' Gornall said, 'and just as we got there, a pair of headlights came on at the German HQ, came out and turned right towards Cyrene. I thought it might be Rommel moving in the vehicle.'[5]

It was a *Panzergruppe* driver, who had been sent on a mission to Cyrene. He spotted four of the commandos diving for cover, but oddly enough, he thought nothing of it. He did not report the sighting until late the following day.

After the car had gone, Keyes told the main party to disperse among the shacks, while he and Jack Terry did a preliminary recce to find out how many sentries were on duty.

Just after they had left, Jim Gornall stumbled clumsily over a pile of tins. 'The Arabs in the huts started gabbling away, obviously shouting "Who's that?"' he said. 'Behind me was a Palestinian Jew, a Corporal, whom I'd never met before, and he shouted at them in Arabic, "Shut up! We are a German patrol and we're doing a night exercise!" I asked him what he said immediately afterwards. It was absolutely pouring with rain, and the Arabs never actually came out of the hut. If they had we'd have silenced them.'[6]

Robin Campbell recorded it differently; in his account he reported the Arabs wouldn't shut up, and a moment later two Arab *carabinieri* arrived – an officer and an NCO – to find out what the noise was about. The officer demanded to know who they were and what they were doing. Campbell blustered in German and Drori repeated in Arabic that they were a German patrol, and asked them to quieten down the man in the hut, who was still shouting. The officer bawled at the unseen shouter, who went silent. Then, wishing them '*Gute nacht*', the two Arab policemen disappeared into the shadows.

Moments later, Keyes and Terry returned. Keyes reported to Cooke and Campbell that they had spotted no sentries at the rear of the house, confirming that the back door would be their best approach. There was a bell-tent in the grounds in the front that he suspected was being used as a guardhouse. Because of the rain, the enemy was staying inside; on reflection, Keyes said, he had decided he didn't need Cooke's party for the assault. He advised Cooke to make a detour to the west to strike the Cyrene road.

Fred Birch collected the men in his party and, without a word, Cooke and his men vanished silently into the streaming night.

D-1

17 November 1941   2330 hours

It was 2330 hours on 17 November, and D1 was just thirty minutes away. From this point, the sequence of events becomes confused. Robin Campbell, Jack Terry and Avishalom Drori all gave their own written versions of what happened to Geoffrey Keyes' biographer, Elizabeth Keyes, and these were supplemented by oral accounts from various members of the team.

Robin Campbell, Keyes' Second-in-Command, was the principal witness on the British side, but his written account, on which most descriptions of the Rommel Raid are based, is in places self-contradictory, and it may be deliberately false. The German reports present a further level of contradiction.

From this moment on, things happened very quickly, in a blur of movement. As with any event, the protagonists, each in a different position, saw and interpreted events in their own subjective way; two people reporting the same incident faithfully will always have different views of what actually happened.

In Elizabeth Keyes' account, Keyes and Terry returned from their first recce, then Keyes went off again and, having spotted a sentry standing in the drive, he went forward alone and killed the guard at the gate, presumably with a knife.

Clearly, knifing a sentry was a possibility. The SOE training manual lays down specific instructions for this technique: attack from the rear. With left forearm, strike violently on left side of opponent's neck and instantly transfer the left hand to cover his mouth and nostrils. Simultaneously with the blow on the neck, thrust the knife into his kidneys.'[1] But the double-edged commando knife, designed by SOE hand-to-hand combat instructor Denis Fairburn, had not yet been issued to 11 Commando; and knife fighting had not been taught as part of commando training. As Jim Gornall said, 'You simply bought your own knife and learned how to use it.'

If Keyes did not use a knife, then unless he used cheesewire – the commandos did carry cheesewire for garroting – he must have shot him. One of Elizabeth Keyes' informants, Lieutenant Ernst Schilling, the officer in charge of the Motor Detachment which provided the guards for the HQ building, stated in a letter to her in 1946 that the sentry *in the house* had been alerted by a shot from the guard tent, 'by which one man had been killed'.[2]

This claim is also dubious. For a start, Schilling wasn't an eyewitness; he was sleeping in a villa nearby and didn't arrive until it was all over. Secondly, Elizabeth Keyes claimed that her brother killed the sentry *then* returned to the main party outside the grounds; just possible if he had used a knife, but improbable if he had shot the man. The general rule in irregular warfare is that since the first shot in any surprise action alerts the enemy, it almost always marks the beginning of the attack. To have shot the guard before the assault party was in place would have been suicide. The SOE training manual states: If there are sentries round the building they must be silently eliminated first, or if they have to be shot, the attack must coincide with this. In this latter case the first shot fired by the sentry killers is the signal for the attack.[3]

Even if Elizabeth Keyes' sequence of events was wrong and Keyes shot the guard at the gate, then sprinted the fifty yards to the door of the house in an Olympic time, the guard in the house would still have been ready for him.

In any case, if Keyes *had* disposed of the guard at the gate by stabbing, shooting or garroting with cheesewire, what happened to his body? The

German reports said that only two guards were present. A German witness, Joseph Hoiss, who said he was sleeping some distance away, said there were always two sentries at the HQ building – they took turns, one sleeping in the tent while the other stood guard in the hall – but both of these men were accounted for in the reports.[4]

Unless the body of an unaccounted third guard simply vanished, Keyes' disposing of a sentry must have been a figment of Elizabeth Keyes' (or Ernst Schilling's) romantic imagination.

Keyes had planned to send three of his men, Andrew Radcliffe of the Royal Army Service Corps, Lance Corporal Bill Pryde and Private John Phiminster of the Cameron Highlanders, to cut the telephone wires to Cyrene once the first shot was fired. It was taboo for wires to be cut prior to any assault, for that would be as much a giveaway as a premature gunshot. The men listened intently as Keyes changed his instructions, ordering them to watch the front of the house, particularly for any sentries who might emerge from the bell-tent while the assault party entered from the rear. Keyes then told the rest of the party to stay where they were until he'd had another look at the house.

This time he went off with a pair of wire-cutters, taking Radcliffe, Pryde, Phiminster and the interpreter, Avishalom Drori, with him. Before they reached the fence, Keyes said Drori was making too much noise and told him to wait there. He went forward with the rest of his party and cut their way through the fence at the back of the house with the wire-cutters. Keyes, Radcliffe, Pryde and Phiminster approached the back door, tried it and found it locked. Keyes stationed his three men outside with instructions to shoot anyone who emerged, and did a quick circuit of the house to discover if any windows were open or accessible. Finding they were all high up and heavily shuttered, he decided that the only way to get in would be by the front door, and slipped back through his hole in the fence to fetch Campbell and the rest of the party.

Outside the grounds, among the huts, he gave his final orders. Charlie Bruce, Charles Lock, Jimmy Bogle and Bob Murray were to position themselves in the Motor-Transport Pool on the southern side of the house. They would cover the assault party from outside the grounds, hold off an enemy relief party if it came, and warn the main party of its approach. Meanwhile, they would set demolition charges on any vehicles they found in the M/T Pool. Frank Varney, the ex-Sherwood Forester from Nottingham, Spike Hughes, Corporal Stephen Heavysides, of the Yorkshire & Lancashire Regiment, and Joe Kearney would join the other three in watching the house, spaced at intervals around its perimeter, with instructions to shoot anyone who came through the windows. The assault party – Keyes, Campbell, Terry and Coulthread, with Drori and Brodie covering – would go through the front door, bump off Rommel and his staff, then pull out. Finally, the covering party would set explosive charges on the house and power-plant, and everyone would beat a hasty retreat. They would regroup here among the huts, which would be the emergency RV. A single whistle-blast would be the signal to make for the fall-back RV at the cave. There was a password so that the covering party could distinguish friend from foe in the darkness and the pouring rain: Keyes reminded them of the challenge, *Island*, and the answer, *Arran* – a tribute to the place where they had trained.

Looking upwards at the six storeys of the house Keyes saw that there was a light on at the top. He waited for it to go out. When it did, he led his ten commandos through the hole he'd previously cut in the fence at the back of the house and Hughes, Kearney, Heavysides and Varney peeled off. At the front of the house there was a gravel drive lined with stone pines leading from the gate, where the guard-tent stood. The front door was an ornate, Italian-style double-entrance of wood, which stood in a wide porch at the top of six low steps. Keyes stationed Brodie and Drori, armed with .303 rifles, outside, and he and Robin Campbell ran up the steps, followed by Jack Terry and Denis Coulthread, both armed with Thompsons. Keyes was probably carrying a Colt .45 automatic, and Campbell a standard Webley .38 revolver, though Campbell's earliest account said that Keyes had a Tommy gun.

Campbell gave several versions of what happened next. In two of them, he simply opened the door for Keyes (because Keyes had a Tommy gun – a two-handed weapon) and in another, he banged on the door and demanded in German to be let in, whereupon the door was opened from inside; Drori corroborated the latter story, saying, 'Captain Campbell knocked at the door and asked in German to open it.'[5]

Joseph Hoiss said that the commandos simply pushed the door open, while, in a statement made years later, Terry said, 'We knocked on the door and a big German opened it.'[6]

Inside the main door was a set of glass doors, beyond which an *Afrika Korps* private, Rifleman Jamatter, was stationed. Jamatter, dressed in a steel helmet and greatcoat, was actually more of a marshal than a guard; his duties were principally confined to receiving visitors and directing them to the correct rooms inside the HQ. Obviously raiders were not expected.

At that moment, according to a German report compiled the following day, a meeting was in progress on one of the upper storeys, between the Chief Engineer of the *Panzergruppe Afrika*, the senior Quartermaster, Captain I.G. Weitz, and two Supply Officers, Lieutenants Schulz and Ampt.[7]

Rifleman Jamatter, a big, powerful man from south Germany, either opened the main door at this point, or saw the commandos, dressed in British battledress and with blackened faces, coming towards him through the entrance. One of them, Keyes, was pointing a Colt automatic at him. Keyes hesitated in shooting Jamatter; probably he had hoped to overpower the sentry silently so as not to alert the house. But all the witnesses agreed that he hesitated long enough for Jamatter to grab the Colt's muzzle and deflect it. The two men began to grapple desperately in the second doorway, with Jamatter bellowing in German and backing into a position against the wall in between the two sets of doors. Campbell implied that Keyes wanted to stab the German but he wasn't able to get his knife out; nor could Campbell and Terry get around Keyes to stab

Jamatter. As the cat was already out of the bag anyway, Campbell said, he squeezed the trigger of his .38 and shot Jamatter several times, wounding him.

The attack was now on.

As Jamatter tumbled to the floor, Keyes told Campbell and Terry to use their grenades and Tommy gun. At the same time, Keyes muttered that his arm had gone numb – either due to the fight with Jamatter, or because Campbell had inadvertently shot him. There was no time to follow this up, because they were now in the eye of the tiger, and events were moving too fast for succinct comprehension. What followed next probably lasted no more than two minutes.

They went through the glass doors and into a large hall with more heavy wooden doors opening off it – all of them shut – and a stone staircase with an Art Deco balustrade on the right. The logical step would have been to run upstairs, as it was most likely that Rommel would be on an upper floor; they had already observed a light up there from the outside. But stairs were difficult and dangerous for an assault party, requiring one man to cover while the other dashed up: the advantage lay with the defenders, who could roll grenades down on them.

The officers meeting upstairs had heard the commotion, according to the German report, and Weitz, assuming the enemy soldiers were after his documents, placed them under lock and key while the others drew and cocked their pistols. Doors creaked and slammed all over the house as officers and men rushed to find out what was happening.[8]

On the ground floor, Campbell said, they heard a man in heavy boots running downstairs, but no one could see him because of the turn in the staircase. When his feet came into view, Terry fired a burst from his Tommy gun at them, and they quickly vanished, though Denis Coulthread claimed that it was he, not Terry, who fired bursts at the man's silhouette on the staircase. Drori too said someone fired sub-machine-gun bursts at a man clattering downstairs, shouting 'What's up there?', but he did not name anyone.[9]

Coulthread spun round to the open main door and noticed the beam of torchlight approaching down the drive. He concealed himself by the door where he would have the drop on any interloper who might try to enter. The man approaching was the other marshal, who had been asleep in the guard-tent, Rifleman Matthe Boxhammer. He had heard the shots and was running to investigate. Boxhammer, 20 years old, was from Malling in Bavaria, and belonged to the Motor Detachment of the Quartermaster's office.

Avishalom Drori, squatting by the main door, also saw the light coming. 'I hid myself in the garden,' he wrote, 'when the man with the torch, who was dressed in a pyjama, was near me I shot him with my rifle. He did not shout nor sigh, but just fell down silently.'[10]

Denis Coulthread peered out of the doorway to find out what had happened and saw Drori standing over an apparently dead German soldier. 'I just stood there,' Drori said to him, 'and he walked on to the end of my weapon. All I had to do was pull the trigger.'[11]

In the key passage of Campbell's text, he said that Keyes had flung open one door and found the room empty but, noticing a crack of light from the door on the left, pointed to it and threw it open. The door opened outwards; inside, he and Campbell saw ten Germans in steel helmets, some sitting, some standing. Keyes fired a double tap or three shots from his Colt .45, while Campbell yelled, 'Wait, I'll throw a grenade in!' Keyes slammed the door shut and hurled his weight against it while Campbell pulled the pin on the No. 36 Mills bomb he had drawn from his pouch.

'Right!' Campbell said, and Keyes flung the door open again. Campbell flicked the grenade in carefully so that it would not rebound off an obstacle. He saw it roll into the middle of the floor, and Terry followed it up with a burst from his Tommy gun into the room.

'Well done!' Keyes grunted.

According to Campbell, these were his last words. As he tried to close the door again, one of the *Afrika Korps* men shot him at almost point-blank range, and he went down.

Coulthread said that he heard someone shout, 'A grenade!' and heard Keyes' Colt .45 clatter on the stone floor. Campbell forced the door closed, and he and Terry threw themselves to one side as the grenade exploded with a concussive thump that shook the whole house.

For a moment there was absolute silence. Campbell saw that the light had gone out inside the room.

Upstairs, according to the German report, the lights had also gone out, and one of the officers telephoned to the barracks, five minutes' walk away, where the lieutenant in charge, Ernst Schilling, had just turned in after checking some nearby offices. When the voice on the other end told Schilling the HQ building was under attack, he thought at first it was a joke. Then two things happened simultaneously: the phone line went dead and Schilling heard shots and an explosion over the drumming of the rain from the direction of the HQ. He immediately called out the guard.[12]

Back in the HQ building, the *Panzergruppe* QM staff, still convinced the raiders were after their documents and would soon be on their way up to the top of the house, posted guards on each of the rooms and were coolly organizing a defence of the staircase. Lieutenant Ampt, one of the Supply Officers, advanced down the stairwell, shone his torch into the hall and saw a body lying in front of the door to the left-hand room. There was still shooting going on, so he retreated.[13]

'I decided Geoffrey had to be moved in case there was further fighting in the building,' Campbell said, 'so between us Sergeant Terry and I carried him outside and laid him on the grass verge by the side of the steps leading up to the front door. He must have died as we were carrying him outside, for when I felt his heart it had ceased to beat.'[14]

These events all took place in a very short space of time, and Campbell wrote his report in 1943. In the intervening period he had lost a leg and spent two years in a German hospital and prison camp. He admitted having a rather bad memory. But his account catalogues a farrago of ineptitude and clumsiness unworthy of trained special forces troops. If Keyes really opened the door, fired, then closed and opened it again, in full view of armed enemy soldiers, he was simply asking to be killed. And Campbell's account, with its suggestion of cricket-pitch civilities ('Wait, I'll throw in a grenade!' 'Right!' 'Well done!') has a stilted quality that sounds unnatural considering the razor-edge peril of the situation – it reads like an account of the way in which stiff-upper-lipped Englishmen ought to behave, rather than the reality of soldiers in close action.

Jack Terry's account, written only three months after the events, is quite different. He did not mention firing a burst at a man on the staircase. He said that he saw the door on the left open a crack, then close again. Keyes, who had been peering into another room, he said, noticed the crack of light and flung the door wide. Terry reported that Keyes opened the door only once, upon which he *walked inside* the room firing his Colt. Terry followed him, and when he saw him fall, fired a burst of deadly .45 calibre rounds from his Thompson around the room. A moment later, he said, Robin Campbell arrived and 'threw grenades (sic) over my shoulder.'

Terry wrote that there were sounds of resistance from outside the house, so he and Campbell dragged Keyes back through the main door, then took up positions ready to throw grenades at anyone who followed. They heard Keyes groaning, and Campbell went to examine his body. 'He came back,' Terry said, 'saying to me, "It's no use worrying about him now, we can't do anything. He's dead."'[15]

Bob Laycock's official report, taken mostly from information given to him by Terry – the only man present who was not killed or captured – also failed to mention a second opening of the door by Keyes. Laycock reported that when Keyes opened the door of the left-hand room, the occupants were waiting for him: 'He was met by a burst of fire and fell back into the passage mortally wounded.'[16] Terry, Laycock said, then emptied two magazines of his Thompson into the room, while Campbell threw in a grenade and slammed the door.[17]

The citation for Keyes' VC, also written by Laycock, told yet another story. Laycock said Keyes had decided on a strategy of rushing into each room separately in order to bluff the enemy into believing there were more of them than was actually the case. He opened the door of the first, empty, room and fired inside, alerting the occupants of the second room, who were ready for him and shot him as he opened the door.

The *Panzergruppe* report, written the following day, mentioned only one room being occupied, and said there were only five men, rather than ten.[18]

No one suggested that Keyes fired into an empty room.

The German report names four men of the *Afrika Korps* – an officer, two NCOs and a private – who were sleeping in the left-hand room, designated Room WuG – an acronym for Administration & Supply – which doubled as an office and dormitory. Another officer, a Lieutenant Jager – a *W class* officer, recruited because of his administrative experience and with no officer training – was asleep in a part of the same room that was partitioned off as an office by a plywood screen.

When they heard the commotion and shots outside in the hall, the four *Afrika Korps* men leapt out of their bunks. One of them, Sergeant-Artificer Kurt Lentzen, an ordnance expert, opened the door thinking that a guard had been playing with a firearm and had shot himself. He shone his torch into the hall in time to see a British soldier coming towards him with a sub-machine-gun (this was later changed to a pistol). The soldier shot him twice as he leapt sideways and back into the room to cock his own weapon, but the shots went low, hitting him in the thigh and the calf. Another of the Germans, Lieutenant Kaufholz, who had stepped up next to Lentzen with a Walther P38 in his hand, fired once at the intruder, but was shot four times, twice in the chest by rounds that passed straight through and struck the radiator behind him, once in the stomach and once in the arm.

Two enemy soldiers then entered the room and threw two hand

grenades. The resulting explosion knocked out everyone in the room except one, Senior Sergeant (actually *Saddle-Master Class 1*) Bartl, and mortally injured a Rifleman Kovacic, who had severe internal wounds in the large intestine. Lieutenant Jager, behind his plywood screen, jumped out of the window, only to be shot and mortally wounded by one of the commandos stationed in the grounds.[19]

Campbell said he left Keyes' body where it was on the grass verge outside the porch, and re-entered the house to find all was quiet. He then, for some unspecified reason, decided to have a look at the back of the house where Keyes had posted a sergeant, before searching the upper floors. He left two men on guard in the hall, then ran round the back of the house. 'While I was approaching,' he wrote, 'the man posted at the back entrance … shot me thinking I was a German.'[20]

Campbell claimed he then sent for Jack Terry, to whom command had now devolved, gave him his grenades and explosives, 'with instructions to use them to the best effect'. He also handed over his map, telling Terry to bug out to the RV after blowing the house, and sounded the whistle for withdrawal.[21]

Elizabeth Keyes added – presumably from Campbell's later testimony – that the two men he left in the hall were Jack Terry and Denis Coulthread, but they both moved back outside when they heard shooting and took up positions by the door with grenades at the ready.[22]

This is intriguing, because Terry maintained that he was actually *with* Campbell when the captain was hit by a stray burst in the right leg. He said that he promptly took cover in the bushes, where he was joined by Brodie. When 'things had quietened down' he went to collect the rest of the party, while Brodie examined Campbell. Before swallowing his morphia tablets, Terry said, Campbell gave the order to finish off the grenades and blow up the power plant.[23]

Avishalom Drori recalled those frantic few minutes differently. He took out Matthe Boxhammer – who was still breathing – and was in position outside the entrance when he heard the gunshots and an explosion, followed by more gunshots. There was silence for a few minutes and, as he approached the porch, he saw Campbell carrying Keyes' body down the steps. 'Can I help?' he said.

'No,' Campbell replied. 'He's dead.'

Drori thought Campbell looked as if he were in pain, and asked if he were wounded, but Campbell answered shortly, 'No.'

Drori pointed to Boxhammer's body, lying nearby, and said, 'I've shot a German.'

'Good,' Campbell said.

'Are we going to retreat, Sir?' Drori asked.

'No,' Campbell said, and went back into the house again.

Drori, like Terry, believed that Keyes was not dead at this point, but was lying near the door with his right hand touching his wound, which was just above the belly. Shortly afterwards he heard Keyes groan; he knew then it was all over for Colonel Keyes.

He stood there for a few minutes, then went to look for the rest of the party, running into Jack Terry, who told him that Campbell had been shot in the leg by accident, then ordered Drori to pull out.[24]

Inside, according to the German report, Lieutenant Ampt and Captain Weitz ventured downstairs to find that the body Ampt had seen outside Room WuG had vanished. It was clear from a broad trail of blood leading to the main door that the body had been dragged outside. Curiously, the main door was now closed. There was a deathly hush, except for groans coming from Room WuG. Ampt and Weitz entered the room to find the floor flooded with water and blood – the explosion had damaged the central heating system. Lieutenant Kaufholz was lying in the bloody mixture, dying from gunshot wounds. Rifleman Kovacic was lying on his bunk with his abdomen split open. Lieutenant Jager had been badly wounded by one of the British soldiers positioned outside. He was barely alive when they found him later outside the south-west corner of the house.[25]

Many points in these reports are irreconcilable, even allowing for the confusion of battle, the delusion of memory and the passage of time. Something is missing.

Campbell's account, written after Keyes had been awarded the VC and become a posthumous hero, is obviously intended to emphasize his glory, but it is as full of holes as a colander.

For a start, neither Terry nor the German report said anything about an enemy soldier coming downstairs and being fired at. Coulthread said that he shot at a silhouette on the stairs, which is not consistent with Campbell's claim that Terry fired at a man's feet. Although Drori supports the notion that someone fired up the stairs, it is likely that he and Coulthread were too far back to see anything; both were naturally anxious to underline their active part in the events. In any case, the hall was dark – or, at the very best, dimly lit with poor visibility: both Lentzen and Ampt had to shine their torches into it.

Campbell said there were ten soldiers in steel helmets and greatcoats in the room, but the German report would not be wrong on this point. His assertion that Keyes opened the door, fired, closed it and opened it again is not only uncorroborated by any other statement, but is also patently ridiculous. Keyes was not experienced in this type of warfare, but he was not stupid; he would not think that once he had fired a few inaccurate shots from his Colt, the enemy – however few in number – was going to wait patiently while his men got their act together, armed and slung in a grenade.

Campbell said he and Terry carried Keyes' body outside; this was disputed by Drori, who said he saw only Campbell carrying Keyes; his claim that Keyes was dead by the time they got him outside is disputed by both Drori and Terry, who said he died later. The timing of the evacuation of Keyes' body is also brought into question by Ampt's claim to have seen an unattended body outside Room WuG while the shooting was still going on.

Both Campbell and Terry mentioned a hush after the grenade (or grenades) went off, but Drori said that he heard shooting, an explosion, then more shooting before, or at the time, Campbell emerged with the body.

Sergeant Jack Terry's account accorded more nearly with the German report. While Campbell maintained that he shot Jamatter as he was grappling with Keyes, Jamatter himself said that, after grabbing the muzzle of Keyes' weapon, he was knocked down by a group of six or eight men, one of whom shot him three times in the back as he tried to crawl away.[26] Terry wrote that the assault-party – of *four* men – entered the house after shooting the doorkeeper.

Neither Terry nor the German account said anything about shooting at anyone on the stairs: Keyes opened fire, fire was returned, Terry opened fire, and Campbell threw grenades: in that sequence. The only discrepancy between the two was that Terry claimed the door opened and was closed almost immediately, while the German report did not make mention of the door being closed.

From both British and German points of view, the most satisfactory scenario would be this: having disposed of Jamatter, Keyes saw the door of Room WuG open and moved towards it, whereupon it was suddenly closed. He flung it open again, advanced, fired two shots at Lentzen, and was shot once by Kaufholz. Terry fired a burst of at least four rounds from his Thompson, mortally wounding Kaufholz, and Campbell threw in one or two grenades. They withdrew, closing the door, and dragged Keyes' body outside. Campbell, Terry and Coulthread went back into the house, and Campbell, suddenly wondering what was going on at the back, left them there, ran around the house and was shot by one of his own men.

This would appear to be the most likely sequence of events, except for one thing: the German official report, written in May 1942 after all the evidence had been carefully sifted, concludes: 'it is fairly certain that *both* [British] officers were shot by their own men.'[27]

This might be dismissed as propaganda, but elsewhere the report emphasizes the coolness and quick-thinking of German noncombatant quartermaster staff – which had impressed even the British, as Elizabeth Keyes wrote: 'Unlike the British main headquarters, the *Afrika Korps* carried no "fat" … all its staff were hand-picked fully trained fighting men.'

This was nonsense, but good for German propaganda: Elizabeth Keyes even added that the survivors of the raid said, 'It was very bad luck that [Geoffrey] should have lost his life "by the slender chance of guard-room sentries having loaded weapons so far behind the line, and using them so accurately at close range."' This is a particularly odd statement given that the commandos' objective had been to kill or capture Rommel, a project Bob Laycock had warned them involved almost certain death. It is doubly strange because no sentry – even if Jamatter and Boxhammer are classed as sentries – fired a single round during the entire incident.

In fact, despite Bob Laycock's dramatic assertion in his report that Keyes was *flung back by a burst of fire*, the total German output of rounds fired during the Rommel Raid was a magnificent total of *one*: a single round from a Walther P38. It was fired at a dark figure by Lieutenant Kaufholz, and witnessed by at least one survivor, Sergeant Bartl, but it was never claimed as a hit.

Laycock said Keyes was a sitting target because he was framed in the doorway against the light in the hall; this was just one of many spurious statements in his report. The light in the hall was either extremely dim – dim enough for two of the Germans to have to shine a torch into it to see anything – or non-existent. Campbell's testimony – in this case not disputed by Terry – was that the light was *on* in Room WuG, and that it did not go out until after the explosion, so the Germans would have been in the light and the attackers in darkness.

Nevertheless, Keyes apparently managed to fire only two shots, both of which went low. Although the German report said that the lights went out upstairs, this was not because the generator was out of action – it wasn't hit until later. The explosion could have caused a connection to short out, but this could not have happened until after Keyes had been shot.

The description of Keyes' wound was inconsistent: Drori said it was just above the belly, whereas Campbell placed it just above the heart. Though it is not clear whether an autopsy was performed on Keyes, the Senior Medical Officer of the *Panzergruppe Afrika* did examine the German fatalities thoroughly. He would have had a good idea what kind of weapon had killed him from Keyes' external wounds. Yet the Germans remained convinced, in spite of their own propaganda, that Keyes had been killed by his own men.

Joseph Hoiss, who claimed to have come on the scene later, said, 'I cannot remember any officer or man from the German Headquarters affirming that he had shot any of the soldiers.'

Something is wrong. Examining Campbell's claim proves it literally *cannot* be true; it indicates that Keyes was shot *after* Terry had fired the burst that mortally wounded Kaufholz, and after Campbell had thrown the grenade. How could Kaufholz possibly have shot Keyes after being hit by four .45 bullets, two of which passed straight through his chest and hit the radiator behind?

And how can Lieutenant Ampt have seen Keyes' body lying apparently unattended in the hall, when there is no British account of Keyes' body being left alone in the house?

Then there is Keyes' mysterious numb arm, which was not in Campbell's original statement but appeared in Elizabeth Keyes' report of the affair: even she suggested that Campbell might have wounded Keyes – she mentioned a chipped elbow.

If Campbell shot Keyes, then the wound he inflicted could have been far more serious than just a chipped elbow: it could have been Captain

Robin Campbell, not any of the Germans, who killed Lieutenant Colonel Geoffrey Keyes. This was obviously the implication of the German report, which was – puzzlingly – not mentioned by Elizabeth Keyes at all.

It is significant that, in his original statement, Kurt Lentzen said clearly that he saw a figure with a sub-machine-gun coming towards him in the light of his torch. He did not mention seeing anyone else at this stage. If Keyes *did* have a Colt pistol, as most of the reports suggested, then it was not Geoffrey Keyes, but Jack Terry whom Lentzen saw, and who shot him a moment later. The fact that the shots that hit Lentzen went low would be more consistent with a sub-machine-gun burst than a double-tap from a pistol.

The inconsistencies in the reports lead to another scenario: Robin Campbell, while attempting to shoot the big German, Jamatter, accidentally shoots Keyes as well, who, for a moment or two, feels only a numb sensation. At that moment, Jack Terry sees the door of Room WuG open and a torch-beam shine out of it, and realizes that they are all in trouble. As he springs towards the door, he is seen by Kurt Lentzen; the Sergeant-Artificer has got up thinking he heard an accidental discharge by a sentry, so his pistol is consequently not cocked. Lentzen dives for cover, but he is too late and Terry's first shots hit him in the leg. Terry springs into the room, by which time Kaufholz, whose P38 *is* cocked, has stepped up. Kaufholz gets off a single wild shot before Terry fires a burst that mortally wounds him.

Campbell, having recovered from the shock of having shot his commander, now enters the room behind Terry and rolls a grenade. At this moment, while Terry and Campbell are momentarily inside the room, Lieutenant Ampt shines his torch downstairs and sees Keyes' body, lying unattended in the hall, and hears shooting still going on in the room. He retreats. A split second later Terry and Campbell withdraw from the room. They hear the grenade explode, then drag Keyes' body out of the house.

Avishalom Drori is standing in the garden, having just shot Matthe Boxhammer. Denis Coulthread is hovering somewhere near the door;

though he claims to have heard Keyes' pistol clatter to the floor, in the darkness he did not see Keyes hit.

Campbell later claims Terry fired at feet on the stairs to explain away the initial burst of fire that wounded Lentzen – who is supposed to have been shot by Keyes. Coulthread says he fired at a man on the stairs so he can stake his claim to have been part of the action. (Brodie, who also says he was in the hall, is not mentioned by anyone else at all; Terry, maintained that only four men entered the house.)

Now, at some stage since the grenade went up, there has been a burst of fire from outside the house. Drori has heard it; so has Terry, who interprets it as enemy resistance. Campbell, who has heard it too, thinks it might be Rommel, escaping from the back door or a window. Leaving Terry and Coulthread on guard in the house, he rushes round the building in a state of high excitement, only to be shot in the right leg by one of his own men.

Terry follows up and finds this second catastrophe: perhaps he and Campbell manage to exchange a quick word, agreeing they must keep this disaster hush-hush, but there isn't enough time to create a cover story: that is why their accounts are so different.

When Terry writes his report three months later, it is still not generally known that Campbell was wounded by one of his own men, so his story is that Campbell was shot by a stray burst, in an incident in which Terry himself came under fire – implying, without actually saying so, that this was enemy action. By the time Campbell comes to write his own report two years later, the fact that his wound was a blue-on-blue incident is well known, and there is no point in denying it.

But the glory of Geoffrey Keyes – the 'first commando VC', the son of Admiral of the Fleet Sir Roger Keyes, personal friend of Winston Churchill – must be preserved at all costs. In his first version, Campbell puts a Tommy gun into Keyes' hands rather than the Colt .45 he substitutes later, predicting rightly that a surviving witness will say that the man who opened fire first had a Tommy gun, and in case the German medical reports confirm that both Lentzen and Kaufholz were hit by sub-machine-gun bullets.

In fact, the Germans cleverly pieced together the forensic evidence and discovered the truth. The assertion that Geoffrey's death was bad luck because no one expected guardroom sentries to have loaded weapons so far behind the lines, and to be able to use them with such accuracy, as recorded by Elizabeth Keyes based on what the survivors of the raid told her, is strangely out of place and nonsensical. Only one shot was fired by the Germans, and that shot did not hit its mark.

As for the burst of fire that Terry and Drori heard after the explosion, this might have been when Lieutenant Jager was mortally wounded. He had been in a partitioned-off part of Room WuG and was protected a little from the blast of the grenade by the plywood screen. Jager was an administrative officer with neither battle experience nor training; he was also newly wed and expecting his first child. He jumped out of the window; it didn't even occur to him that there might be an enemy soldier posted outside. But there was: Spike Hughes, the truculent ex-London postie, the old man of the squad, who was waiting with a Thompson, and had orders to shoot to kill. He plugged Jager with three .45 calibre shots in the stomach as he emerged from the window.

Round at the front, or inside the hall, Campbell heard the shooting. His first thought was that someone had bagged Rommel. He rushed round to the side of the house where the shooting had come from, forgetting the password in the process, and was also potted by Spike Hughes, who was edgy after shooting Jager and expecting enemies from all sides.

Jim Gornall supported this sequence of events; he said it was well known among the survivors of the raid that it was Spike Hughes who had shot both Jager and Campbell with his Tommy gun.[28] Both men were certainly shot by sub-machine-guns, which were carried by only a few of the commandos. Terry and Coulthread had Thompsons, but neither could have shot Jager or Campbell; all the evidence concludes it was indeed Spike Hughes.

Jager was shot at the south-west corner. Although Campbell said he was shot at the back of the house, where Keyes had posted a sergeant, none of the reports, British or German, said where Campbell's body was found. And there was no sergeant posted at the back of the house – the only sergeant in the party apart from Jack Terry was Sergeant Charlie Bruce, who at that point was at the M/T Pool.

Given the German certainty that Keyes was killed by one of his own men, there is enough evidence to suggest that Robin Campbell – ex-BBC sub-editor, ex-Reuter's man, son of a baronet, who was classed as *a very good type* by his recruiter – was the man who shot Geoffrey Keyes: the first commando VC was actually killed by his own Second-in-Command.

But there might be another – even more bizarre – possibility. The only person alive at the time of writing, who might have been able to throw light on the mystery, was Jack Terry, who adamantly refused to talk to me. For many years he maintained a stubborn silence about the Rommel Raid.

In 1997, while attending a memorial service for the commandos on the fifty-sixth anniversary of their foundation, at Spean Bridge in Scotland, Terry agreed to give an interview to the press. 'Over the years,' the reporter wrote, '[Terry] has neatly sidestepped the conversation when the subject [of the Rommel Raid] has been raised, even with his wife, Joan, and their grown up family of five sons and two daughters.'[29] But Terry did go on to talk to the journalist about that night forty-six years ago. In a terse version of what happened in the HQ, he revealed a different sequence of events from any claimed hitherto. 'When we first got in,' he told the reporter, 'we looked at a couple of rooms that were empty, then found a room that was full of Germans. Keyes was hurled back against the door with a burst of fire. I was at his side. We dragged him out and [then] chucked in a grenade. It wasn't until we got outside that we knew he was dead.'[30]

The truth is that even if Jack Terry breaks his silence completely and gives us a detailed description of what he thought took place, we will never know for certain what exactly happened in that house at Beda Littoria just after midnight on 18 November 1941. Ultimately, reality is itself unknowable, because we do not live in an objective world. History is not objective; witnesses see what they want to see, memory is selective, historians interpret facts in different ways.

The only true conclusion is that, *whatever* happened there, the truth is not to be found in any of the official reports. Bob Laycock's report and his citation for Keyes' VC were almost entirely specious from beginning to end. In his official report Laycock claimed that two men came downstairs and were put to flight by Terry, but Terry did not mention this at all. Laycock said the light went out in the room downstairs *before* the shooting, when Campbell says it went out *afterwards*. Laycock incorrectly stated that no enemy emerged from the guard-tent, but claimed that two men – not one – came running towards the house. He claimed Keyes was shot by a burst of fire when he opened the door of the room for the first time, when we know the Germans fired only one shot, and that it is unlikely to have hit Keyes. He wrote that Terry fired two magazines into the darkened room; Terry himself said he shot off only a burst, into a room in which the light was on. And he said that Campbell was shot while attending Keyes, when Campbell himself, and Jack Terry, wrote that he was shot while circling the house.[31]

In short, Laycock's report to the Eighth Army bears very little relation either to what actually happened or to the information given to him by Sergeant Jack Terry. There is hardly a single statement in any of his accounts that is verifiably accurate.

The men offered to carry the injured Robin Campbell back to the beach-head, but he refused. He knew that it would be an impossibly demanding task for them to haul him eighteen miles over the escarpment, at night and in pouring rain. They had had difficulties enough on the way in; now they were exhausted and despondent.

'It suddenly became obvious to me,' he wrote later, 'that I should have to be left behind when the others withdrew and that I must fall into the hands of the Germans. My first thought was, "but this can't be happening to *me!*" After this first wild recoil I was able to examine my situation more calmly. I had quite expected to be killed, and I was only wounded in the leg. I was flooded with a sense of relief. There was nothing more I could do and I began to feel almost serene (perhaps the morphine I had taken helped) and only slightly apprehensive about what the Germans would do to me.'[32]

The guards from the barracks five minutes away had been alerted by the Germans; they were now moving towards the HQ, and there was no time to spare. Joe Kearney, the ex-forest ranger from St Johns, and Denis Coulthread were carrying gelignite charges, but the Bickford match-head igniters had been ruined by the rain and wouldn't work. Spike Hughes had a Brasso-Tin incendiary bomb, which ignited itself when the head was crushed. He suggested that Kearney should throw his gelignite charge through the open window Jager had just jumped out of. Hughes would then chuck the incendiary in afterwards and they would have to hope it would set off the gelignite. They both hurled their devices in, but nothing happened – even the incendiary failed to go off.

Meanwhile, Jack Terry, Brodie and Denis Coulthread were trying to force their way into the electric-light plant at the back of the house. They could hear the generator humming away maddeningly inside, but, frustratingly, could do nothing to smash open the steel door. Brodie examined his charges; the fuse-heads were damp.

'Try a grenade,' Terry said. Brodie noticed an exhaust pipe directly connected to the generator, emerging from the concrete wall of the hut, and Coulthread rammed three gelignite charges down it. Finally, Brodie pulled the pin on a grenade and dropped it into the pipe. There was a four-second delay on the grenade and it went off with a deafening *boom!* when they were only twenty yards away. Only one of the charges had exploded, but it was enough to wreck the generator. In the house, the rest of the lights went out.

Terry, Brodie and Coulthread ran back to the RV among the Arab shacks outside the grounds, where Jim Gornall had once stumbled over a pile of tins and awoken some Arabs – it had happened only a few minutes previously, but now it felt like that had been in a different life. Terry blew his whistle. Hughes, Coulthread, Brodie, Kearney, Varney, Drori, Heavysides, Pryde, Phiminster and Radcliffe were all present and correct, but Charlie Bruce and his party of three weren't there. Terry blew the whistle again, but there was still no sign of them, so he gave the order to bug out back to the RV at the cave.

Bruce, Lock, Bogle and Murray were busy setting up gelignite charges with time-pencils on the vehicles in the M/T Pool, on the other side of the building, and throwing a grenade through the window of the Town Hall. They didn't hear Terry's whistle, but they got away only a few minutes afterwards, before the German guard arrived.

Whether the charges went off or not is another moot point. Terry and his group claimed to have heard them explode twenty minutes after leaving, but the German report mentions no damage to vehicles in the M/T Pool. Possibly all Terry and his men heard was the detonation of the grenade thrown through the Town Hall window by Charlie Bruce.

The night was pitch-black and the rain was still bucketing down as it had been throughout the entire operation. A sea-mist that suddenly descended on them cut down visibility even further. Spike Hughes, who was tail-end Charlie, told Terry they ought to lie up until first light, other-wise there were going to be casualties simply from falling down the escarpment. No sooner had he said it than Terry himself – at the head of the party – suddenly vanished over the edge of a cliff, losing his precious Thompson in the process. He managed to cling on to a bush and was hauled back by the others, but Spike's point was proven and Terry decided that they would stay where they were – only about a mile from Beda Littoria – until daylight. He doubted if even the most resolute searchers were going to come looking for them here in this weather. They sat huddled together, soaked to the skin, in the darkness and the rain, feeling exhausted and depressed. Elizabeth Keyes wrote that this was because they had lost Keyes' zest and exuberance; it might have been partly the case, but more likely it was because – now they had seen the target – they began to realize just what kind of wild goose chase Keyes had led them on. Had Sergeant Jack Terry – who still believed that Rommel had been at the HQ, and that the raid had therefore failed – been privy to certain other secrets, he might have had even more reason to feel depressed.

D1

18 November 1941 About oooo hours

At midnight on 17 November, about the time Geoffrey Keyes was grappling in the hall of the HQ with Rifleman Jamatter, a *High Priority* signal was decrypted at a secret office of British Intelligence at GHQ Cairo. The signal was from MI6 in London. *Ultra* at Bletchley Park had just decoded a message from German Army Enigma which revealed that Lieutenant General Erwin Rommel was on his way back to Libya and would arrive the following day, 18 November. He had spent the past three weeks in Rome.

On 7 October, Rommel had written to his wife, Lucie, asking what she thought of his leave plans. 'I should be able to get away to Rome for a week at the beginning of November,' he wrote. 'I've got a lot of business to clear up there.'[1]

Six days later he had written again saying that he hoped they would meet in Rome on 1 November. 'Enquire about the trains, please, and let me know what time you are getting there. I'll arrange things so that I can be there on time. I'm hoping that the situation will permit me to stay until the 15th. But you must bring along a civilian outfit for me (brown suit).'[2] Rommel wanted to remain in Rome until 15 November because that was the date of his fiftieth birthday.

Despite the Führer's prohibition, Rommel was still determined to attack Tobruk, and he had scheduled his offensive for 21 November. Jake Easonsmith had been right in thinking that the redeployment of the Trieste Division was part of the build-up for that attack. Rommel had been encouraged by German successes in Russia at the beginning of

October, which increased the threat to the Middle East and made a British offensive in Libya less likely.

'An attack in Libya would be a risky business [for the British],' he wrote to Lucie on 12 October, 'and would not have any direct effect on things in Russia. Once we've taken T. [Tobruk], there'll be precious little hope for them here.'[3]

However, the Italian Supreme Command still believed, quite rightly, that Auchinleck was preparing an invasion for November. The 'business' Rommel had to clear up in Rome was to persuade the Italians that they were wrong: he wanted to obtain their support and get back to Libya before 20 November, in time to begin his move on Tobruk. Auchinleck, who had been trying his damnedest to lure Rommel into an offensive by pretending that he was reinforcing the Ninth Army in Palestine, had known weeks previously via *Ultra* that the Desert Fox was planning an attack on Tobruk about 21 November, which was why he and Cunningham had scheduled *Operation Crusader* for 18 November.

Rommel flew to Rome on 1 November as planned, with his friend Johannes von Ravenstein, GOC, 21st Panzer Division. When he arrived, he went directly to the office of Lieutenant General Enno von Rintelen, the German military attaché in Rome, and launched into one of his infamous tirades. Rommel blamed von Rintelen for abetting the rejection of his plan for an offensive against Tobruk, and he spared nothing, raging at the attaché and even branding him a coward.

Once he had warmed up on the hapless von Rintelen, he telephoned Colonel General Jodl, High Command Operations Officer in Berlin, and told him he was completely disgusted that Jodl was against his attack on Tobruk. Jodl broached the possibility of a British offensive, but Rommel said even if the British were to advance, von Ravenstein's 21st Panzers would hold them off while he fell on Tobruk. Jodl asked if Rommel could guarantee there would be no danger. Rommel, who did not believe there would be such an advance anyway, gave his personal pledge, and Jodl finally capitulated.

Rommel had won: the attack on Tobruk would go ahead after all, and was rescheduled for 23 November.

Satisfied now that he had got his way at last, Rommel settled down to enjoy a holiday with his wife. At midday on 15 November, while Keyes and his party were lying up in the wadi near Bay 1, Rommel and von Ravenstein joined their wives for lunch at the Hotel Eden. Lucie and the Countess von Ravenstein had that morning been sightseeing together and were full of excited chatter about St Peter's and the Coliseum.

Rommel listened politely to their talk for a few minutes, then turned to von Ravenstein and said, 'You know, I have been thinking about what we ought to do with those infantry units ... '[4]

Later, they were invited to see a film at the Italian Supreme Command, *On To Benghazi,* showing Italian units putting British troops to flight during the *Sonnenblume* offensive – without the help of the *Afrika Korps*. 'Very interesting and instructive,' Rommel commented dryly afterwards. 'I often wondered what happened in that battle.'[5]

Rommel left Rome two days later, on 17 November, but his aircraft developed engine trouble and was diverted to Athens, where he stayed overnight. When the raiding party attacked the HQ in Beda Littoria, he was some four hundred miles away. He did not hear about *Operation Crusader* until his flight touched down in Libya on the afternoon of 18 November, and even then he did not believe it was a major offensive, dismissing it as a reconnaissance in force.

Even if Rommel had returned to the combat zone on 17 November, Keyes and his commandos would not have found him at Beda Littoria. The house Keyes had attacked was actually the HQ of Colonel Schleusener, the Chief Quartermaster of the *Panzergruppe Afrika,* who was billeted there with a dozen of his officers and men, none of them higher in rank than major. There were more than one hundred officers and three hundred men of the *Panzergruppe* billeted in the Italian villas within a quarter-mile radius of the building, most of them clerks, drivers and orderlies. But although it has since been claimed that Rommel had never used the house, in his account of the Winter Campaign of 1941, Lieutenant General Fritz Bayerlein, Rommel's Chief of Staff, writes: 'During the night of the 17–18 November, British Commandos, in a raid of great audacity, tried to wipe out what they supposed to be Army Head-quarters in Beda Littoria – two hundred miles behind our front – as a prelude to their offensive. The place they attacked was actually occupied at the time by the Quartermaster staff, who lost two officers and two other ranks. *It is interesting to note that Rommel had in fact formerly had his HQ in this house.* He himself had had the first floor and his ADCs the ground floor. The British must have received knowledge of this through their Intelligence Service.'[6]

So knowledge was not lacking; it was the dissemination of the infor-mation that left much to be desired. Bayerlein does not mention when Rommel had occupied the house, but on 28 June, he had written to Lucie saying that she shouldn't worry about his health as he was now in a place lying six hundred feet above sea-level – almost exactly the altitude of Beda Littoria. By October, however, Rommel had moved to a *Casa Cantoniera*, an Italian road-surveyor's post, near the main coast road at Gambut, a little east of Tobruk, and nearer his own front line. There is evidence that this was not the first time since leaving Beda Littoria that he had changed base. On 26 August he wrote to Lucie: 'I returned to my *new HQ* in the evening and moved into my two rooms. Bagged two more bugs, alas, this morning – though they were outside the net. There are endless swarms of flies and my flycatcher is going to come in very useful.'[7]

When John Haselden brought the intelligence that Rommel's HQ was in Beda to GHQ, probably in September, it was already out of date. If Hussain Taher confirmed that Rommel was still there on 19 October, during Haselden's final recce, then either he was telling Haselden what he wanted to hear, or he simply didn't know.

The Chief Quartermaster of *Panzergruppe Afrika*, Colonel Schleusener, who slept in the building but was in hospital in Derna at the time of the raid, suggested that since both he and the *Panzergruppe* Chief Medical

Officer were of the same build as Rommel and wore the same type of uniform, either of them might have been mistaken for their C-in-C. Other unconfirmed reports suggest that the HQ had been identified from Army Enigma by *Ultra*. Tommy Macpherson said GHQ had doubted the accuracy of Haselden's reports for some time before the raid took place; if so, they did not make this known to either Bob Laycock or Geoffrey Keyes.

What is unforgivable is the fact that no attempt was made by G(R) or any other branch of British Intelligence to ascertain whether Rommel was likely to be at Beda Littoria when the raid was put in. This would have been easy enough to do, for it is now known that on 2 November, Army Enigma revealed to *Ultra* that Rommel had left for Rome the previous day, and by 14 November, when the commandos were last in contact with GHQ, no word had been received of his return.

British Intelligence knew, before the commandos even embarked on their submarines, that Rommel was not in North Africa at all.

D1

18 November 1941   0000–0030 hours

For Roy Cooke's party, the raid was not yet over. While Jack Terry and his men were withdrawing from the German HQ, Jim Gornall was shinning up a wet telegraph pole, a mile down the road to Cyrene, cursing silently to himself as he tried to cut ten telephone lines with a pair of pliers. 'We had no wire-cutters,' he said, 'only this pair of pliers. I got a hook up and cut all the lines, which took about fifteen minutes. Actually, I thought it was a ridiculous waste of time.'

The Cyrene crossroads, where Cooke's party was to blow up the cable mast, was ten miles from Beda Littoria, but once the job was done the party would have to bug out back to Bay 1 at Khashm al-Kalb, a distance of almost thirty miles. Although the men didn't know it, John Haselden had promised Cooke that he would send Tony Hunter's LRDG patrol, stationed near Slonta, to pick the party up, but the patrol never came.

Cooke told his party that they would nab the first vehicle they saw coming in either direction. The rain continued to beat down unmercifully. 'It was unbelievable,' Gornall said. 'The rain was so heavy you could have cut it with a knife. It never stopped the entire time.'[1]

The commandos had already had an exhausting climb up the escarpment earlier in the evening, and the rain, the mud and distance had begun to take its toll. Shortly afterwards, Terry O'Hagen, who had been limping along with one foot unshod after losing his plimsoll on the escarpment, asked for a rest. Cooke halted the party for ten minutes, but as soon as they started off again, O'Hagen fell behind. Cooke realized that he would never be able to keep up, and told him to return to Bay 1, detailing Corporal Kerr to go with him. He asked Fred Birch to give them his compass, and told them to hand over the explosives they were carrying. In exchange he filled them up with grenades.[2]

'Righto,' he said. 'Make your own way back to the beach, but on the way be sure you muck up any transport that you can find.'[3]

Instead of going directly overland to the coast, Kerr and O'Hagen retraced their tracks to Beda Littoria and hid out in the Arab market there. They were picked up by an Italian sweep later the same day.

'They shot off and that left only Cooke, myself, Macrae, Paxton, and the Sergeant [Fred Birch] to do the job,' Jim Gornall said. 'The worst thing was that they'd told us there was often an armoured car stationed at the crossroads to protect the cable mast, and we didn't know how we were going to deal with it if there was.'[4]

They were still looking for a vehicle to hijack, and six miles further on came across two petrol tankers parked on the side of the road by what appeared to be a farm. Fred Birch thought that they were unable to start the trucks because there was no starting handle, while Gornall remembered that they decided not to touch them anyway: if the farm was inhabited, it would have raised the alarm. Instead, they marched on into the pouring rain and a bitter north-westerly wind.

Twenty minutes later they saw a pair of headlights coming towards them from the direction of Cyrene, gleaming like cats' eyes in the darkness. 'Cooke said, "We're having this!"' Gornall said. 'He said, "Gornall, take the torch and flag it down." I thought, well they'd better not see me armed, so I gave someone the Tommy gun I'd now swapped for my rifle, and I stood in the road. As it came, I switched on the torch and waved it down. The others were hidden along the road skirting. The vehicle was approaching and I saw it slowing down and I was waving the torch. I heard a shout – there were probably two people in the thing, the driver and a passenger – I heard a shout and the revving of the engine, and it came straight towards me. I just flung myself to the side and as I did, the lads opened up. It got maybe ten yards and shot over to the right-hand side of the road. The lights went up in the air – it got maybe thirty yards off the road, then stopped. The lights were still on but the engine died.'[5]

Birch remembered jumping out of the ditch and firing his Tommy gun through an open window, head high, and more shots as the car careened away from them. 'The car ran off the road and stopped,' he said. 'We approached slowly and carefully, but there was no one in it. The left-hand door was open. We tried the starter and it wouldn't work, and we couldn't push it out of the ditch.'[6]

There was no sign of the passengers – an Italian captain and his driver, who were both unarmed. They had clearly fled, and there was no indication that anyone had been hit. Cooke and Birch tried hot-wiring the ignition, but there was no response – obviously something vital in the motor had been wrecked. Cooke told his men to smash the headlights, and they pressed on towards their objective.

It was another four or five miles to the crossroads, but when the five-man party arrived they were relieved to see that there was no armoured car waiting for them. It was 0330 hours and still raining, although the rain had slackened off slightly by this time. They took cover, and Birch collected the explosives they had been carrying – four sticks of gelignite each. He and Cooke then went to recce the cable mast, a structure of four massive wooden poles with cross-members, carrying a complex array of terminals and wiring, with lines going off in four directions, to Derna, Slonta, Bardia and Benghazi.

The plan was to place massive cutting charges on the four poles and topple the whole structure. While the other three lay on watch on a low ridge, Cooke and Birch set up the explosives, laying charges on each pole, joined together by cordtex fuse and two twelve-inch lengths of Bickford igniting fuse. Birch struck the match-head igniter against the match-box, and he and Cooke sprinted back to Gornall, Paxton and Macrae.

'They got down beside us,' Gornall recalled, 'but nothing happened. The fuses that they'd used had got wet while we were coming ashore and they'd forgotten to check them. Or they were still usable when they left the beach, but had been ruined by the rain.'[7]

'All matches for setting off the charges were soaked,' Cooke said, 'even inside the oilskin pouches – it had rained for some sixteen hours pretty solidly. [It was] very worrying, because it was getting light and there were one or two posts around us.'[8] Cooke and Birch returned to the mast and had another go, this time using a No. 36 grenade as a detonator, pulling the pin and laying it under one of the charges. The grenade had a seven-second delay, and the two men ran 'like the clappers of hell' and dropped down again beside the others. The Mills bomb misfired. They returned and put in another grenade. This time it exploded with a dull crump and a puff of smoke, but the gelignite didn't go up. Cooke started to feel both very foolish and 'nearly frantic with the wind up and frustration and nerves, cursing pretty profusely.'[9]

'What the hell do we do now?' he said.[10]

It was at this point that Gornall remembered the self-igniting thermite incendiary he'd bagged on *Torbay* thinking it might come in useful. 'I've got a Brasso-Tin incendiary bomb in my pouch here,' he said. 'Would that be of any use?'

For Cooke it was the answer to a prayer. 'Bless his heart,' he wrote later. '[Gornall] had been watching me running about with grenades, trying to strike matches that wouldn't and so on [and he] sort of metaphorically took the straw out of his mouth.'[11]

'Just the job,' Cooke said.[12]

'Cooke and I returned to the poles,' Birch went on with the story. 'I attached two new lengths of Bickford fuse and a detonator to the cordtex, struck the incendiary on a stone, laid it on the fuse, and retired. We had only gone five yards when the incendiary burst out and the whole place was lit up over an area of about two hundred yards diameter. On reaching the low bushes about a hundred and fifty yards away, we threw ourselves down and after sixty seconds the charge went off, and we heard wires dropping on the road. We knew the job was done.'[13]

When the smoke cleared, it became obvious that the cable mast hadn't toppled over. It was listing, but was held in place by a single pole. Birch thought that the charge on the fourth pole had misfired, probably because the blast from the incendiary had cut the cordtex lead. An Italian report completed the same day said a bomb exploded under the telegraph wires, and a report made by Colonel Schleusener, the Chief Quartermaster of the *Panzergruppe Afrika*, when he was a POW in 1946 claimed that only one pillar of the cable mast was damaged.[14]

The official German report held that the cable mast had lifted off the ground but settled down in the same place, and that communications had been interrupted but not put out of action permanently.

Incidentally, Schleusener said that the pillars of the mast were concrete, Elizabeth Keyes said steel, and eyewitnesses Jim Gornall and Fred Birch said they were wood.[15]

Whatever the case, it was almost light and high time to make themselves scarce. They planned to cut directly across the escarpment to the coast, and then follow it west to Bay 1. The rain was again streaming down savagely as they began the long tramp back to the final RV.

'We had to find a place to lie up,' Gornall said. 'And we suddenly realized we were walking through a cemetery with these ancient tombs all over the place – dome-shaped Arab tombs. Cooke said, "That one will do!" and there was a small doorway, so we all crawled in. Inside it was black as the ace of spades. Obviously it had been raided and there was a jumble of rubble.'[16]

Inside, the tomb was divided into four chambers, each one large enough to stand up in, and the commandos removed their equipment and soaking battledress, laying out their maps, wallets and notebooks to dry. They ate chocolate, raisins and sweets from their rations, then cleaned their weapons methodically.

It was still freezing, even inside the tomb, and all day they dozed fitfully, huddling together for warmth, unaware that a German recce party from Beda Littoria had followed in their footsteps, found the shot-up car, and the damaged cable mast, and footprints in the mud around it from Cooke's brothel creepers, which they identified as being from British crêpe-soled shoes. The Italian command had already picked up O'Hagen and Kerr, and had mobilized two infantry battalions with tracker dogs to beat the *maquis* and look in every cave on the escarpment for the rest of the party.

Cooke and his four men, still bedraggled and exhausted, set off at last light. The weather had cleared up slightly, but was still overcast. They descended the escarpment, boxed round a deep ravine, and began to climb down again. By 0830 hours on the morning of 19 November Cooke reckoned they were within five miles of Bay 1. There was no particular urgency to get there, as they still had another twenty-four hours to make the final RV. The rain had stopped. While it had been raining they had at least been safe from the air, but now they had to find cover in case a spotter plane came over. Luckily they ran into a family of Bedouin herding their goats, who lived in some caves nearby.

'A young Arab, who seemed to be the chief … took us to a cave cut out of rock below ground level,' Fred Birch said. 'Then he told us to sit down and sent an old woman out to boil some water. We explained that we were *Inglesi* and wanted to get to the sea, and he asked if we were *paracadutisti*. Thinking it was easier to say yes, we nodded our heads. He said, "*Inglesi buono, Italiani non buono*", and made a gesture of cutting his throat, then lifted his shirt and showed us two bullet wounds in his chest and another in his neck. "*Italiani bang-bang*," he said.'[17] He told them in pidgin Italian that Italian troops had been searching the area the previous day and might be back again today.

After they had drunk coffee and eaten stew and chapattis, the Arab got out a pocket-watch and indicated by gestures that the commandos should sleep till noon, after which he would guide them to the beach. It was now about 0950 hours, and Cooke's party was shattered after the long night march.

They had just laid down to rest when there was a shout from outside the cave, where the Arab chief had posted a lookout. He dashed outside and a moment later called 'Shawish!' – the Arabic word for sergeant. Fred Birch, the only sergeant in the team, hurried outside in time to see two Italian soldiers in full battle order and steel helmets, rifles at the ready, advancing down the slope about six hundred yards away. Birch rushed inside with the news, and Cooke told them to prepare for a fight. The young Arab told them to stay where they were. Picking up his Italian rifle he pointed to himself, then outside, and said, 'Bardayn bang-bang Italiani mafeesh,' which Cooke took to mean he intended drawing the enemy off.

The Arab vanished through the cave entrance and the commandos waited tensely. A few minutes later they heard the pop of the Arab's rifle, answered by a volley of at least twenty rounds. Birch looked at Cooke. 'There's more than two of them out there!' he said.

'Let's see!' Cooke said.

The two of them crept outside and saw the enemy now advancing in company strength. The place was surrounded. The Arabs were hidden in the maquis, taking pot-shots, and rounds were sizzling back and forth. Crawling back into the cave, Cooke and Birch hoped they hadn't been spotted – that the Italians would either be drawn off by the Bedouin or would simply look in the cave and carry on. A few seconds later, though, two Italian soldiers came right inside. Cooke fired three shots from his Colt .45 – a double-tap and a single shot – and both soldiers went down. One was mortally wounded and didn't get up again, but the other was only winged and ran out screaming.

'Watch out for grenades!' Birch yelled, and no sooner had he shouted the warning than the Italians started shovelling in money-box bombs. The first landed three feet from Birch's head, followed in quick succession by four more, all of them exploding at once with a tremendous roar, filling the cave with choking smoke and dust. Another four grenades followed; Macrae yelled that he'd been hit by shrapnel, and Gornall was bleeding from splinters in the face.

'I was kneeling behind this rock, and one of the money-box grenades dropped about a yard away,' Gornall recalled. 'I put my arm over my face and it went off. I finished up with these three splinters in my face – I just rubbed them and found they were bits of tin, that's all. If it was 36s they'd been throwing, we'd all have been dead without doubt, but these were just a loud bang and shock.'[18]

By now Cooke had realized that if they stayed where they were, sooner or later they would all be killed. 'It's hopeless,' he told the others. As if to emphasize his words, two more grenades bounced through the entrance and blasted off.

Cooke threw his Colt down and said he was going out. 'If they shoot me,' he said, 'you'd better dash out. Get as many as you can and go down fighting!' He walked out with his hands held high, to a terrific din of voices. A minute later Birch heard Cooke saying, 'Come out with your hands up!' The four of them walked out, straight into the muzzles of two Breda machine-guns trained right on the cave entrance. Had they tried to run for it, Birch realized, they'd all have been dead meat.

They were searched and their hands tied behind them, and a medical orderly gave them each a swig of Cognac. They were held until 1500 hours, when the rest of the Italian unit arrived, then marched about six miles over the escarpment to Cyrene, where they were put in a guard-room.

Next morning they were taken to Apollonia in a truck, together with half a dozen Arabs. Here Cooke was separated from them and they were thrown in a cell. 'The crafty buggers put two spies in there,' Gornall recalled. 'They claimed to be South African officers, but they were Eyeties who spoke English. We thought it was odd, because they had separated our officer from us, yet they'd apparently put us in with two South African officers. They were listening to what we said, but we were wary because we'd been trained not to trust anyone. Anyway, when we were interrogated the next day, one of them was behind the desk in Italian uniform, asking the questions. All I gave was my name, rank and number.'[19]

The following day they were sent to Benghazi, where they ran into Kerr and O'Hagen, who had been picked up in Beda Littoria on 18 November. Gornall was put into a large hangar-type building that was full of Allied servicemen, many of them RAF. He'd been given some cigarettes by Cooke, who had in turn been thrown them by an RAF officer as they marched past.

That night, during an RAF raid on Benghazi, another party was marched in. 'I was lying on a top bunk smoking a cigarette,' Gornall said, 'when I heard a voice saying, "Give us a fag, mate!" I thought, "Bloody hell, am I hearing things?" It was Billy Morris, who had been with me on the Litani job. He'd left 11 Commando for the SAS, and had been on the practice jump when two of them had been killed – the next one in line. The storm that had jiggered up our operation had jiggered up the SAS operation as well. Billy Morris had been with Eoin McGonigal, an 11 Commando officer, on the Tmimi raid, and they jumped into the storm and were scattered all over the place. Billy Morris told me that he'd last seen McGonigal in his parachute harness, dead, with his body up against a wrecked Messerschmitt 109. He'd landed, but had been dragged by the storm and killed.'[20]

D1

18 November 1941 0030–0630 hours

In Beda Littoria, the German patrol arrived at the HQ only minutes after the commandos had left to find Lieutenant Jager dying outside the open window at the south-west corner of the house. They found Keyes' body near the front entrance, and Campbell, still alive, propped up against a tree in the grounds. Since neither Keyes nor Campbell had been wearing badges of rank, the Germans assumed at first that Campbell was the leader of the commando group. Campbell claimed later that the Germans had discussed whether they should finish him off, but had decided against it and taken him inside for medical treatment. After they had bandaged him up, they attempted to interrogate him, but he growled at them in German that they would get nothing out of him, and they didn't.

The Germans and Italians had to piece together what had happened. First of all, since news had come in that day of the capture of Bonnington and his SAS men in the Bombay that had crash-landed west of Tobruk, they assumed that Keyes' party had been parachuted in – the two men evidently hadn't shaved for a couple of days, leading to the conclusion that they had been hiding on the escarpment for some time, and had chosen the night of 17 November because the foul weather had given them cover.

Awad and Idriss, Keyes' Bedouin guides, had waited on the escarpment until first light, but having missed both Terry's and Bruce's parties in the darkness, returned to the town to find the place in a hullabaloo. Platoons of both German and Italian troops were scouring local buildings – where they found Kerr and O'Hagen – and preparing to move north towards the coast. Awad asked a local Arab what was going on, and the man replied, laughing, that the British had attacked Rommel's house, but unfortunately Rommel wasn't there.

Awad said he had returned to Karm al-Hassan, where he picked up Bob Fowler and guided him back to the beach. The Italian report, written that day, concluded that the natives helped the British with shelter and information and they consequently took reprisals. Fingers must have been pointed at Awad, who told Elizabeth Keyes in 1945 that he had his cows confiscated and had been forced to flee to the desert. Awad's testimony is also flawed: Bob Fowler, who – like O'Hagen and Kerr – was bagged on 18 November, claimed to have left the cave that morning, and to have reached the coast alone. He had been carrying Keyes' camera with him, which he buried in a mess-tin when he got there. Fowler was subsequently spotted by a Bedouin who pretended to befriend him and instead led him straight to the Italians.

During the night of 17/18 November Jager, Kaufholz and Kovacic all died. Boxhammer's body wasn't found till morning – on examination by the Chief Medical Officer he was found to have a single bullet in his stomach. Campbell was sent to hospital in Derna that morning, and on 19 November, at 1600 hours, Keyes and the four German dead were buried with full military honours in the local Catholic churchyard. There was a rumour that Rommel himself had attended the funeral, but this is impossible as the Desert Fox was with his troops on 19 November, fighting for his life against a British offensive he had never believed would happen.

There is another legend: that Hitler had issued orders proclaiming that all British commandos should be shot on sight, but that Rommel had been so impressed with the courage of the men sent to kill him that he tore it up. This too is a myth – the notorious *Kommandobefehl*, decreeing death to all captured British commandos, was not signed by Hitler until the following year, on 14 October 1942. As for Rommel, when he heard about the raid, he was not impressed, but indignant that the British would believe he kept his operational HQ two hundred and fifty miles behind his own front line.

D1–D2

18–19 November 1941

Sergeant Jack Terry's party started off at first light. They descended the escarpment and, pressing on without a halt, made the RV with Laycock in the wadi near Bay 1 at 1700 hours that afternoon. They had missed their original route and the fall-back RV, the cave at Karm al-Hassan where their boots, blankets and spare stores were hidden. The trek back had not been entirely uneventful. At a point a little more than halfway they had been stopped by a ten-man patrol of the Italian Libyan Arab Force. Drori had explained in Arabic that his party was German. The Arab troops had let them pass, but Terry wasn't convinced that they had bought it; he suspected the enemy patrol might be following their tracks out of sight.

When they arrived at the wadi they were greeted enthusiastically by Bob Laycock, Sergeant John Nicholl, Bren gun party George Dunn and Larry Codd, and medic Ed Atkins. Exhausted and mentally drained, they threw themselves into the cover of the *maquis* and ravenously devoured the meal of bully-beef and hard tack biscuits Dunn and Codd had prepared. Laycock was distressed to hear the bad news about Keyes and Campbell, but in view of his earlier prediction of certain death, it did not come as a complete surprise. He was concerned about the twelve men who were still missing – Roy Cooke's group, Charlie Bruce's team and Bob Fowler – but there was no time to brood over it. There was an hour of light left, and he wanted to be able to re-embark that night.

Leaving Terry in the wadi with his men, he went down to the beach with Ed Atkins to recce the conditions. He had been doing this at intervals over the past three days while the raiding party had been away; at first he had hoped that the commandos on *Talisman* would still be able to get off. In fact, *Talisman* was already on her way back to Alexandria: Miers had ordered her to withdraw on the morning of 16 November – the day after the commandos had moved to their targets. *Torbay* had remained in place off the headland, waiting for them to return.

On the beach Laycock was met by 'Farmer' Pryor, the still-shoeless SBS man, who had some infuriating news to impart. Pryor and John Brittlebank had helped Campbell hide the deflated rubber dinghies and the Mae Wests in a cave by the beach on the night of 14 November. Now they had disappeared. The SBS men had been told by some friendly Bedouin that they had moved the boats because they thought the cave where they were hidden wasn't suitable. The problem was, the tribesmen had gone off without showing them the new hiding place, and the pair had searched for them in vain.

Laycock was furious: now they were without dinghies or Mae Wests for the embarkation. In spite of this latest setback, he remained reasonably confident that they would get away. The wind was still up, but there was less swell than there had been for the past couple of days, and if *Torbay* could send a *folbot* with a grass line, then as long as they could be supplied with another lot of Mae Wests, the men could be towed to the submarine even without dinghies.

While Laycock was on the beach, a runner arrived from Jack Terry to say that his lookouts had spotted a Bedouin who had obviously seen them; he had sprinted away in a suspicious manner. Terry, faced with a problem that was to become a perennial one for special forces troops – whether or not to kill noncombatants who compromised them in the field – had refrained from giving the Arab a bullet. Laycock approved of this: the last thing they needed was a blood-feud with the local tribes.

But Jock Haselden had warned them that some of the coastal Bedouin were hostile and might sell them out to the Italians. He sent Atkins back with instructions that Terry should move the men down to the cave on the beach where Pryor had originally concealed the dinghies, so they would at least be away from the place where they had been spotted by the Bedouin.

By the time Atkins reached the wadi, Charlie Bruce had arrived at the RV with Charles Lock, Jimmy Bogle and Bob Murray. Unlike Terry's party, they *had* found the cave at Karm al-Hassan on the way back, but Bob Fowler and all their stores had vanished. Laycock had given instructions that three men should stay in the wadi, move the stores further down and post a lookout in case Roy Cooke's party came back.

At last light, 1819 hours, Laycock saw *Torbay* through his binos, fully surfaced, standing a quarter of a mile off Bay 1. Miers had given instructions that he should use 'F' procedure – one-way signal traffic from beach to boat, in order not to compromise *Torbay's* position in the darkness. Laycock flashed the recognition signal – four dashes repeated three times – and requested a resupply of Mae Wests and a *folbot* with a grass line. There was no response, and Laycock was stuck in the agonizing position of not knowing whether Miers had not been able to read his signals or was simply observing 'F' procedure. He realized that this wasn't going to work, so, having waited to make sure there was no hostile movement, he began flashing again: *There are no enemy anywhere near. If you cannot launch folbot, flash three times.* Again the message went unanswered.

At this point, Laycock gave up and, leaving a man to watch, went down to the cave to tell the men that re-embarkation was probably out until tomorrow. No sooner had he said this than 'Farmer' Pryor came in to report that the Bedouin who had moved the dinghies had come back and the boats had now been retrieved.

Much later, at about 2330 hours, the lookout returned to say that *Torbay* had commenced signalling with her Aldis lamp.

Laycock hurried back to the beach, and for some minutes conducted a farcical exchange of messages with *Torbay*, which began with Miers signalling that the sea was *too rough tonight*, and that he had already sent an unmanned dinghy with a supply of lifejackets, food and water. Laycock interpreted this signal as saying 'too rough for embarkation' and signalled *Thank-you – good night.*

Just as he was leaving the beach, *Torbay's* Aldis lamp started flashing again, asking how many Laycock's party were and how many Mae Wests were needed. Laycock replied that they were twenty-two, and signalled *have now found boats and Mae Wests.*

According to Miers' log, the first part of the signal was clear, but the second came through as *have no boats and Mae Wests. Good night.*

There was a long pause. On the beach Laycock and his party had just discovered the rubber dinghy with the life-jackets, food and water sent from the sub – Miers' had judged the drift so perfectly that it had hit the beach just twenty yards from Laycock's position. He signalled that it had come in. *What luck your operation?* Miers then enquired.

Though there was no news from Cooke, Laycock must have been aware that the raid had been an utter catastrophe – they had neither snatched nor taken out Rommel, they had not destroyed the house, and the jury was out on the power-plant and the Motor Transport Pool. There had been minimal enemy casualties in return for the loss of two British officers of field-rank. Laycock knew that the process of spin-doctoring would have to begin now, so he signalled back: *Good work – messed up their HQ but sad casualties. Keyes killed, Campbell, Cooke and 6 ORs missing. Raiding party not pursued.* He need not have bothered – Miers was completely baffled by his rendering of this text, which according to his log, came through as: *Goodness only knows. Some killed in camp and missing from HQ.*[1]

The ambiguity of the message coupled with the fact that the raiders had apparently lost their dinghies and lifejackets alarmed Miers and, as he wrote in his log, 'seemed to make the statement that "no enemy were anywhere near here" extremely thin.'[2]

He felt the commandos were in considerable danger, and signalled: *As you will be in danger by day, am prepared to close the spit west of the bay at dawn so that you can swim. Otherwise try again tomorrow night.*[3]

Laycock interpreted this as: *If there is danger tomorrow and you would like to swim I am prepared to close point west of beach. Otherwise try again tomorrow night.* Laycock missed the *at dawn* bit of the message entirely; he thought that Miers was suggesting they swim out now.

In his report, Laycock said he was tempted, but on close consideration, he realized that the men were exhausted and that swimming out in rough seas would be risky. 'I came to the conclusion,' he wrote, 'that the troops in their exhausted condition would almost certainly be drowned in attempting to swim from a rocky foreshore against surf, wind and sea.'[4] However, it appears this close consideration did not take Laycock very long, for Miers' log noted that the 'answer came prompt' (ie immediately): *Try tomorrow night.*[5]

Evidently Laycock mishandled the situation badly; this probably cost most of his party their freedom. Elizabeth Keyes said in her book that 'neither side could make head or tail of one another's signals.'[6] Her implication was that both sides were equally to blame, but the Royal Navy signaller on *Torbay* would certainly have known his job; Laycock, on the other hand, was unable to read *Torbay's* signals correctly because his knowledge of the Morse code was imperfect. As for his own signals, they could not be properly read by *Torbay* for the same reason. Laycock tried to explain this away by stating that he had only a standard British Army torch, a cylinder of Bakelite with a head set at right-angles that could be stood on its end. The torch had a button on its side for sending Morse signals, but the button was missing, so he had to send by laboriously switching the torch off and on. Even if this were true, it should not have hampered anyone who knew his Morse code properly, and it would not explain why Laycock was unable to read the signals from *Torbay*.

Laycock's poor knowledge of Morse code was serious, for it is evident that Miers thought the commandos had no dinghies, and didn't understand the signal that they had been found, otherwise he would not have made the offer to close the beach so that they could swim out to the submarine. He did think it too rough to embark that night, but the wind was Force 4 and moderating, and he noted in his log that the met report suggested an improvement by the following day. By first light the commandos would have been more rested and since they had their dinghies (and now three lifejackets each), they would have stood a good chance of getting back on *Torbay*.

If Laycock had understood Miers' offer, it would have been obvious that *Torbay* had not grasped his own message telling them the dinghies had been found, which he should have repeated. Elizabeth Keyes said that Laycock was concerned because he believed that six of the men from *Talisman* had been drowned already; in fact, just one man had died, Peter Barrand, and Laycock did not mention Barrand's death in his report at all.

All the accounts clearly agree that the sea was much calmer the following morning, and if Laycock's signalling had been up to scratch, the entire party would almost certainly have got away at dawn.

Laycock returned to the cave, ordered the stores brought up and told the men to stand down. After making sure that Terry had organized sentries, he turned in, with instructions that he was to be roused an hour before first light. When he awoke, his first thought was about defence. He inspected the caves with 'Farmer' Pryor and posted three sentries where they would have a commanding view. Three men were still occupying the wadi, and Laycock now sent detachments out as flank pickets to the west and east.

All was quiet until about noon. The wind had dropped and the sea was calmer; the commandos could have easily re-embarked in peace. SBS officer Pryor was lying with some of the commandos near the old fort on the beach, watching with fascination an old Bedouin ploughing about half a mile away: he had a camel and a donkey harnessed in the same team. Suddenly there was the crack and thump of a .303 from the western pickets, followed by a whole salvo of returning fire.

Pryor and the men with him dashed for the cover of the fort, seeing their comrades from another cave, divided from them by a small stream, running out and taking up firing positions in the nearest cover. Craning his neck from the fort, Pryor saw a troop of red-turbanned *carabinieri* crawling towards them over the brow of a knoll. Everyone was now shooting back at them, and their progress was slow and cautious.

Laycock, watching them through his binos, thought they didn't present a serious threat, but asked for volunteers to cut across the escarpment and outflank the enemy to the west and assess their strength. Avishalom Drori, Charlie Bruce and John Nicholl volunteered. Drori went off alone, making a small circle, while Bruce and Nicholl went off together, making a larger one. As the three men were working their way through the *maquis*, 'Farmer' Pryor asked Laycock to give him a man with a Tommy gun; he said he would outflank the enemy to the seaward side. Though Pryor never knew the name of the man who went with him, a process of elimination suggests that it was George Dunn's Number Two on the Bren, Lance Corporal Larry J. Codd. Pryor and Codd (if it was indeed him) ran west along the beach in a hail of fire, crossed the stream and, dodging from rock to rock, worked their way to within two hundred yards of the *carabinieri*. 'I looked round,' Pryor said, 'and saw that my man had managed to get his Tommy gun jammed solid. I poked it about a bit and banged it, but couldn't budge it. Rather cross, I said, "Well try and clear it for God's sake! – I'm going on!" and very foolishly I went on for another fifty yards, bound for another patch of rocks. When I got there I saw there were some more Eyeties on the hill further west, and there were my six lying there having target practice at me.'[7]

Pryor considered rushing them, but decided that would be suicide. Instead, he turned back – and was shot through the thigh while withdrawing, leaving his Tommy-gunner behind the rock with his weapon still jammed. At 1400 hours Laycock gave the order to fall back to the east and go into escape and evasion: it was every man for himself.

Drori meanwhile had managed to get behind the Italians and had concealed himself there. After a while he heard Laycock calling to him to withdraw, and made for his position. 'Before I reached him,' he said, 'he was already running, leaving me behind. The Italians, who up to that point had hardly fired a shot, opened with a barrage of fire. I did not attempt to catch up with the running men but hid myself in the bush.'

Drori saw the white flag Atkins put up on the beach, but it was some time before the *carabinieri* closed in on him and Pryor. He said they shot dead one of the commandos, and seriously wounded another.

Pryor said he had heard that the Arabs shot dead his Tommy-gunner at point-blank range, but all the members of the raiding party are accounted for as POWs. It is more likely that the Italians had found the body of Peter Barrand, who had been drowned off *Talisman* on 15 November. The body had probably been washed ashore, where it had been found and buried locally by the *carabinieri*, so giving rise to the rumour that they had killed one of the commandos.

Spike Hughes, who had been inside one of the caves, had heard bullets zipping past, but he had not been aware of what was going on until Laycock's order to run came through. He dived out of the cave and clambered up the escarpment, where he met George Dunn, Bob Murray, Joe Kearney, Denis Coulthread, Jimmy Bogle, Corporal Stephen Heavysides and Lance Bombardier Brodie, who had made their way there in ones and twos. Despite Laycock's instruction to split into groups of no more than three, they decided to head south together towards Mekili, where they thought they were mostly likely to be picked up by British troops.

Bill Pryde said that while the battle was going on, Frank Varney had come rushing into the cave where he was taking cover with Radcliffe, Phiminster and Lock. Varney passed on the escape order, but as the cave was facing west towards the advancing Italians, this presented a problem. They decided to run for it one by one. Four of them got out without a scratch despite the rounds fizzing past them, but Radcliffe was hit – only a flesh wound, but a bloody one. Together, the five men made their way south towards the escarpment, where they hid among the *maquis* for most of the day. At one point an Italian patrol passed only thirty yards from their hiding-place, but no one spotted them. At last light they examined their supplies and discovered that the sum total of their remaining rations was one tin of bully-beef. In spite of this, they decided to make for Hunter's LRDG patrol at Slonta.

Jack Terry had retired to the position originally held by the eastern picket when the *carabinieri* had started advancing, but he waited there patiently for Bob Laycock, who soon came hobbling up, having injured his knee. They began to run east, with Italian rounds winging past their ears; none of them found a mark. Having outrun the enemy, they decided to go for the fall-back beach, Bay 6, where a submarine would come in on the nights of 20 and 21 November.

Sergeant John Nicholl and Sergeant Charlie Bruce decided to stick together and walk east towards Tobruk. John Brittlebank, the SBS man, who had now lost his partner, 'Farmer' Pryor, headed for the hills alone.

D3

20 November 1941

In the early hours of 20 November, Jake Easonsmith's LRDG patrol of six Chevrolets and two fifteen-hundredweight Bedfords, was laagered in a depression between two sand hills, three miles south-east of a crossroads on the Triq al-'Abd. Easonsmith had placed hurricane-lamps on top of the two ridges – for once he wanted to make the place unmistakable. At around 0100 hours, the desert silence was suddenly broken by a chorus of voices singing a well-known music-hall song:

> Roll out the barrel,
> Let's have a barrel of fun!

It was the signal agreed with the SAS, and moments later ten exhausted figures limped into the camp: Jock Lewes with Pat Riley, Johnny Cooper and seven other men of Lewes's stick, who had just trekked for thirty-six hours from their DZ, having abandoned their attempt to reach the target.

Their navigation had been excellent – they had headed south-west, knowing they would hit the five-mile-wide track sooner or later. As the day wore on the clouds cleared and the air warmed up, raising morale slightly. Water had been no problem as there were puddles everywhere from the previous night's torrential rain. They were not moving tactically but in a ragged bunch, secure in the belief that the enemy would not search for them here, so far from the combat zone, and that they would see any vehicle approaching from miles away. Every two hours they grabbed a ten-minute rest, taking off their packs and devouring chocolate and hard tack biscuits. In the afternoon Johnny Cooper had spotted a signpost in the distance; when they reached it, they found that it pointed west to Benghazi and east to Sollum: they had found the Triq al-'Abd.

The only difficulty now was to decide whether the RV was to the east or the west. Lewes decided to turn west, calculating that they had been blown further east than anticipated. They marched on resolutely, their muscles aching with strain, across undulating sand, through warrens of blasted limestone hills, across endless plains of black clinkers looking like the aftermath of some primaeval planetary impact. The old caravan way was littered with the bleached bones of camels that had fallen out of camel-trains over centuries, which only added to the sense of desolation; here and there were little nests of burned-out tanks and soft-skinned vehicles – even wrecked aircraft – souvenirs of the battles that had recently ebbed and flowed along this route.

Night came. Cooper recalled, 'the sky was full of stars. There were so many that I became a little confused. However, I fixed my gaze on one that seemed to look different from the other twinkling specks in the sky.'[1]

He pointed this anomaly out to Lewes, who looked at it through his binos, and said, 'There are two lights on twin hillocks about a hundred yards apart on a small escarpment. This must be the RV.'[2]

Easonsmith's New Zealanders welcomed them round the fire, handed out mugs of tea laced with rum and produced a bully-beef stew in short order. Before dawn, David Stirling and Bob Tait also staggered in. They had been lucky enough to run into one of Easonsmith's outlying pickets manned by Captain David Lloyd Owen, who had seen Paddy Mayne and his party the previous night. Stirling and Tait stopped to rest with Lloyd Owen for a while. Over a welcome mug of tea laced with whisky, Stirling told Lloyd Owen about the disaster: '[He] was not in any way down-hearted,' Lloyd Owen said. 'He was even then turning over in his mind all the mistakes that had been made and the lessons that he could learn from this abortive attempt. He was so certain that he could succeed and nothing was going to stop him – if he was given another chance.'[3]

The official birthday of the SAS Regiment is 17 November – the day before *Operation Crusader* – and much has been made of the lessons learned from that first mission. Success develops its own mythology and the Regiment's later successes and subsequent elevation to legendary status were to temper the débâcle of the Gazala/Tmimi raids with a rosy-tinted hue. Even Stirling's biographer entitled his chapter on this episode *Case Proven*, when all that had really been proven was that Stirling's conception was utterly wrong. His epiphany had been based on a perfect ignorance of the Sahara, which could have been alleviated had he talked to the LRDG experts. The result of that ignorance was the loss of two-thirds of L Detachment, forty out of sixty-two highly trained men, for absolutely zero result: not a single Messerschmitt Bf 109 had been destroyed. It is very difficult to see, despite the layers of adulation, exactly what case had been proven.

'He knew the concept was right,' his biographer wrote. 'Both he and Mayne had gone right up to the enemy's protected flank without incident.'[4] But this in itself was hardly something new. The LRDG had been doing that – and more – since September 1940, with spectacular results, and had not lost anywhere near as many men, even by aggregate. Stirling was a dreamer who had come up with a wonderful but totally impractical idea: anyone has the right to be wrong and to change his mind, but few are privileged to learn their lessons at the expense of forty lives.

It was as they sat there, Lloyd Owen said, that an idea came to him. 'Surely the answer,' he told Stirling, 'is for the LRDG to convey the SAS parties to within a few miles of their targets. We would then lie off while you do whatever you have in mind, and we could always return a day or so later to collect you again.'[5]

It was the obvious solution, but to depend on the LRDG would mean

Stirling would have to admit that his Parashot idea was wrong – and to accept that the LRDG had pre-empted his concept of the SAS. Lloyd Owen's remarks sounded unacceptably patronizing to the Laird of Keir. Mumbling that the LRDG cars were too slow, and showing open signs of doubt about Lloyd Owen's claims that the LRDG was a better concept than Stirling's Parashots because mobility was the key to desert power, Stirling finished his tea and took Bob Tait on to Jake Easonsmith's RV.

Lloyd Owen never doubted that his suggestion had sunk in, 'as [Stirling] had never at that stage travelled with one of the LRDG patrols,' he wrote, 'he had no idea whether my claims were true. He did not know how very reliable were our methods of navigation, or how good were our communications. He had no idea then of how safely we could range across the desert and rely on our superior speed and knowledge to outwit the enemy.'[6]

At Easonsmith's RV, Stirling found Lewes's stick subdued. Pat Riley was concerned about the loss of his close friend Jock Cheyne, with whom he had swapped parachute-harnesses before the drop. For months afterwards Riley wondered if the exchange had contributed to Cheyne's fate. In the few hours of darkness that remained, they snatched some sleep. Lewes, Riley and Stirling shared the same tarpaulin.

'At some point in the night,' Riley said, 'David leaned across me and said to Jock, "I think that's the end of parachuting for us." Jock's reply was affirmative.'[7]

Although Paddy Mayne's stick had passed Lloyd Owen's position before Stirling, they did not arrive at Easonsmith's until later – Mayne had spotted the hurricane-lamps on the hillocks but had wisely decided to lay off for a while to make certain this was the LRDG and not the *Afrika Korps*. At first light, when Easonsmith gave the order to move to cover, he had the lamps removed and replaced by a smoking fire, which finally brought Mayne in.

Mayne was shattered to find that his close friend Eoin McGonigal was missing. They had been inseparable since their time in the Royal

Ulster Rifles together, and Mayne could not get over the loss. The SAS were staggered by the attrition they had suffered.

'The missing men were all close buddies,' Cooper wrote, 'with whom we had shared the hardships of training and life at close quarters in camp. We noticed too the worried expressions on the faces of the officers as they sat together discussing the operation.'[8]

No one else came in that morning. Bonnington's stick had been captured after crash-landing in the Bombay. McGonigal had been killed, and the rest of his men – including Jim Gornall's friend Billy Morris – captured. Sergeant Yates, who had been leading the remainder of Stirling's stick, had got as far as the Triq al-'Abd. Faced with the same choice as Lewes, he had turned east instead of west – and marched straight into the hands of the Axis.

Easonsmith waited at the RV eight hours longer than scheduled, in case more survivors showed, but in the afternoon Lloyd Owen arrived to say that his patrol had done a recce of the entire area and seen no one. Easonsmith decided they could delay no longer, and withdrew to the fall-back RV in the Wadi al-Mra. The following day he sent his Chevies out to search for the others, covering an eight-mile radius, but every truck came back empty. He hung on until noon on 22 November, then pulled out.

Not long afterwards an Italian Savoia-Marchetti 79 aircraft spotted them and came in for a strafing run with its machine-guns rattling. No one was hit, but the Savoia vanished, to be replaced forty minutes later by a German Heinkel bomber. Fortunately the Heinkel missed the patrol and dropped its payload on some derelict trucks instead. Easonsmith's party continued to move in fits and starts, now stopping to take cover as hostile aircraft zoomed overhead, now speeding on to make up time.

Despite his early misgivings about the LRDG, Stirling could not help but notice the ease and skill with which Easonsmith handled the patrol: seeing the LRDG in action for the first time, he began to understand how his brainwave could be done. During the two hundred-mile journey back to the LRDG base at Siwa, he talked to the men, noted their perfect navigation, their skill in camouflage, their ability to improvise solutions to mechanical problems, the way they used the ground and, above all, Jake Easonsmith's almost uncanny ability to read the minutiae of the desert.

By the time Easonsmith had dropped Stirling and his men off at Jaghbub Oasis near Siwa, to be picked up later by air, Stirling had revised his initial response to Lloyd Owen. 'He told us he was very impressed by the LRDG's ability to move about in the desert,' Johnny Cooper said, 'and reasoned that their patrols could drop us off. We would then walk in silently in three-man patrols, complete our sabotage and return to a pre-arranged RV. We had to admit to ourselves that we had failed on our first operation but we had learnt many valuable lessons for the future.'[9]

This was the only positive result of the Gazala/Tmimi raid: it forged a partnership between the SAS and the LRDG in which Stirling's unit was able to serve an apprenticeship with the desert experts. By the following year, the SAS were operating in their own vehicles, not as an LRDG Mark II, but as a unique combination of the Commando and Long Range Desert Group traditions which laid the foundations for the modern SAS.

D9

26 November 1941

David Stirling arrived at General Cunningham's new HQ at Maddalena the following day, on 26 November, to find the Eighth Army on the verge of panic. *Operation Crusader* had fared badly: the planned entrapment of the *Panzergruppe* had failed. Cunningham had intended to mass his forces at Gabr Salih, a point in the desert, the only significance of which was that it provided a landmark, hoping to lure Rommel into a battle in which his armoured forces would be knocked to bits by superior numbers. The Tobruk garrison would then sally out and strike Rommel from the rear. But Cunningham had made a fundamental mistake in occupying a position that Rommel had no reason to fight for, then compounded that mistake by allowing his forces to disperse when Rommel failed to take the bait. At midday on 19 November, just at the time the men of 11 Commando heard the first shots fired by the advancing *carabinieri*, the green 22nd Armoured Brigade, under Major General Willoughby-Norrie, had charged a fortified position at Bir Gubi occupied by the Italian Ariete Division. The 22nd – made up of three Yeomanry Regiments who were the epitome of the old cavalry mentality – attacked with neither artillery cover nor infantry support. They believed that cavalry-type élan would be enough to send the Eyeties packing, but they were wrong. The Eyeties fought with resolve and panache, despite their inferior tanks, and by last light the British had lost forty brand-new Crusaders. The veteran 7th Armoured Division had also left Gabr Salih to attack Gambut.

Astonishingly, the Desert Fox, for all his much-vaunted mystical qualities, still refused to believe that this was a true offensive: he had ordered
his units to take no action. He was saved by his deputy, Lieutenant General
Ludwig Cruewell, commanding the 15th Panzer Division, who ignored
Rommel's orders and moved on Gabr Salih. This, of course, was what
Cunningham had wanted in the first place – except that by now he no
longer had superior numbers of tanks there. It was defended only by the
4th Armoured Brigade with a hundred and twenty-three Honey tanks,
of which Cruewell proceeded to make mincemeat. The remnants of the
22nd Armoured, limping back from defeat by the Ariete to help the 4th
Armoured, arrived too late: they had been decimated by Cruewell's
panzers and were now preparing to pull out to Tobruk.

Cunningham, faced with losing all his tanks, badly wanted to retreat.
Auchinleck, as strong-minded as Rommel, refused to consider it. He
believed Cunningham was cracking under the strain, so, on 25 November,
he decided to relieve the Eighth Army leader of his command.

The order had not yet been presented to Cunningham when Stirling
arrived on 26 November. The GOC asked to see him, so Stirling was
taken to a small tent where, for five minutes, Cunningham questioned
him intensely about traffic movements on the Gazala-Tobruk road.
Stirling said later that he was 'struck by the strain and fatigue on the
general's face.'[1]

He was still at Maddalena that afternoon when his patron, Major
General Neil Ritchie, flew in with his boss, the Chief of the General
Staff, Middle East Command, Lieutenant General Sir Arthur Smith.
Smith was carrying a letter from Auchinleck, which he solemnly handed
to Cunningham: it said, very simply, that the C-in-C had decided to
relieve him because he had begun to think defensively. Neil Ritchie, until
recently Deputy Chief of the General Staff, was Cunningham's replacement.

Stirling saw Ritchie after lunch and found him, in contrast with Cunningham, genial, smiling and confident and, as one PR officer described

him, 'A huge, handsome man, most extraordinarily smartly turned out and fairly oozing energy and vigour.'[2]

In spite of this glowing appraisal, Neil Ritchie was even less equipped to fight a major offensive than Cunningham: '[Ritchie's] fatal amalgam of over-confidence and underestimation of the enemy,' psychologist Norman Dixon wrote 'produced a deadly military endeavour.'[3] Though highly popular, he was far too junior and inexperienced an officer for this command, and even if he had been more experienced, he was too slow and ponderous to match Erwin Rommel. His campaign was ultimately to prove disastrous for the British: he, too, would be sacked by Auchinleck, the following June.

Meanwhile, Cunningham collected his personal kit and flew back to Cairo with Arthur Smith, who regarded him with both sympathy and admiration. 'He was a grand chap,' Smith said. 'How sad it was that at this critical time and because of his health he lost his grip. He was not himself – he was not Cunningham.'[4]

Stirling was lucky that Ritchie was now in the driving seat, but that alone might not have been enough to save the SAS if another member of the Silver Circle Club had not intervened. Brigadier Sir John Marriott, Scots Guards was a well-known socialite and a member of the Randolph Churchill and Evelyn Waugh set. He had personally escorted the King's brother, the Duke of Gloucester, on his official tour of the Western Desert. His wife, Maud – known as Momo – was the daughter of an American financier and, reputedly, the smartest woman in Cairo. She was also commonly believed to be Randolph Churchill's mistress; her parties, attended by generals, commandos and celebrities, were considered the most select of all Cairo's wartime events.[5]

Stirling ran into Marriott at Eighth Army HQ that same day; his advice was blunt and to the point: 'I should make yourself scarce for a while,' he said. He suggested that Stirling take the remnants of his unit to Jalo Oasis, a hundred and fifty miles south of Benghazi, which had been captured recently by a mobile force under the command of Brigadier Denys Reid.

Marriott recommended Stirling to Reid via the old boy network, and Stirling quickly shifted L Detachment there – carefully eliminating all reference to its presence from wireless traffic in case it should be ordered back to Kabrit and oblivion.

Meanwhile, Stirling busied himself with Mayne and Lewes: working with the LRDG they planned an attack on Agedabia airfield. The débâcle at Gazala / Tmimi would be plastered over as if it had never happened; before anyone even realized that the SAS was still around, they would present Ritchie with a success.

19 November – 25 December 1941

At 1820 hours on the night of 19 November, Crap Miers brought *Torbay* to the surface in Bay 1 once more, but he had received no signal from Bob Laycock – although he didn't know it, Laycock and Jack Terry were hiding from the Italians in the *maquis*. Then Miers' sharp-eyed lookout spotted a light in the old fort. On the off-chance that Laycock's torch had given out, Miers decided to send in his last serviceable *folbot*, manned by Tubby Langton, the ex-Cambridge rowing blue, and Corporal Cyril Feeberry, the ex-Grenadier Guards boxing champion. He instructed Langton to approach with extreme caution; they were to pull out at once if they spotted anything in the least suspicious. If he found Laycock's party, Langton was to return with a grass line and tow the men to the boat. If this was impossible, he was to tell Laycock that the commandos would have to swim for it at first light the following morning, 20 November.

There was a heavy sea running and the *folbot* capsized in the surf; luckily it was still seaworthy. Langton and Feeberry managed to stumble to shore and empty it out. Leaving the craft on the shingle, they separated and, leopard-crawling on all fours, they moved off two hundred yards in different directions. Suddenly Langton heard low voices and spotted the glow of cigarettes. He froze and turned his ear towards the voices – they were hard to make out, but he thought they were speaking Italian. The glowing cigarettes were the clincher: Langton thought no commando would be smoking so openly at night, on an enemy beach, prior to re-embarkation.

Langton and Feeberry returned to the RV, where they decided to relaunch the *folbot*, paddling slowly along the beach in the hope of spotting the commandos. A moment later a blue light flashed out of the darkness. This was the signal agreed with Laycock, and Langton at once began flashing a series of Ts back.

Just then a huge roller hit them, capsized the *folbot* and sent them crashing into the beach. Langton's paddle was wrenched out of his hands and carried away and the *folbot* was holed, though he and Feeberry managed to salvage the craft herself, the Tommy gun and their stores. They upended and drained the canoe cautiously, knowing they must be in full view of enemy troops; at any moment they expected a salvo of gunshots to crackle out. Miraculously, nothing happened. A minute later they were making for the boat, with Feeberry paddling alone; the damaged canoe was steadily filling with water. It took five minutes to reach *Torbay*, and the *folbot* was on the brink of sinking when she was hauled aboard the sub.

Langton knew that Feeberry had saved them both. 'I have no hesitation in saying,' he wrote later, 'that his strength, presence of mind and courage on this occasion saved us from a very nasty situation.'[1]

Things looked bad for Laycock and his party, but Miers stayed in the area, surfacing again at last light the following day, but spotting no signals. Before diving twelve hours later, his watch saw movement in the dunes around Bay 1, where it looked as if artillery was being dragged into position. Miers was tempted to engage the battery with his quick-firing gun, but there were enemy aircraft about and it was too dangerous to stay surfaced. The next day the watch spotted a Caproni CA 309 Ghibli aircraft landing near Khashm al-Kalb. Miers realized there was now no hope of finding the commandos. He could still do something useful: he could pot the Ghibli. When he surfaced at sunset on 21 November the aircraft had been moved under cover of the scrub, but it was still faintly visible by telescope. It was a very difficult target, but he ordered his gunnery officer to have a go. The four-pounder was laid and brought to bear, firing a salvo of ranging shots until, after twenty minutes, a shell fell directly on the aircraft, which exploded in a rush of flame. This was the first time an aircraft had ever been engaged on the ground by a submarine: 'Our contribution to the offensive,' Miers wrote in his log.[2]

By 1650 hours, *Torbay*'s crew was at diving stations and Miers set a course back to Alexandria. They arrived on 24 November carrying with them the news of *Operation Flipper*'s failure, and the loss of Geoffrey Keyes.

Two days later, on 26 November – the day Alan Cunningham was relieved of command in favour of Neil Ritchie – George Dunn, Bob Murray, Joe Kearney, Lance Bombardier Brodie, Jimmy Bogle, Corporal Heavysides and Denis Coulthread were nearing Mekili. Since the enemy had bumped them on 19 November they had been heading south, walking by day and resting by night, and had covered eighty miles. All they had seen of the enemy was a few vehicles on the horizon, and they had been helped by the Bedouin, who had brought them goats, and even entertained them in their tents.

However, by the morning of 26 November they had not eaten for three days. Believing Mekili was a small native village held by a handful of Italians, they decided on a bold plan to raid it, grab what food they could and make off. They still had the Bren gun, although George Dunn revealed they had no more than a dozen rounds left between the lot of them.

In fact, Mekili was actually held in strength by the Italians who were now in a high state of alertness: the commandos had no idea that the LRDG had raided Mekili earlier that day, dropping a couple of shells on the fort from a Bofors gun. As soon as the group saw Mekili in the distance they dropped into cover to wait for last light, but thirty minutes later Dunn spotted movement on a ridge near the fort. A convoy of three light tanks, three motorcycles and a truck with a Breda gun mounted on it, carrying a platoon of infantry, came speeding directly towards them in a pall of dust.

It soon became obvious that they had been seen, because the motorcyclists worked behind them while the truck halted two hundred yards to their front and the infantry deployed. They had no chance. Dunn and his comrades realized they had no options left against so many, and laid down their weapons, stood up silently and waited to be captured.

They were bundled into the truck and taken before the Italian CO, to whom they gave their names, ranks and numbers. The Italians were bemused to find three artillerymen (Dunn, Kearney and Bogle) with four infantrymen (Heavysides, Coulthread, Hughes and Murray), all so far behind their lines without motor transport, and questioned them intently: they got nothing. Dunn was confident that, with sixty miles now between them and Beda Littoria, they would not be connected with the raid on what they still believed to be Rommel's HQ.

Finally the Italians threatened to turn them out into the desert without food and water unless they talked. 'We said that would be OK,' Dunn said, 'as we weren't hungry any more and there was lots of water about.'[3]

Frank Varney, Bill Pryde, Andrew Radcliffe, and John Phiminster had been making for the LRDG at Slonta. On 21 November they had been 'befriended' by some Bedouin, who let them rest in a cave. The next thing they knew, the cave was surrounded by Italians. They were taken back to the beach, where they were searched and their watches and kit confiscated. Soon they were shipped to the holding centre in Benghazi where they met up with Ed Atkins, Bob Fowler, and Charles Lock. Like Fowler, Lock had been betrayed by the Bedouin. He had walked by night on 20 and 21 November; the following night he had met with some Arabs, who, like the Bedouin who had betrayed Varney Pryde, Phiminster and Radcliffe, showed him into a cave. Moments later, without warning, a grenade was lobbed into the cave and had exploded, wounding him in the leg. The *carabinieri* who captured him took him to Apollonia, where his wounds were treated; he arrived in Benghazi on 26 November.

Sergeants Charlie Bruce and John Nicholl walked down the coast and had almost reached the Tobruk perimeter when they were captured by an Italian patrol. Avishalom Drori, who had watched John Pryor and Ed Atkins captured and loaded on mules, had been betrayed by a local Bedouin and taken prisoner by the *carabinieri*. They told him that they had been about to withdraw just before the commandos had run.

Bob Laycock and Jack Terry had approached Bay 5 on the nights of 20 and 21 November, but they had been prevented from getting near by Italian patrols on the beach. After that, they gave up and headed east into the Jebel. Laycock calculated that they would stand a better chance of survival if they simply hid out and made use of the Jebel's natural cover – the formidable *maquis* and the labyrinth of caves – while they waited for the Eighth Army to arrive. 'It afforded just the sort of cover which made it easy for us to avoid being picked up by the numerous patrols that were being sent for us,' Laycock said later. 'But living behind enemy lines is very unlike any other form of soldiering. One can never feel quite at one's ease. One is continually on the alert since there is danger on every side.'[4]

Thirst was never a serious problem, but hunger gnawed them – sometimes they had nothing to live on for several days but arbutus berries and mushrooms. Occasionally Bedouin gave them bread and – once – a goat. They ate every bit of it but for the horns and hooves, and buried its entrails, coming back for them later. One thing they never managed to get rid of was a constant craving for sugar.

They never lit a fire during the day, but if they found a cave, they would take the risk and light one at night; they shared their single Arab blanket in relative comfort. Once, they got careless: Laycock left his Colt .45 and field-glasses at the mouth of the cave they were occupying and they both dozed off inside. They awoke with a shock to find that someone was in the cave with them – a Bedouin. Laycock groped frantically for his weapon – in vain.

Fortunately for them, the Bedouin turned out to be friendly. Terry and Laycock, aware that there was a hefty price on their heads, were constantly amazed at the help they received from the Arabs: 'Terry and I owe the fact that we were able to keep alive entirely to the Senussi,' Laycock wrote, 'for we managed to make friends with about a dozen of them – we used broken Italian and signs.'[5]

Unlike their colleagues, Laycock and Terry were never betrayed to the enemy, but Laycock feared the *carabinieri*: unlike the Italian and German units looking for them, they were excellent trackers. However, they came only by day, and Laycock was usually able to spot them miles away with his field-glasses. After sunset the commandos would move back into the wadis the *carabinieri* had cleared during the day. To fill in the vacant hours, Laycock read aloud to Terry from the only book he had with him – *The Wind in The Willows* by Kenneth Graham – which had originally belonged to John Pryor. Terry was not greatly impressed by the story, but endured Laycock's readings as there was simply nothing else to do.

The most infuriating thing for Laycock was his inability to get accurate information about the advance of British forces. The weeks passed and on Christmas Eve 1941, near Cyrene, they were excited to see what they believed were British troops in the distance. They decided not to approach them in the dark, so spent the night in a cave with three Bedouin, hardly able to believe that their wanderings were about to end, but, as Laycock wrote, 'dreading the almost unbelievable disappointment that would have resulted had they turned out to be Germans.'[6]

They were unable to sleep, waiting for daylight to come, and at first light they crawled to within a stone's throw of the troops. They were dressed in British battledress, with Italian overcoats and Arab headcloths … It was not until he spoke to them that Laycock finally accepted that they were British.

It was Christmas Day, 1941. Bob Laycock and John Terry had survived forty-one days behind enemy lines.

It is generally believed that Jack Terry and Bob Laycock were the only survivors of the Rommel Raid. In fact there was a third: the SBS man, John Brittlebank, who somehow managed to survive quite alone in the Jebel. Though Terry and Laycock were not yet aware of it, he had been picked up by British forces only the previous day. Laycock and Terry were rushed back to Ritchie's HQ at Tmimi, arriving the same evening at 2120 hours. When they got there, an immediate signal was sent to GHQ informing the C-in-C and Oliver Lyttelton, the British Minister in Cairo, of Laycock's survival. 'Feel it would interest [you] to know that Laycock arrived today at 9.20 pm for his Christmas Dinner,' the message read.

'Please state,' the answer came back, 'why Laycock was one hour twenty minutes late for Christmas dinner.'[7]

The first thing Jack Terry did on arrival was to wolf down a jar of marmalade to assuage his craving for sugar. When he was asked how it felt to be back behind his own lines again, the ex-butcher's boy from Nottingham reflected a moment on the tedious hours he'd spent listening to *The Wind In The Willows*. 'Thank God,' he said, 'I won't have to hear any more about that bloody Mr Toad!'[8]

36

The Aftermath

At Western Desert HQ Bob Laycock sought out the Brigadier General Staff responsible for the raid only to find that he knew nothing about it: there had been a complete shake-up since early November, when the commandos had left on their ill-fated mission. Laycock was ill for a few days, but when he recovered in early January, he sat down to compose a report that not only left a great deal out, but exonerated himself from any blame for what had gone wrong.

The BGS saw the opportunity for a PR coup despite the complete failure of *Operation Flipper*, and asked Laycock to submit names for awards. Laycock recommended both Geoffrey Keyes and Jack Terry for the VC. Keyes, the dead son of an Admiral of the Fleet, got his; Jack Terry, the living ex-butcher's boy, did not. He was given a DCM instead, in spite of the fact that he had faced precisely the same odds as Keyes and had *succeeded in* bringing the survivors safely back to the beach – where they were skewered by Laycock's incompetence. The BGS's actual opinion of the results of the raid is scrawled on the cover of Laycock's report: 'I doubt whether this operation achieved anything very great.'[1]

The standard argument supporting all special forces operations is that even if unsuccessful, vital enemy resources are bound to be hived off from the front lines to protect vital areas. This is generally true, but a perusal of the *Panzergruppe* War Diary shows that this was not the case with the Rommel Raid, because within a few days Axis forces became concerned with the British offensive and the minor threat of commando raiders was forgotten.

The Rommel Raid was born of one man's ambition to achieve glory and, as so many times in British history, it was rescued from ignominy by the valour and determination of the ordinary enlisted men, none of whom played a part in its planning, nor were even told the nature of their mission before they embarked. Given the prevailing conditions, it might have succeeded had the intelligence been correct. Not only was there a failure of intelligence, there was a failure to *disseminate* the intelligence actually available.

No one can deny the incredible courage of the men who took part in the raid: this itself remains an inspiring example to posterity. But courage must be used to some end. The fact that British Intelligence knew that Rommel was not in North Africa at the time of the raid and did not inform the raiding party meant that the courage and lives of many brave young men was squandered to no avail.

Epilogue

Sergeant Jack Terry DCM, Royal Artillery, later transferred to the Special Air Service Regiment and served on other raids in North Africa under Captain Bill Fraser, the ex-11 Commando officer who was one of the first recruits for the SAS. Terry fought with the *maquis* in Europe after D-Day and was awarded the Resistance Medal; he had already received his Distinguished Conduct Medal for his part in *Operation Flipper*. He left the army in 1945 and fulfilled his long-term ambition of joining the Nottingham Police, with whom he served for twenty-eight years until his retirement. He fathered five daughters and two sons. At the time of writing he still lives in Nottingham.

Lieutenant Colonel Robert (Bob) E. Laycock DSO, Royal Horse Guards, was whisked back to Britain within weeks of his return to take charge of the new Special Service Brigade, responsible for training and organizing all commandos. He was awarded the Distinguished Service Order in 1943. In 1944 he took over from Lord Mountbatten as Chief of Combined Operations, a major general at the age of 36. After the war he was knighted and became Governor of Malta and in 1960 he was awarded the ceremonial rank of Colonel Commandant of the Special Air Service Regiment. He died in 1968.

Bombardier John Brittlebank DCM, Royal Artillery, returned to the SBS. His story of escape and evasion in the Jebel al-Akhdar has hitherto remained untold. In September 1942 he was captured after making an attack on Crotone Harbour in a *folbot* using an experimental torpedo. Prevented from making the RV with his submarine, Brittlebank and his partner, Captain Wilson, paddled for Malta, two hundred and fifty miles away. They were seized by the Axis when they were obliged to put into a beach for repairs. Brittlebank revealed nothing about his mission under interrogation, even when he was told he would be shot at dawn the following day. For this, and his part in the Rommel Raid he was awarded a Distinguished Conduct Medal.

Captain Robin Campbell, General List, had his leg amputated and spent two years in military hospital and prison camp in Germany before being repatriated in 1943. There is an unconfirmed story that Campbell actually met Erwin Rommel during his term as a POW. He died in 2001.

Lieutenant (later Captain) Royston (Roy) Cooke, Royal West Kent Regiment, was sent to Torre Tresca Prison Camp in Italy, from which he and another officer promptly escaped. They were recaptured shortly and the following day an Italian Divisional Commander, General Nicolo Bellomo, asked them to demonstrate how they had got out. When they did so, Bellomo panicked, and for some reason gave the order to open fire: Cooke was shot in the buttocks and his comrade killed. In 1945, General Bellomo was convicted of murder and shot by firing squad. Cooke died of polio in the 1950s.

Gunner James (Jim) Gornall MM, Royal Artillery, was imprisoned in the Italian 'bad boys' POW camp at Garvi Castle in Italy, and later moved to a camp in Germany. He escaped and, with the help of the Resistance, managed to get back to Britain. He returned to a Royal Artillery Anti-Aircraft Unit and served as a professional soldier for thirty years, attaining the rank of sergeant. He ran the Army

Recruiting Office in Chester before retiring there. For his part in the raid he was awarded the Military Medal.

Bombardier Joseph (Joe) Kearney, Royal Artillery, escaped from POW camps in Italy and Germany and was recaptured four times. On his fifth attempt, in April 1945, he was picked up by US forces. After the war he returned to St John's, Newfoundland, where he took up his job as an official with the Natural Resources Department. He married in 1947 and had three children He died in 1987.

Corporal Charles Lock, London Scottish, escaped from German custody during a train crash and made his way across Europe to Odessa, where he embarked on a ship bound for Glasgow. His first act when he arrived was to visit Ruth Pridham Black, the girl he had met while training on Arran and vowed to wed. They married and had two children. After the war, Lock returned to his family's retail business in Deal, which he converted into an electronics outlet, specializing in radio and TV. Now 93, he lives quietly in Walmer.

Lieutenant Commander (later Rear-Admiral) Anthony Cecil Capel 'Crap' Miers RN VC, DSO, was awarded the Distinguished Service Order for his part in *Operation Flipper* and later won a Victoria Cross for his bold attack on Axis ships in Corfu Roads in March 1942, when *Torbay* was pursued back to sea and had no fewer than forty depth charges dropped on her. The entire crew received gallantry awards; all the men were received at Buckingham Palace. Miers was, years later, accused by the British press of war crimes for machine-gunning the survivors of a ship he had sunk.

Captain (later Lieutenant Colonel) John E. 'Jock' Haselden MC and bar, Intelligence Corps, completed his task on *Operation Flipper*, cutting the telephone lines on the Slonta Road, and returned to Siwa with the LRDG in December 1941. Haselden was awarded the Military Cross and bar for his part in the reconnaissance for *Operation Flipper* and the operation itself. He was later appointed Western Desert Liaison Officer for the Eighth Army, an SOE post coordinating regular operations with the G(R) network among the Senussi. After Tobruk fell to the Axis in 1942, he planned and led an audacious commando-style raid on the port, but was killed in action there.

Lance Corporal Malcolm Edward 'Spike' Hughes, Manchester Regiment, returned to the Post Office after the war, where he worked until he passed the Civil Service examination in 1956. He was posted to the headquarters of the Post Office Savings Bank in Hammersmith, where he worked as a clerical officer until his retirement at sixty, after which he was employed by an asbestos manufacturing company in Rickmansworth. When asked why he had joined the commandos, his reply was always, 'Because I didn't know any better at the time.' He lived in Watford until his death in 1984, aged 83.

Captain Antony (Tony) Hunter MC, Royal Scots Fusiliers, was captured by the Italians on 22 November after dropping off Haselden and his team. Hunter had gone off on foot with two men to search for Corporal Porter, a missing crew member who had not returned from observation duty. They were attacked by twenty Italians in trucks armed with a Breda gun. The rest of Hunter's patrol was sent back to Siwa and another patrol, under Second Lieutenant Croucher, was dispatched to pick up Haselden. When Croucher reached the RV on 1 December he found not only Haselden but Hunter as well – he had escaped from the Italians and joined up with the G(R) crew. Hunter was later awarded the Military Cross for his many courageous exploits with the LRDG.

Captain (later Major) Robert (Bob) Melot, General List, Haselden's comrade from G(R), worked among the Senussi until the end of the

North Africa campaign, then transferred to the SAS. He was killed in a motor accident while serving with the Regiment in Europe in 1944.

Corporal (later Squadron Sergeant Major) Cyril Feeberry DCM, Grenadier Guards, the SBS *folbot* man on *Torbay*, became Squadron Sergeant Major of the Special Boat Section when it was reformed in 1943 under Major George Jellicoe. He was awarded the Distinguished Conduct Medal for his many distinguished actions, including his part in the Rommel Raid.

Lieutenant (later Lieutenant Colonel Sir) Thomas (Tommy) Macpherson MC and two bars, Cameron Highlanders, spent two years in prison camps in Italy and Germany, including the notorious Garvi Castle. He made several attempts to escape and finally succeeded in 1944, stowing away on a Swedish ship bound for Britain at Danzig. Only six weeks after returning to Scotland he was recruited into the SOE and was parachuted into France before D-Day with one of the famous Jedburgh Teams consisting of two officers and a W/T operator. He fought with the French Resistance, at one point capturing an entire Armoured Division single-handed, and won the Military Cross three times. He was knighted after the war, and now divides his time between London and an estate in northern Scotland.

Warrant Officer Charles (Charlie) West, RAF, the pilot of the Bombay carrying Lieutenant Bonnington's stick on the Tmimi/Gazala raid, came out of his coma after twelve days. He recovered from his injuries so fully that he escaped from his POW camp, and subsequently fought with distinction among the partisans in northern Italy.

Captain James M. Ratcliffe DSO, George Medal, Middlesex Regiment, the SBS officer who commanded the recce for the Rommel Raid, was a POW at Montalbo Camp in Italy. He escaped and fought among the partisans in the Balkans, winning both the Distinguished Service Order and the George Medal.

Captain (later Lieutenant Colonel Sir) David Stirling DSO, Scots Guards, led the SAS to great success in the North Africa campaign. He was captured in Tunisia in 1943 and sent to the Italian 'bad boys' camp at Garvi; he attempted to escape from here and other camps four times. He was later imprisoned at Colditz, and though he never managed to escape successfully, was awarded a Distinguished Service Order for his gallant conduct as a POW. On returning to Britain he was appointed Second-in-Command of the SAS Brigade until its disbandment in 1945. The SAS Regiment he had created became a Territorial unit, 21 SAS Regiment (Artists, Volunteers) in 1947, amalgamating the traditions of all wartime special-forces units – LRDG, SOE, SAS, SBS and Army Commandos – with that of a 19th-century infantry battalion, The Artists' Rifles. In 1950, the Regiment saw action in the Malayan Emergency as the Malayan Scouts (SAS), and was eventually reformed as a regular unit, 22 SAS Regiment, in 1952. A third TA unit, 23 SAS Regiment (Volunteers) was added to the SAS Group in 1959. All three regiments are now included with the SBS as part of the UK Special Forces group. David Stirling was knighted, and died in 1990.

Lieutenant John 'Jock' Lewes, Welsh Guards, never lived to see the world change, or to witness the meteoric rise of the unit he had played such a major role in creating. He was tragically killed after an SAS raid on Nufilla only six weeks after the Gazala/Tmimi drop, on 30 December 1941, when his patrol was attacked from the air.

Lieutenant (later Lieutenant Colonel) Blair 'Paddy' Mayne DSO and three bars, Royal Ulster Rifles, distinguished himself in many raids in North Africa, the Mediterranean, and Europe, and was awarded the Distinguished Service Order four times. He led the Special

Raiding Squadron during the war in the Mediterranean and commanded the 1st SAS Regiment from January to October 1944. He left the army in 1945 and joined the South Atlantic Survey, but found the job tedious. He returned to Northern Ireland and took up his pre-war career as a solicitor. He never went back to major league rugby. Mayne was killed in a motor accident in Ulster on 15 December 1955.

Lieutenant (later Captain) William (Bill) Fraser MC, Gordon Highlanders, was excluded from the Tmimi/Gazala raids because of injuries sustained in training, but took part in subsequent SAS raids, in one of which he was responsible for destroying twenty-two enemy aircraft on the ground. For this and other actions he was awarded the Military Cross.

Captain (later Major) John Richard 'Jake' Easonsmith MC, DSO, Royal Tank Regiment, became CO of the LRDG just before it was converted into a Mediterranean seaborne raiding unit. He was killed in action on the island of Leros in October 1942.

Lieutenant Eric 'Judy' Garland MC and bar, Yorkshire & Lancashire Regiment, the first officer across the Litani River, flew Spitfires as an RAF officer in Italy, and later worked as a pilot in East Africa. He now lives in the Isle of Mann.

Lord Roger Keyes, 1st Baron Keyes of Zeebrugge, was sacked as Director of Combined Operations with responsibility for the recruitment and deployment of the commandos by his friend Winston Churchill in 1941: his work was sound, but he had offended too many senior officers. He died in 1945, and is buried at Dover.

Corporal (later Lieutenant Colonel) John (Johnny) Murdoch Cooper DCM, MBE, Scots Guards, won the Distinguished Conduct Medal for gallantry with the SAS, and was later awarded an MBE. After the war he served with 22 SAS Regiment, then the Sultan of Oman's Armed Forces, until his retirement as a lieutenant colonel in 1979. Until recently he lived in Portugal, where he died in 2000.

Lieutenant Colonel Henry 'Kid' Cator, MC, Royal Scots Greys, commanded the 1st SAS Regiment when it was reorganized in 1943 until it was taken over by Blair Mayne in 1944.

Sergeant Ernie Bond OBE, Scots Guards, who survived the Bombay crash with Bonnington's stick, joined the Metropolitan Police after the war and became a Scotland Yard officer and later commander of the Bomb Squad. He retired an Assistant Commissioner of Police, with an OBE.

Sergeant (later Major) Pat Riley DCM, Coldstream Guards, became Squadron Sergeant Major of L Detachment and was eventually commissioned. He too joined the police after the war, but finding it tedious, rejoined the army. He retired in Sussex with his wife, Kay.

Corporal (later Warrant Officer Class 1) Bob Bennett MM, BEM, Grenadier Guards, helped the SAS reform during the Malayan Crisis in 1948. He won both the Military Medal and a British Empire Medal while serving with the Regiment.

Sergeant (later Major) Jim Almonds MM, Coldstream Guards, took charge of Jock Lewes's patrol after Lewes was killed in December 1941, guiding them safely back to their own lines. He retired from the army with the rank of major, after serving as Military Adviser to the Emperor Haile Selassie. For his brave actions with the SAS he was awarded the Military Medal.

Private Reginald (Reg) Seekings MM, DCM, Cambridge Rifles, went to live in Rhodesia after the war but returned to Britain after

UDI. He won both the Military Medal and the Distinguished Conduct Medal during his time with the SAS.

Warrant Officer First Class (later Lieutenant) Lewis Tevendale DCM, Gordon Highlanders, also joined the police after the war, in Whitehaven, Northumberland, and served there for many years. For his many courageous actions at the Litani River, he was awarded the Distinguished Conduct Medal, and was later commissioned.

Lieutenant General (later Field Marshal) Sir Archibald Wavell, took the post Lieutenant General Sir Claude 'The Auk' Auchinleck had vacated as C-in-C India, until 1943, afterwards becoming Viceroy of India. He died Earl Wavell of Cyrenaica and Winchester, on 24 May 1950.

Lieutenant General Sir Alan Cunningham was admitted to hospital on his return to Cairo in 1941 and was found to be suffering from overstrain. He was never again given operational command. He was transferred to the Staff College in Northern Ireland, but returned to the Middle East as High Commissioner of Palestine in 1945 until 1948. He died in 1983.

Lieutenant General (later Field Marshal) Sir Claude 'the Auk' Auchinleck was relieved of command in August 1942 by Winston Churchill, who blamed him for losing Tobruk. When his replacement, Lieutenant General Bernard Montgomery, defeated Rommel decisively at el-Alamein later that year it was largely due to the new organization Auchinleck had created. Auchinleck returned to his old post of C-in-C India in 1943, taking it back from Wavell. He held it until he retired, as a field marshal, in 1947. Auchinleck died in Marrakech, Morocco, on 23 March 1981.

Major General Neil Ritchie was relieved of his command by Auchinleck in June 1942 after a disastrous campaign. In spite of this, Ritchie, who epitomized the anti-intellectual ideal of the British Army, was fêted in Britain and invited to Buckingham Palace. In 1944 he served as a corps commander in NW Europe under General Bernard Montgomery and, after the war, became Managing Director of an insurance company in Canada. He died in Canada in the 1980s.

Lieutenant (later Captain) Evelyn Waugh, Royal Marines, eventually got his wish to serve with a Household unit and, despite his suede shoes, was transferred to Bob Laycock's own Royal Horse Guards when *Layforce* was disbanded. After the war he became one of Britain's best known and most distinguished authors – Mark Amory called him 'one of the best five novelists in the English language of the century'. His Sword of Honour trilogy, *Men At Arms* (1952), *Officers & Gentlemen* (1955) and *Unconditional Surrender* (1961) is a fictionalized account of his experiences in the commandos. The cryptic dedication to Bob Laycock in *Officers & Gentlemen*, believed by some to be ironic, runs: 'To Major General Sir Robert Laycock KCMG, CB, DSO, *that every man in arms should wish to be*'. Waugh married and had six children. He died in 1966.

Erwin Rommel, the Desert Fox, remains the single most famous general of the Second World War – on any side. He exceeded his ambition to become Generaloberst – a colonel general – by attaining the supreme rank of Feldmarschall in 1943. In July 1944 he was accused of being part of a conspiracy to assassinate Adolf Hitler; he was offered an ultimatum: trial for high treason, or immunity for his family and a state funeral if he committed suicide by taking poison. He died on 14 October 1944, and was given a state funeral. His complicity in the conspiracy plot has never been proven.

Operation Flipper: Nominal Roll

Beach Party (8)

Lieutenant Colonel **Robert E. Laycock,** *Royal Horse Guards* – Escaped

Sergeant **John Nicholl,** *Parent Unit Unknown* – Captured

Bombardier **George Dunn**, *Royal Artillery* – Captured

Lance Corporal **Larry J. Codd**, *Corps of Royal Signals* – Captured

Private **E.C. Atkins**, *Bedfordshire & Hertfordshire Regiment* – Captured

Lieutenant **John M. Pryor**, *Bedfordshire & Hertfordshire Regiment* (**Special Boat Section**) – Wounded & Captured

Bombardier **John Brittlebank**, *Royal Artillery* (**Special Boat Section**) – Escaped

Extra Man (left at RV)

Private **Robert Fowler**, *Cameron Highlanders* – Captured

Assault Party – German HQ (6)

Lieutenant Colonel **Geoffrey C.T. Keyes**, *Royal Scots Greys* – Killed

Captain **Robin F. Campbell**, *General List* – Wounded & Captured

Sergeant **Jack Terry**, *Royal Artillery* – Escaped

Lance Corporal **Denis Coulthread**, *Royal Scots* – Captured

Lance Bombardier **A. Brodie**, *Royal Artillery* – Captured

Corporal **Avishalom Drori**, *51 Middle East Commando* – Captured

Covering Party – German HQ (7)

Lance Corporal **William Pryde**, *Cameron Highlanders* – Captured

Corporal **A.E. Radcliffe,** *Royal Army Service Corps* – Wounded
& Captured

Private **John A. Phiminster**, *Cameron Highlanders* – Captured

Lance Corporal **Frank Varney,** *Sherwood Foresters* – Captured

Bombardier **Joseph Kearney**, *Royal Artillery* – Captured

Lance Corporal **Malcolm Edward 'Spike' Hughes**, *Manchester
Regiment* – Captured

Corporal **Stephen Heavysides**, *Yorkshire & Lancashire Regiment* –
Captured

Outside Covering Party – German HQ (4)

Sergeant **Charles Bruce,** *Black Watch (Royal Highland Regiment)* –
Captured

Corporal **Charles Lock**, *London Scottish (Gordon Highlanders)* –
Wounded & Captured

Private **James Bogle**, *Gordon Highlanders* – Captured

Private **Robert Murray**, *Highland Light Infantry (City of Glasgow
Regiment)* – Captured

Cyrene Crossroads Party (7)

Lieutenant **Roy Royston Cooke**, *Royal West Kent Regiment* – Captured

Sergeant **Frederick Birch**, *Liverpool Scottish (Cameron Highlanders)* (7 &
51 ME Commando) – Captured

Corporal **John Kerr**, *Cameron Highlanders* (7 & 51 ME Commando) –
Captured

Gunner **James Gornall**, *Royal Artillery* – Captured

Lance Bombardier **Terence O'Hagen**, *Royal Artillery* – Captured

Gunner **P. Macrae**, *Royal Artillery* – Captured

Private **Charles H. Paxton,** *Cameron Highlanders* – Captured

Sources

Published Works

Barnett, Correlli, *The Desert Generals* London 1960

Beevor, Antony, *Crete, The Battle & the Resistance* London 1991

Bennet, Ralph, *Ultra & Mediterranean Strategy 1941–45* London 1980

Bierman, John & Smith, Colin, *Alamein – War Without Hate* London 2002

Bradford, Roy & Dillon, Martin, *Rogue Warrior of the SAS: Lt Col Blair 'Paddy' Mayne* London 1987

Brown, George A., *Commando Gallantry Awards of the Second World War* London 1991

Carrell, Paul, *Foxes of the Desert* London 1960

Chapman, Paul, *Submarine Torbay* London 1989

Cooper, Artemis, *Cairo in the War 1939–45* London 1989

Cooper, Johnny with Kemp, Anthony, *One of the Originals* London 1991

Cowles, Virginia, *The Phantom Major* London 1960

Dixon, Norman, *The Psychology of Military Incompetence* London 1998

Edelmaier, Hans, *Das Rommel Unternehmen* Salzburg 2000

Evans-Pritchard, E.E., *The Senussi of Cyrenaica* London 1944

Fergusson, Bernard, *The Watery Maze – The Story of Combined Operations* London 1961

Foot, M.R.D., *SOE 1940–46* London 1984

Fraser, David, *Knight's Cross, A Life of Field Marshal Erwin Rommel* London 1993

Greene, Jack & Massignani, Alessandro, *Rommel's North African Campaign September 1940–November 1942* Cambridge, Mass. 1994

Gordon, John W., *The Other Desert War* London 1987

Hinsley F.H., *British Army Intelligence in the Second World War, Volume 2,* London 1981

HMSO, *The SOE Syllabus: Lessons in Ungentlemanly Warfare* London 2001

Hoe, Alan, *David Stirling – The Authorised Biography of the Creator of the SAS* London 1992

James, Malcolm, *Born of the Desert – with the SAS in N. Africa* London 1945

Kemp, Anthony, *The SAS at War 1941–45* London 1991

Kennedy–Shaw, William B., *The Long Range Desert Group* London 1953

Keyes, Elizabeth, *Geoffrey Keyes of the Rommel Raid* London 1956

Ladd, James, *Commandos & Rangers of the Second World War* London 1978

Ladd, James D., *SAS Operations* London 1986

Lansborough, Gordon, *Tobruk Commando* London 1956

Lattimer, John, *Alamein* London 2002

Lewes, John, *Jock Lewes, Co-Founder of the SAS* London 2000

Lewin, Ronald, *The Life & Death of the Afrika Korps* London 1977

Liddell Hart, Basil, Ed., *The Rommel Papers* London 1953

Lloyd Owen, David, *The LRDG – Providence Their Guide* London 1980

Lodwick, John, *The Filibusters* London 1950

Lodwick, John, *Raiders from the Sea: The Story of SBS in the Second World War* London 1956

Mackenzie, William, *The Secret History of the SOE* London 2000

Maclean, Fitzroy, *Eastern Approaches* London 1949

Marrinan, Patrick, *Colonel Paddy* London 1960

Mather, Carol, *When the Grass Stops Growing* London 1997

McLuskey, Fraser, *Parachute Padre* London 1951

Messenger, Charles, *The Commandos 1940–1946* London 1985

Mitcham, Samuel W. Jr., *Triumphant Fox* New York 1984

Moorehead, Alan, *African Trilogy, The Desert War 1940–43* London 1944

Neillands, Robin, *The Raiders: Army Commandos 1940–46* London 1969

Newsinger, John, *Dangerous Men: The SAS & Popular Culture* London 1997

Pitt, Barrie, *The Crucible of War Volume I: Wavell's Command* London 1980

Pitt, Barrie, *The Crucible of War Volume II: Auchinleck's Command* London 1980

Pitt, Barrie, *Zeebrugge – 11 VCs Before Breakfast* London 1958

Popiakoff, Vladimir, *Private Army* London 1950

Saunders, Hilary S., *The Green Beret – The Story of the Commandos, 1940–1945* London 1949

Smith, Peter C., *Massacre At Tobruk* London 1987

Timpson, Alastair, *In Rommel's Back Yard* London 2000

Walsh, R. Raymond & Walsh, Jean, *Commandos Roll of Honour* London 1999

Warner, Philip, *The SAS – The Official History* London 1971

Warner, Philip, *The Secret Forces of the Second World War* London 1985

Waugh, Evelyn, *Officers & Gentlemen* London 1955

Waugh, Evelyn, *Diaries* (ed. Michel Dove) London 1976

Wellsted, Ian, *SAS with Maquis* London 1994

Windmill, Lorna Almonds, *Gentleman Jim* London 2001

Wynter, H.W., *Special Forces in the Desert War 1940–43* London 2001

Young, Desmond, *Rommel* London 1950

Other Works – Unpublished

Bews, David & Cashmore, Stephen, *Caithness Archives*: unpublished MS

Birch, Frederick, *Personal Diary From Fred Birch: Schoolboy to Soldier*: School Project

Butler, H.H., *Personal Report on the Litani River Action 1941*

Campbell, Captain R.F., *Personal Account of the Rommel Raid, 25th November 1943*: Lord Roger Keyes Papers

Campbell, Captain R.F., *Report in the Imperial War Museum*

Extract from Narrative of HMS Torbay: November 1942 Lord Roger Keyes Papers

11 Commando War Diary, Public Records Office

Haselden File WO 210/727, Public Records Office

Hoiss, Joseph, *Report of the Raid on the Prefettura at Beda Littoria in November 1941: July 25th 1979*: Lord Roger Keyes Papers

Hughes, Alice, *Malcolm Edward Hughes – A Personal Account by His Daughter Alice*: Private Communication with the author

Keyes, Elizabeth, *Geoffrey Keyes & The 11th Scottish Commando*: unpublished MS, Lord Roger Keyes Papers

Keyes, Geoffrey, *Letter 13/11/41*: Lord Roger Keyes Papers

Keyes, Geoffrey, *Personal Diary 1941*: Lord Roger Keyes Papers

Keyes, Geoffrey, *Precis of Orders by Lieutenant Colonel R.R. N Pedder HLI & Report on Litani Action*, 21 June 1941

Lappin, Graham, *Black Hackle: The Story of the No 11 Scottish Commando*: Unpublished MS

Laycock, Bob, *Report on Operation Flipper* PRO WO201/720

Layforce War Diary: Public Records Office

Lock, Charles, *War Diaries, Letters and Papers*: Mary Louise Guiver Papers, Private Collection

Macpherson, Thomas, *Notes on Left Flank Operations of Litani Landing 1941*, Sir Thomas Macpherson Papers, undated

Macpherson, Thomas, *Reconnoitring the Rommel Raid – A Personal Account:* Sir Thomas Macpherson Papers, undated

More, George, *Report by Capt G. More RE on Operations by Z Fighting Party on 9. 6. 41 & 10. 6. 41 near the Litani River:* 20 June 1941

Ross, Dr Hamish, *Interview with Sir Thomas Macpherson. 20 Dec 2001*: Transcript

Terry, Jack DCM, *Report on the Attack on Rommel's HQ*: February 4th 1942 LRK Papers

Tevendale, RSM L., Gordon Highlanders, *Account of Action Taken by No 1 Troop and Cdo HQ in Action on Monday 9th June 1941*

Notes

GKOTRR = *Geoffrey Keyes of the Rommel Raid* Elizabeth Keyes 1956

LRK Papers = Lord Roger Keyes Papers (Private Collection)

STM Papers = Sir Thomas Macpherson Papers (Private Collection)

1 Crusader Day 2

1 John M. Pryor quoted in Elizabeth Keyes *GKOTRR* 1956 *P156*

2 *Ibid*

2 Crusader Minus 18 Months

1 Charles Messenger *The Commandos* 1985 *P26*

2 Correlli Barnett *The Desert Generals* 1960 *P103*

3 David Fraser *Knight's Cross* 1993 *P271*

4 Charles Messenger *Commandos* 1985 *P27*

5 Barrie Pitt *Zeebrugge* 1958 *P222*

6 Elizabeth Keyes *GKOTRR* 1956 *P130*

7 David Bews & Stephen Cashmore *Caithness Archives* Unpublished MS

8 D.D. Drummond *in a letter to the author May 2003*

9 Malcolm Hughes *A Personal Account by His Daughter, Alice* – Private Communication with the Author

10 A.A. Archibald *in a letter to the author May 2003*

11 Elizabeth Keyes *GKOTRR* 1956 *P136*

12 Graham Lappin *Black Hackle: The Story of the No 11 Scottish Commando* Unpublished MS *P3*

13 Elizabeth Keyes *GKOTRR* 1956 *P137*

14 *Ibid P145*

15 Jim Gornall *in conversation with the author March 2003*

16 D.D. Drummond *op.cit*

17 *Ibid*

3 Crusader Minus 11 Months

1 Geoffrey Keyes *Personal Diary 1941* LRK Papers

2 Evelyn Waugh *Officers & Gentlemen* 1955 *P47*

3 Alan Hoe *David Stirling* 1992 *P84*

4 Carol Mather *When the Grass Stops Growing* 1997 *P89*

5 *Ibid P51*

6 Bob Laycock *Papers* Liddell Hart Centre for Military Archives, King's College, London

7 Carol Mather *WTGSG* 1997 *P23*

8 Evelyn Waugh *Diaries* ed. Michel Dove 1976 *P439*

4 Crusader Minus 8 Months

1 Samuel Mitcham *Triumphant Fox* 1984 *P124*

5 Crusader Minus 7 Months

1 Antony Beevor *Crete* 1991 *P221*

2 *Ibid P218*

3 *Ibid P223*

6 Crusader Minus 6 Months

1 H.H. Butler *Personal Report on the Litani River Action 1941*

2 Thomas Macpherson *Notes On Left Flank Operations* STM Papers

3 *Ibid*

4 Lewis Tevendale *Account of Action on Litani River* STM Papers

5 Gerald Bryan *Report on Litani River Action 1941* STM Papers

6 *Ibid*

7 *Ibid*

8 Lewis Tevendale *op.cit*

9 *Ibid*

10 Blair Mayne *in a letter to his brother 15 July 1941* quoted in Graham Lappin *Black Hackle: The Story of the No 11 Scottish Commando* Unpublished MS P3

11 *Ibid*

12 Jim Gornall *in conversation with the author March 2003*

13 Elizabeth Keyes *GKOTRR* 1956 P190

14 Jim Gornall *in conversation with the author March 2003*

15 *Ibid*

16 Geoffrey Keyes *Personal Diary 1941* LRK Papers

17 *Ibid*

18 Jim Gornall *op.cit*

19 Thomas Macpherson *Interview with Hamish Ross 2002* STM Papers

20 Jim Gornall *op.cit*

7 Crusader Summer 1941: I

1 Erwin Rommel *Rommel Papers* 1953 P146

2 *Ibid* PP148–9

3 Correlli Barnett *The Desert Generals* 1960 P103

4 David Fraser *Knight's Cross* 1993 P273

5 *Ibid* P43

6 *Ibid* P209

7 *Ibid*

8 Crusader Summer 1941: II

1 John Lattimer *Alamein* 2002 P27

2 Quoted in Robin Neillands *The Raiders* 1969 P92–3

9 Crusader Summer 1941: III

1 Alan Hoe *David Stirling* 1992 P45

11 Crusader August/September 1941

1 Sir Thomas Macpherson *Introduction to Das Rommel Unternehmen* 2002 (in German)

2 Elizabeth Keyes *GKOTRR* 1956 P58

3 *Ibid* P20

4 *Ibid* P193

5 Sir Thomas Macpherson *Interview with Hamish Ross 2002* STM Papers

6 Bob Laycock *quoted in Special Forces in the Desert War* 2001 P416

7 Bob Laycock *Memo to C-in-C Auchinleck 17 October 1941 File 24* Liddell Hart Centre for Military Archives, King's College, London

8 Sir Thomas Macpherson *in conversation with the author March 2003*

12 Crusader September/October 1941

1 Bob Laycock *Memo op.cit*

2 Carol Mather *WTGSG* 1997 P29

3 *Ibid*

4 Alan Hoe *David Stirling* 1992 P74

5 *Ibid* P47

6 Johnny Cooper *One of the Originals* 1991 P19

7 Bradford & Martin *Rogue Warrior* 1987 P24

8 McLuskey *Parachute Padre* 1951

9 Bradford & Martin *Rogue Warrior* 1987 xiv

10 & preceding Geoffrey Keyes *Personal Diary 1941* LRK Papers

13 Crusader Minus 39 Days

1 Gordon Lansborough *Tobruk Commando* 1956 P43

2 William Kennedy-Shaw *The Long Range Desert Group* 1953 P119

3 E.E. Evans-Pritchard *The Senussi of Cyrenaica* P196

14 Crusader Minus 29 Days

1 David Lloyd-Owen *The LRDG – Providence Their Guide* 1980 P138

2 H.W. Wynter *Special Forces in the Desert War* 2001 P82

15 Crusader Minus 33 Days

1 Alan Hoe *David Stirling* 1992 P86

2 Lorna Almonds Windmill *Gentleman Jim* 2001 P70

3 Bradford & Martin *Rogue Warrior* 1987 P30

4 Alan Hoe *David Stirling* 1992 P86

16 Crusader Minus 30 Days

1 Sir Thomas Macpherson *Introduction to Das Rommel Unternehmen* 2002 (in German) P6

2 *Ibid*

3 Sir Thomas Macpherson *RRR – A Personal Account* STM Papers

4 *Ibid*

5 *Ibid*

6 *Ibid*

7 *Ibid*

8 *Ibid*

9 *Ibid*

10 *Ibid*

11 *Ibid*

12 Ralph Bennet *Ultra & Mediterranean Strategy*

13 Sir Thomas Macpherson *Introduction to Das Rommel Unternehmen* 2002 *(in German) P7*

17 Crusader 1–9 November

1 Elizabeth Keyes *GKOTRR* 1956 *P204*

2 Charles Lock *Personal Diary* Mary Louise Guiver Papers

3 *Ibid*

4 *Ibid*

5 Sir Thomas Macpherson *Introduction to Das Rommel Unternehmen* 2002 *(in German) P4*

6 Charles Lock *op.cit*

7 & preceding Bob Laycock *Report on Operation Flipper PRO/WO201/720*

19 Crusader Minus 8 Days

1 Paul Chapman *Submarine Torbay* 1989 *P87*

2 *Ibid*

3 Sir Thomas Macpherson *Introduction to Das Rommel Unternehmen* 2002 *(in German) P4*

4 Elizabeth Keyes *GKOTRR* 1956 *P207*

5 Lord Roger Keyes *in conversation with the author* March 2003

6 Elizabeth Keyes *GKOTRR* 1956 *P58*

7 *Ibid*

8 Jim Gornall *in conversation with the author* March 2003

9 *Ibid*

10 Paul Chapman *Submarine Torbay* 1989 *P90*

11 Jim Gornall *in conversation with the author* March 2003

12 Elizabeth Keyes *GKOTRR* 1956 *P204*

13 Antony Miers *HMS Torbay Log 13 November 1941*

14 Geoffrey Keyes *Letter 13/11/41* LRK Papers

20 Crusader Minus 4 Days

1 Jim Gornall *in conversation with the author* March 2003

2 *Ibid*

3 *Ibid*

21 Crusader Minus 4 Days: 1900 hours

1 Elizabeth Keyes *GKOTRR* 1956 *P210*

2 *Ibid*

3 *Ibid*

4 *Ibid*

5 Antony Miers *HMS Torbay Log 14 November 1941*

6 *Ibid*

22 Crusader Minus 3 Days: 0040 hours

1 Jim Gornall *in conversation with the author* March 2003

2 *Ibid*

3 Michael Willmott *HMS Talisman Log 15 November 1941*

4 Elizabeth Keyes *GKOTRR* 1956 *P211*

5 Charles Lock *Account of the Landing at Crab Bay* Mary Louise Guiver Papers

6 *Ibid*

7 Michael Willmott *HMS Talisman Log 15 November 1941*

8 *Ibid*

9 Charles Lock *op.cit*

10 *Ibid*

11 *Ibid*

23 Crusader Minus 3 Days: 0500–0600 hours

1 Elizabeth Keyes *GKOTRR* 1956 *PP218–19*

2 Jim Gornall *in conversation with the author* March 2003

3 *Ibid*

4 Robin Campbell *Report on the Rommel Raid 1943* LRK Papers

5 *Ibid*

24 Crusader Minus 2 Days: 0600–1800 hours

1 Robin Campbell *op.cit*

2 *Ibid*

3 Jim Gornall *in conversation with the author* March 2003

25 Crusader Minus 2 Days: 1830 hours

1 Philip Warner *The SAS* 1971 *P25*

2 Alan Hoe *David Stirling* 1992 *P99*

3 *Ibid P24*

4 *Ibid*

5 Johnny Cooper *One of the Originals* 1991 *P24*

6 Alan Hoe *David Stirling* 1992 *P100*

7 Philip Warner *The SAS* 1971 *P25*

8 Alan Hoe *David Stirling* 1992 *P100*

9 Johnny Cooper *One of the Originals* 1991 *P25*

10 *Ibid*

26 Crusader D-1: 0600 hours

1 Jim Gornall *in conversation with the author March 2003*

2 Robin Campbell *Report on the Rommel Raid 1943* LRK Papers

3 Alan Hoe *David Stirling* 1992 *P100*

4 Jim Gornall *in conversation with the author March 2003*

5 *Ibid*

6 *Ibid*

27 Crusader D-1: 1800 hours

1 Alan Moorehead *African Trilogy* 1944 *P23*

2 Jim Gornall *in conversation with the author March 2003*

3 Fred Birch *Personal Diary: From* Fred Birch, Schoolboy to Soldier, School Project

4 Jim Gornall *op.cit*

5 *Ibid*

6 *Ibid*

28 Crusader D-1: 2330 hours

1 HMSO *SOE Syllabus* 2001 *P367*

2 Ernst Schilling To Elizabeth Keyes *28 April 1946 GKOTRR 1956 P266*

3 HMSO *SOE Syllabus* 2001 *P275*

4 Joseph Hoiss *Report of the Raid on the Prefettura at Beda Littoria* 1979 LRK Papers

5 Avishalom Drori 'The Raid on General Rommel's HQ' *in Das Rommel Unternehmen P216*

6 Jack Terry DCM *Glasgow Herald 11/11/96*

7 Report To Chief of Staff *Panzergruppe Afrika 18/11/41*

8 *Ibid*

9 Avishalom Drori – The Raid on General Rommel's HQ *in Das Rommel Unternehmen P216*

10 *Ibid*

11 *Ibid*

12 Ernst Schilling To Elizabeth Keyes *28 April 1946 GKOTRR 1956 P266*

13 Report To Chief of Staff *Panzergruppe Afrika 18/11/41*

14 Robin Campbell *Report on the Rommel Raid 1943* LRK Papers

15 Jack Terry DCM *Report on Operation Flipper February 1942* LRK Papers

16 H.W. Wynter *Special Forces in the Desert War* 2001 *P282*

17 *Ibid*

18 Report To Chief of Staff *Panzergruppe Afrika 18/11/41*

19 *Ibid*

20 Robin Campbell *Report on the Rommel Raid 1943* LRK Papers

21 *Ibid*

22 Elizabeth Keyes *GKOTRR 1956 P285*

23 Jack Terry DCM *Report on Operation Flipper February 1942* LRK Papers

24 Avishalom Drori 'The Raid on General Rommel's HQ' *in Das Rommel Unternehmen P216*

25 Report To Chief of Staff *Panzergruppe Afrika 18/11/41*

26 *Ibid*

27 *Oberkommando der Panzerarmee Afrika Report on Raid In Beda Littoria 21 May 1942*

28 It seems just as likely that Jager was shot from inside the room by Terry, as he tried to get out of the window. Malcolm Hughes readily admitted to his family after the war that he had shot one of his own officers 'who had forgotten the password', but apparently never claimed to have shot a German officer.

29 Jack Terry DCM *Glasgow Herald 11/11/97*

30 *Ibid*

31 H.W. Wynter *Special Forces in the Desert War* 2001 *P282*

32 Robin Campbell *Report in the Imperial War Museum*

29 Crusader D1: About 0000 hours

1 Erwin Rommel *Rommel Papers* 1953 *P151*

2 *Ibid P152*

3 *Ibid*

4 & preceding Samuel Mitcham *Triumphant Fox* 1984 *P139*

5 *Ibid*

6 Fritz Bayerlein in *Rommel Papers* 1953 *P156*

7 *Ibid P149*

30 Crusader D1: 0000–0030 hours

1 & preceding Jim Gornall *in conversation with the author March 2003*

2 Roy Cooke quoted in Elizabeth Keyes *GKOTRR* 1956 *P241–2*

3 *Ibid*

4 Jim Gornall *in conversation with the author March 2003*

5 *Ibid*

6 Fred Birch *Personal Diary*

7 Jim Gornall *op.cit*

8 Roy Cooke quoted in Elizabeth Keyes *GKOTRR* 1956

9 *Ibid*

10 Jim Gornall *in conversation with the author March 2003*

11 Roy Cooke quoted in Elizabeth Keyes *GKOTRR* 1956 *P241*

12 Jim Gornall *in conversation with the author March 2003*

13 Fred Birch *Personal Diary*

14 Lieutenant Col. Schleusener *Statement Made While a POW* 1946

15 Jim Gornall *in conversation with the author March 2003*

16 *Ibid*

17 Fred Birch *op.cit*

18 Jim Gornall *op.cit*

19 *Ibid*

20 *Ibid*

32 Crusader D1–D2

1 Antony Miers *HMS Torbay Log 19 November 1941*

2 *Ibid*

3 *Ibid*

4 Bob Laycock *Report on Operation Flipper* PRO/WO201/720

5 Antony Miers *HMS Torbay Log 19 November 1941*

6 Elizabeth Keyes *GKOTRR* 1956 *P244*

7 John Pryor quoted in Elizabeth Keyes *GKOTRR* 1956 *P241–2*

33 Crusader D3

1 Johnny Cooper *One of the Originals* 1991 *P21*

2 *Ibid P27*

3 David Lloyd Owen *Providence Their Guide* 1980 *P61*

4 Alan Hoe *David Stirling* 1992 *P105*

5 David Lloyd Owen *Providence Their Guide* 1980 *P61*

6 *Ibid*

7 Alan Hoe *David Stirling* 1992 *P104*

8 Johnny Cooper *One of the Originals* 1991 *P29*

9 *Ibid P30*

34 Crusader D9

1 Correlli Barnett *The Desert Generals* 1960 *P103*

2 *Ibid*

3 Norman Dixon *The Psychology of Military Incompetence* 1998 *P127*

4 Correlli Barnett *The Desert Generals* 1960 *P118*

5 Artemis Cooper *Cairo in the War 1939–45,* 1989 *P183*

35 Crusader Plus

1 George A. Brown *Commando Gallantry Awards of The Second World War* 1991 *P67*

2 Antony Miers *HMS Torbay Log 21 November 1941*

3 Elizabeth Keyes *GKOTRR* 1956 *P254*

4 Bob Laycock *Papers* Liddell Hart Centre for Military Archives, King's College, London

5 *Ibid*

6 *Ibid*

7 Charles Messenger *The Commandos* 1985 *P115*

8 *Ibid*

36 The Aftermath

1 Bob Laycock *Report on Operation Flipper* PRO/WO201/720

Index